Chinese Economists on Economic Reform – Collected Works of Zhou Xiaochuan

T0330902

This book is part of a series which makes available to English-speaking audiences the work of the individual Chinese economists who were the architects of China's economic reform. The series provides an inside view of China's economic reform, revealing the thinking of the reformers themselves, unlike many other books on China's economic reform which are written by outside observers.

Zhou Xiaochuan (1948–) has been Governor of the People's Bank of China since 2002 and is one of the most influential economists in the world. He holds numerous other important positions, including Governor of the International Monetary Fund for China and Vice-Chairman of the National Committee of the Chinese People's Political Consultative Conference. Before his important work as a banker, he was, in the 1980s, a major contributor to the process of analysing policies to do with the structural reform of the Chinese economy.

The book is published in association with **China Development Research Foundation**, one of the leading economic and social think tanks in China, where many of the theoretical foundations and policy details of economic reform were formulated.

Routledge Studies on the Chinese Economy

Series Editor
Peter Nolan
Director, Centre of Development Studies;
Chong Hua Professor in Chinese Development; and
Director of the Chinese Executive Leadership Programme (CELP),
University of Cambridge

Founding Series Editors
Peter Nolan, *University of Cambridge* and
Dong Fureng, *Beijing University*

The aim of this series is to publish original, high-quality, research-level work by both new and established scholars in the West and the East, on all aspects of the Chinese economy, including studies of business and economic history.

Routledge Studies on the Chinese Economy – Chinese Economists on Economic Reform

1 **Chinese Economists on Economic Reform – Collected Works of Xue Muqiao**
   Xue Muqiao, edited by China Development Research Foundation

2 **Chinese Economists on Economic Reform – Collected Works of Guo Shuqing**
   Guo Shuqing, edited by China Development Research Foundation

3 **Chinese Economists on Economic Reform – Collected Works of Chen Xiwen**
   Chen Xiwen, edited by China Development Research Foundation

4 **Chinese Economists on Economic Reform – Collected Works of Du Runsheng**
   Du Runsheng, edited by China Development Research Foundation

5 **Chinese Economists on Economic Reform – Collected Works of Lou Jiwei**
   Lou Jiwei, edited by China Development Research Foundation

6 **Chinese Economists on Economic Reform – Collected Works of Ma Hong**
   Ma Hong, edited by China Development Research Foundation

7 **Chinese Economists on Economic Reform – Collected Works of Wang Mengkui**
   Wang Mengkui, edited by China Development Research Foundation

8 **Chinese Economists on Economic Reform – Collected Works of Yu Guangyuan**
   Yu Guangyuan, edited by China Development Research Foundation

9 **Chinese Economists on Economic Reform – Collected Works of Zhou Xiaochuan**
   Zhou Xiaochuan, edited by China Development Research Foundation

10 **Chinese Economists on Economic Reform – Collected Works of Li Jiange**
   Li Jiange, edited by China Development Research Foundation

Zhou Xiaochuan

Chinese Economists on Economic Reform – Collected Works of Zhou Xiaochuan

Zhou Xiaochuan

Edited by China Development Research Foundation

Routledge
Taylor & Francis Group

LONDON AND NEW YORK

CDRF 中国发展研究基金会
China Development Research
Foundation

First edition of *A Collection of Zhou Xiaochuan's Works on Economic Reform,*
written by Zhou Xiaochuan,
ISBN: 978-7-80234-207-1
published 2008 by China Development Press.

This edition published 2017
by Routledge
2 Park Square, Milton Park, Abingdon, Oxon OX14 4RN

and by Routledge
711 Third Avenue, New York, NY 10017

First issued in paperback 2017

Routledge is an imprint of the Taylor & Francis Group, an informa business

British Library Cataloguing in Publication Data
A catalogue record for this book is available from the British Library

Library of Congress Cataloging in Publication Data
Names: Zhou, Xiaochuan, 1948- author.
Title: Chinese economists on economic reform. Collected works of Zhou
    Xiaochuan / Zhou Xiaochuan; edited by China Development Research
    Foundation.
Description: Abingdon, Oxon ; New York, NY: Routledge, 2017. |
    Series: Routledge studies on the Chinese economy; 9 | Includes
    bibliographical references and index.
Identifiers: LCCN 2016011587| ISBN 9781138669864 (hardback) |
    ISBN 9781315617954 (ebook)
Subjects: LCSH: Economic development–China. | China–Economic
    conditions–2000- | China–Economic policy–2000-
Classification: LCC HC427.95 .Z4679 2017 | DDC 330.951–dc23
    LC record available at https://lccn.loc.gov/2016011587

ISBN 13: 978-1-138-48198-5 (pbk)
ISBN 13: 978-1-138-66986-4 (hbk)

Typeset in Times New Roman
by Sunrise Setting Ltd, Brixham, UK

Contents

viii   *Contents*

10 Elevating our accounting standards   164
    (April 11, 2001)

11 Capital adequacy ratios and the need to take corrective action   170
    in time
    (September 12, 2003)

12 Several issues to do with reform of State-owned banks   175
    (April 16, 2004)

13 Promoting further development of capital markets by improving   184
    corporate governance
    (December 1, 2004)

14 Improving legal systems and reforming China's "financial
    ecosystem"   190
    (December 2, 2004)

15 China's corporate bond markets: experiences and lessons learned   208
    (October 20, 2005)

    Major works by Zhou Xiaochuan   215
    Index   216

Illustrations

Figure

Tables

Brief biography of Zhou Xiaochuan

Zhou Xiaochuan was born in January 1948. He graduated from the Beijing Institute of Chemical Technology in 1975, and he earned a PhD from Tsinghua University in economic systems engineering in 1985.

Between 1979 and 1985, he was a major contributor to the process of analyzing policies to do with the structural reform of China's economy. From November 1986 to September 1991 he served on the State Commission for Restructuring the Economic System. During this period, he was a member of the leading group in the State Council that evaluated structural reform proposals (1986–7), and was concurrently deputy director of the China Economic Restructuring Research Institute.

From December 1986 until December 1989, he served as Vice-Minister of the Department of Foreign Trade and Economic Cooperation.

From 1991 to 2002, he served in the following positions: Vice-President of the Bank of China; Director of the State Administration of Foreign Exchange; Deputy Governor of the People's Bank of China; President of the China Construction Bank; and Chairman of the China Securities Regulatory Commission.

Zhou Xiaochuan is currently the Governor of the People's Bank of China and has served in this position since December 2002. Since January 2003, he has concurrently served as Chairman of the Monetary Policy Committee and he also now serves as President of the China Society for Finance and Banking. He is the Vice-Chairman of the 12th National Committee of the Chinese People's Political Consultative Conference (CPPCC).

Zhou Xiaochuan is the Governor of the International Monetary Fund (IMF) for China. He is a member of the committee to study sustainable long-term financing in the IMF, and is a member of the World Bank's Commission on Growth and Development. He is a member of the board of the Bank for International Settlements (BIS), as well as being the Chairman of the Asian Advisory Committee to the BIS. He is a Director of the African Development Bank, a member of the G30 (Group of Thirty), and a member of the Fifty Chinese Economists' Forum.

He was on *Business Week*'s Stars of Asia list in 2001 and 2004. He was named Central Bank Governor of the Year for Asia by *Emerging Markets*, which is published by *Euromoney*, in 2005 and 2006. He was honored as the CCTV (China Central Television) "China Economic Person of the Year" in 2004.

Zhou Xiaochuan was one of the first among very few economists to receive a special stipend from the Chinese government in recognition of his contributions. He has published some 100 articles and more than ten books, inside China as well as abroad. Among the articles, the paper on "Rebuilding the relationship between banks and enterprises," was awarded the "Sun Yefang Economic Sciences Scholarly Article" award in 1994. His article on "Moving toward an open economic economy" won the "An Zijie International Trade Award" in 1994. His article on "Social security: economic analysis and policy recommendations" won the "Sun Yefang Economic Sciences Award" in 1997.

In addition to primary responsibilities as noted above, he is the professor and PhD supervisor at the School of Economics and Management of Tsinghua University and at the Graduate School of the People's Bank of China.

Foreword

This series of books is authored by economists who were witnesses to and direct participants in China's "reform and opening up" over the past three decades. Nearly three generations of Chinese economists are represented, for they include both older and younger economists. Articles that were selected display the characteristics of the period in which they were written. Most exerted a direct impact on China's economic-reform policies, whether they were policy recommendations, theoretical works, or research reports. Most of these works are being published for the first time.

The China Development Research Foundation organized and published this series in Chinese in 2008, to commemorate the 30th anniversary of the start of China's "reform and opening up" and to further promote this historic social transformation. Authors and their descendants responded enthusiastically to the proposal. All the articles were edited and finalized by the authors themselves, except for those of the late Xue Muqiao and Ma Hong, which were edited and finalized by members of their families.

This series has been broadly welcomed in China. I am confident that this English edition will be helpful in giving foreign readers a better understanding of China's economic-reform policies.

I gratefully acknowledge the contribution of the World Bank, the Ford Foundation, and the Cairncross Foundation, who supported the translation and publication of this series in English. I would like to thank Justin Yifu Lin, Pieter Bottelier, Peter Geithner, David Dollar, and other experts for their valuable support and candid comments. My gratitude also goes to Martha Avery for her excellent translating and editing.

Wang Mengkui
Chairman
China Development Research Foundation

Preface by the author[1]

Since 1950, 13 economies in the world have grown at an average rate of 7 percent or more over a span of 25 years or longer. Given this growth rate, these economies have doubled every ten years.

In April 2006, the World Bank set up a *Commission on Growth and Development*. In May 2008, the group published a report that evaluates strategies for sustainable growth and comprehensive and coordinated economic development. This was the work of 21 influential policy makers and experts dealing in economic and financial issues. The report focused on the reasons behind this kind of fast economic growth, as well as its consequences and internal dynamics. I was fortunate to be one of the members of the Commission. As a participant in the process of discussing and drafting the *Report*, I learned a number of things about formulating policies. The process gave me a deeper understanding of policy design and the policy strategies that countries can take at different stages of their development.

Given that China is in the midst of astonishingly fast economic growth and development, we are even more appreciative of how essential it is to conduct research on development, as well as on the theory and practice of reform in general. Such research is one of the reasons China's economy has grown in a stable manner—China has been able to draw on the successful experiences of others.

After the Third Plenary Session of the 11th Central Committee of the Communist Party of China (December 1978), there was tremendous debate surrounding the statement, "*Practice is the sole criterion for testing truth,*" and regarding the call to "*Emancipate your mind, seek truth from the facts.*" The traditional form of a centrally-planned economic system was subjected to criticism and reconsideration. This process of debate had the effect of creating a solid foundation of social consensus on shifting our economic model towards a socialist market economy.

Two major discussions were carried out in the course of this debate. One related to "the purpose of socialist production," which began prior to the Third Plenary Session of the 11th. This debate served to clarify the idea that the purpose of socialist production is to satisfy the daily needs of people. This changed the over-emphasis on heavy industry that had been the practice in the past. It put greater emphasis on production of consumer goods and on reform of the process by which such goods are circulated. The second debate related to "material incentives." That is, it focused on incentive policies. Both of these debates were instrumental in helping us formulate policy strategies for China's reform and development.

Now that we are on the verge of completing 30 years of reform and opening up, it is highly important that we evaluate our early experience in the whole process. We should do this in a serious and concerted way, for it is especially important that the younger generation among us, who did not experience all of this, understand it. At the same time, other developing countries should be able to benefit from an objective and fact-based summation of China's experience. They too should benefit from clear-minded analysis.

In 2007, the African Development Bank convened its annual conference in Shanghai. Over 2,000 representatives attended, and quite a few expressed an interest in learning about China's development experience. This year, the African Development Bank held its conference in Mozambique, and China held a separate group discussion on rural finance. China has a long way to go in terms of its own rural finance, but quite a few African nations felt that we had considerable experience and lessons to offer.

In the late 1970s and early 1980s, our experience of reform and development was not limited solely to agriculture but could more accurately be described as a "troika." It included the household responsibility system in rural areas with contracts that were linked to production. It included "opening up" reforms with respect to foreign investment and foreign trade, and it included allowing people to produce consumer goods and stimulating microeconomic activity to distribute such goods.

As early as 1979, China enacted a law called the "*Law on Sino-foreign joint venture enterprise operations.*" This set forth rules on enterprise structure, and more "open" or liberal operating methods. In the early period of reform, China adopted reforms that were referred to as "light industry reforms" aimed at production of consumer goods. These included a whole series of "opening" (liberalizing or deregulating) measures that enabled the market to determine prices. This provided the experience and momentum for pushing forward later reforms.

As we look back on 30 years of reform and opening up, we feel how vitally necessary it is to conduct more sustained research into all these issues. Theoretical approaches and practical experience are constantly changing and evolving. Many new challenges are now appearing and the coming 30 years may well be different from the past. Globalization is occurring at tremendous speed, opportunities are arising from the information revolution, the global financial system is becoming utterly interdependent, urbanization and social development are changing the landscape… all these topics influence population, education, healthcare, and our ecological environment. All require profound reflection and further research. We must constantly reevaluate our actual experience and refresh our theoretical understanding. Only on that basis can we design better policies for the future.

Zhou Xiaochuan
May 30, 2008

Note

1 This was a speech given by the author at the release of the World Bank's "Growth Report," produced by the World Bank's Commission on Growth and Development.

1 Reform of central planning

Orientation, methods, and limits[1]

(1991)

The essence of economic structural reform involves creating a more effective system. In the final analysis, the idea is to realize a more effective structure through the actual results of economic development.

If one posits that the primary focus of reform is to improve the centrally-planned economy, then the question becomes how to do that: through what means and in what direction? Under predetermined orientations and methods, how large is the potential for any improvement (or will there be a limit to improvement)? In comparing the theoretical models of an improved system with models of other systems, what will the "nature" of the systems be? What can we derive from the process that will contribute to how we approach the subject?

Strictly speaking, this work should be highly mathematical and quantified in order to ensure the validity of hypotheses and subsequent comparisons. In this article, I approach the subject in layman's terms. I avoid the use of any mathematical expressions although I will use a few mathematical terms.

Moving a step further, since the subject is already too large for an article, I reduce its scope by putting in some assumptions. Specifically, this article focuses on how centrally-planned economies seek to arrive at equilibrium through "the plan," and how they seek to arrive at the desired proportionate relationships of everything in the plan. Among all the proportionate relationships that are to be realized by the plan, how do we arrive at the optimum proportions and optimum growth? Can we, and indeed how do we, arrive at the desired end-result "nature" of a socialist economy? That is, to the greatest degree possible, how do we satisfy the material and cultural needs of the people? Finally, as compared to other systems, what are the results of such a system after reforming and improving it?

I mainly adopt the following three assumptions:

1 I assume that the work of central planning can receive timely and effective information as needed to execute planning decisions. This is based on the assumption that we have sufficient modern telecommunications and computer technology.
2 I assume that the behavior and motivations of our cadres stay aligned with those of the central government. That is, I assume that our hierarchical form

of organization, Party cadres who are organized in hierarchical teams, will stay aligned with the central government.

3 I assume that we may employ some primary theoretical concepts when we make comparisons to market-economy systems. For example, those would include Pareto optimality, the first theorem of welfare economics, the Turnpike theorem, and so on. I assume this even though some of these concepts might be disputed.

Given the above, this article focuses on a subject that has not received much attention within China. That is, it looks at how a planned-economy system can improve the functioning of the system apart from using the standard methods of information transfer and motivating cadre teams.

Moving from a non-equilibrium type of plan to an equilibrium-type plan

Given the experience of centrally-planned economies, and particularly the experience of China's own planning work, it is not such an easy thing to arrive at equilibrium when trying to organize a plan for the many things that need to be incorporated. We always say that the superiority of a "planned system" can be found precisely in the way in which it is "done according to the proper proportions by operating through a plan." Nevertheless, one still must answer the question about what the proper proportions might actually be. One must answer this with respect to proportionate relationships among all different industries, as well as the goods each industry produces.

This article argues that, at the very least, three different levels of requirements must be met in answering this question. At the lowest level, the system must be able to achieve basic balance in proportions. That is, it must not lead to waste of resources, or a situation in which the objectives of the plan cannot be achieved. The next level up is that the system must be able to satisfy ultimate demand (which includes both consumer and investment demand), while still maintaining a stable balance in the proportionate relationships. That is, it requires that the system minimize the use of mandatory arrangements to allocate final products. Instead, the autonomy of the consumer to make decisions himself determines final allocation of goods, or the enterprise itself makes decisions on how to upgrade technology and so on. The third and highest level requirement is that the system must benefit long-term growth. It must be able to accommodate the proper proportionate relationships of the international division of labor.

In our actual experience, the way we achieve a balanced-type plan, or aim for it, is through the use of "industry-linked equilibrium tables," and the use of "work meetings of upper levels of cadres and lower levels of cadres." The first is a primitive kind of input–output matrix that is highly incomplete. Meanwhile, the latter seeks to resolve equilibrium through a computing process that involves "work" among government levels. In China, that usually means that the budgeting process for the plan "goes up and down twice." It is transmitted from the government level of the central government with its departments to provincial and municipal levels, and then back up, two times. This is a process that involves an initial trial resolution and ultimately moves toward an equilibrium resolution. At the same time, it involves negotiating among upper and lower levels of government.

In terms of substance, this planning process seeks to move toward quantified sets of equations in order to satisfy an equation such as "domestic production + imports = intermediate goods consumption + ultimate demand + exports." In this equation, ultimate demand is divided further into consumers and end-users, and ultimate users into investment in basic infrastructure (capital construction), and investment in technological reform.

In point of fact, our traditional planning methods are fundamentally defective. First, the technology required for "industry-linked equilibrium tables" is backwards and unscientific from start to finish. That includes the whole process, from information gathering and processing, pooling of data, checking and collating, down to how complete the statistics are, so various input–output matrix techniques must be substituted for the data. In addition to needing to set up an input–output matrix for A, however, you also need one for B. On the basis of consolidated or pooled balancing techniques for the A matrix, you should use social accounting matrix (SAM) technology. This in turn requires that you reevaluate the usefulness of the statistical systems of actual production. What's more, you also need to put the supply and demand for tertiary industries into the mix, including their statistics and planning systems.

Second, since the "planning work method" (budget formulation) by which annual plans are submitted and approved is a process that goes through at least "two ups and two downs," that is, two iterations or more, it is fundamentally impossible to come up with a balanced result. All one can do is attempt to move a few steps in the direction of equilibrium. At the same time, this primitive sort of "work method" wastes an inordinate amount of time and effort.

In the meanwhile, there is a great deal of ad hoc "glossing over" of discrepancies. As a result, the process of going from a primitive plan to a plan that is in equilibrium must be changed to a process that uses linear matrix equations. There is no other way to ensure equilibrium if we want to use a plan.

Both of the above two methods for improving our planning work, however, require that those doing the work have sound knowledge of input–output models, and that they have a grounding in linear algebra and applied computer technologies. Some people may argue that a plan does not need to be absolutely seamless. Indeed, they say that we generally should "leave a little room for improvement" in our plan. We should let it be a little flexible for when we need flexibility. This is called "an active approach to balancing the plan."

In fact, however, if we cannot even get to the lowest requirements for a balanced plan, we cannot remotely hope to maintain the authoritative nature of the central plan. We cannot explain why our proportionate relationships should be considered reasonable. We cannot maintain any rationale for the way we set plan prices. Ultimately, we have no way to explain the superiority of the planned economy.

It is precisely these "loopholes in the plan" and our so-called "proactive balancing act" that are leading to the inevitable demise of the entire planned economy.

In the course of reform, one thing has already become a thorny issue, namely how to handle the way in which people decide how to use end-products. How do we maintain the autonomy of the final end-users' decision-making, whether that is the consumer or the enterprise? How do we estimate that end-use demand? At present, work of this kind is done using the lowest level of technology and is highly unsatisfactory. One of the most difficult problems is that we still have mandatory arrangements while also allowing for autonomy in decision-making. Given that the market is still not able to play its complete role, yet the end-user is not given full autonomy, it is hard to estimate what choices there might be if end-users were in fact given full autonomy. This relates to the issue of whether or not end-use demand systems can be predicted at all. Second, highly complex non-equilibrium quantitative economic techniques must be used to estimate all the variables.

Our traditional planning mainly uses regression techniques for lateral comparisons, and time-sequence projections. (In fact, very few people have a grasp of how to do this.) When it comes to China's planning for durable goods, the mistakes are staggering. Because of this, people engaged in planning work must be very skilled in solving special econometric problems.

In trying to achieve equilibrium, we attempt to have a balanced import and export structure that then helps satisfy the right proportions. Importing and exporting supposedly can help balance out oversupplies and undersupplies of the plan in general and therefore make the work of planning a great deal easier. International exchange is carried out under a market system, however. An import–export structure that is balanced in terms of actual goods is not the same as being balanced in terms of value. Whether or not a balance in value can be achieved by such an approach carries with it considerable risk. It is also doubtful whether or not this kind of making up of balances as a way to adjust overall structure does indeed arrive at the optimum situation.

Another problem with this kind of planning model is that it is hard to have the system itself provide incentives for upgrading technology and conserving scarce resources. In the actual functioning of our system, we simply have to admit that this problem is rather relevant to the way things stand today.

Going from equilibrium to optimization

Some people view a market economy as being the root cause of an anarchistic process that leads to periodic crises. It is therefore viewed as the root of all evil, whereas a planned economy is far more intelligent. It uses a planned approach and carries things out according to proper proportions. In both theory and practice, however, the actual situation is that the market is not so bad. Classical market economics allows the market to allocate resources in ways that achieve what is called a Pareto optimum. That is, scarce resources are used in the most efficient way because of the way the market itself functions.

As economics developed, the appearance of macroeconomics and game theory have gone further in demonstrating how to ensure a Pareto equilibrium and not allow an economy to stagnate in a condition of what is called a Nash equilibrium. (In simplified terms, a Nash equilibrium arrives at equilibriums that are sub-optimal. I do not present a mathematical treatment in this article.)

This kind of system is a major challenge to a centrally-planned economic system. After all, when we declare that our plan can balance things out according to proper proportions, and that this must necessarily win out over market economies, we must answer the question, "exactly what proportions?" We must demonstrate what kind of equilibrium we achieve. Is it indeed optimum, the best choice of all? Unless our planning work is shifted in the direction of "the optimum equilibrium," and "the optimum proportions," we are unable to answer these questions. In theoretical terms, at the very least, we lose the argument to a market economy.

Let us assume that in actual practice we have two State Planning Commissions. They both operate according to traditional planning methods in coming up with the plan. Both of these may be able to come up with "equilibrium," and to reach what is said to be "proportionate relationships that are in balance," but the two may be entirely different. With the same logic, now suppose a country "N" has a State Planning Commission that comes up with a whole variety of plans that are all in equilibrium. Country N still must use some criteria or other by which to determine which is best. (One could call this a function that describes the ideal end result or an "object function.") From a purely methodological viewpoint, it is impossible to ensure that the optimum plan is included within these equilibrium plans, all derived by traditional planning methods.

From traditional methods of planning, as well as the method by which we currently operate, one can see that it is fairly easy to come up with a balance or equilibrium if that is at a low level of growth. We can use China's 6th Five-Year Plan as an example. During the 6th Five-Year Plan period, China's gross national product (GNP) actually grew at the high rate of 9.8 percent. By plan indicators, however, it was to grow at a rate that "aimed for 5 percent but tried to stay above 4 percent." The very real problem we face is that if we make our plan according to a growth rate of 8 to 9 percent, we will find it very hard to achieve any kind of balance by using our current planning methods. It will definitely be necessary to "leave some gaps here and there" so that we can fudge things, and this will incur criticism.

In order to gloss over or conceal our technical problems, in the past our approach was to "leave a little room" in the plan to make up for things. This "theory of how to operate" was a self-contradiction, however. When the actual rate of economic growth is twice that of planned growth, the actual proportions in the economy will be very considerably different from those that are in the plan. (This goes for disparities among macroeconomic indicators as well as among departments.) Has the planned economy actually been able to achieve what we declare to be its intended results? Have we in any way achieved proper proportions by the use of a plan? Exactly what kind of proportions have we achieved?

I recommend that we admit the truth. Due to the primitive nature of our planning processes, and our inability to make full use of modern scientific methods, our central plan is incapable of allowing our economy to reach its full potential. Nor can it arrive at an optimum equilibrium. Indeed, our planning may be leading us far in the opposite direction. This means that we are either holding back the potential for economic growth, or we are deviating from the planned proportions as set forth by the plan. It means that we are finding it hard to be competitive in a world economy. Instead of relying on specious excuses, we should try to move forward.

Fortunately, modern mathematical tools and computer science now provide us with the ability to improve our planning in the pursuit of an optimum equilibrium. They allow us to arrive at optimum proportions. I refer to linear programming and specifically to the large-scale linear programming that matured as a science in the 1970s. From the perspective of economic planning, these tools can help optimize a given variable under the constraints of other variables such as economic conditions, productivity, proportionate relationships and so on. Any given target (such as economic growth) can be optimized (or minimized). The logic behind linear programming also indicates that many results can come from applying different constraints, but only one is the optimum result.

What kind of "object function" should central planning adopt as its goal? The simplest method would be to try to maximize national income, for example. That is, we would optimize the aggregate value of the ultimate end-products of each department (which have corresponding demand in other departments). If we also take the dynamic results of investment into account, we could convert the future capacity of national income into net present value. We could then add that to current national income in order to achieve a more complete object function. One of the requirements of linear programming is that the object function and the constraining variables must all be linear functions. If we use this kind of scientific approach, our planning work could perhaps not only achieve greater equilibrium relationships but we could seek to optimize the end result. That would then improve the competitiveness of our planned-economy system overall.

What this means, however, is that decision makers engaged in planning must understand linear algebra. They must have an understanding of operations research and econometrics and be able to carry out input–output modeling. The regrettable thing is that some of our planning personnel seem far more adept at finding verbal excuses than at learning anything scientific or new.

Going from an arbitrary way of setting prices to abiding by the law of value

The two sections above discuss equilibrium and an optimum equilibrium, which can be expressed in terms of physical goods. Given a condition in which physical goods are in balance, planning solutions can, in theory, ensure the equilibrium of the aggregate value of such things as finance, credit, and foreign exchange. The implication of this, however, is that we not only accommodate severe distortions in the pricing system but we also arrive at equilibrium only through the use of mandatory controls. We achieve our predetermined "proportionate relationships" in this way. (The real problem is that the "object function" is measured in terms of value.)

However, socialist economic theory quite correctly says that we must respect the law of value. An important reason for this is that the behavioral patterns and interests of individuals and enterprises are different from the interests of any one government department. Severely distorted prices may skew microeconomic behavior as a result of these interests. This forces the government to rely on ever more stringent commands to get things back in balance, with generally unfavorable results.

Another problem, and one that is seldom discussed, is the way in which planning personnel receive wrong information as the result of a system that does not in fact abide by the law of value. Planners then unwittingly continue to reinforce deviations from the plan. To give an example: let us say that one unit of product B is required to produce one unit of product A. This relationship holds at the normal situation in a given place. Since the plan sets the price of B at an overly low level, however, the enterprise is inclined to use two units of B to make one unit of A. The Planning Commission may, in principle, have increased the pressure it puts on enterprises to conserve B, but in reality these pressures are not effective. The result is that it takes, on average, 1.5 units of B to product one unit of A. Now, when the Planning Commission, or an accounting department, is collecting data for putting into the overall "production relationships equilibrium table," they write in the figure 1.5 and not 1. All planning work that then relies on this figure is subsequently skewed.

The way distorted prices affect actual behavior is then transmitted into the plan. As technical parameters are assembled for planning purposes, many do not reflect the actual cost of what Marxism refers to as the concept of socially necessary labor. The parameters do not reflect the actual underlying costs. From an econometric perspective, such parameters do not represent rational economic choices.

If we are to respect the law of value, our primary task must be to find a way to use rational pricing methods. Influenced by traditional central-planning theory, the first thing people are inclined to do is adopt a pricing formula that simply adds an average profit figure to costs. Meanwhile, they define this "average profit" depending on the factors to which they attribute the greatest importance. They come up with such things as a "dual-channel price," and a "three-channel price."

It is highly unfortunate that such concepts are not only illogical but also fatally flawed. First, cost "collection" (data gathering) should be done on the basis of the rationality of actual consumption. It should not be done on the basis of distorted prices, or the distorted structure of production entities. (Both of these reflect the current state of the planned economy.) Price determination by using distorted structures is neither helpful to society nor is it reasonable in terms of a technical economy.

Second, things that are produced with the goals of "socialist production" in mind are ostensibly produced to satisfy the material and cultural needs of people.

As everyone knows, however, the current state of our planned economy has a strong disconnect between supply and demand. Therefore, it is a mistake to apply a hypothetical "average profit" to our method of setting prices before we have straightened out our structural problems. Moreover, this concept by which we "add on an average profit" does not work for pricing such things as oil, coal, and other resource-type products. There are many other highly apparent problems with it as well. The best result can only be that we let this concept die a natural death.

Before getting into more technical considerations, I would like to look at the subject of setting prices from a higher vantage point. First, we admit that prices have a strong influence on the decision-making of both consumers and enterprises—this is a given. (I include in "prices" the economic levers that relate to prices.) We hope that pricing will guide consumers and enterprises in directions that realize the public goals of society at large. For example, to the greatest degree possible, we hope prices lead to sustainable growth of the national income. If social objectives are achieved, this will, in and of itself, lead to the greatest degree of satisfaction in people's material and cultural lives.

Maximizing these objectives, however, must necessarily be done within the constraints of a whole set of economic conditions and balanced relationships. It must comply with objective laws and must maintain stable, coordinated, and "fittest" proportionate relationships. Some people may feel that adhering to such principles is overly abstract. Approaching the subject in this way does not address actual operating techniques. The dual solution in mathematical modeling (that is, shadow pricing) makes it clear that putting these principles into actual practice is absolutely correct and necessary. Prematurely diving into technical details may well lead to an unconscious violation of more fundamental principles in an economic system.

For example, take the linear programming model that seeks to maximize national income. Our primitive solution arrives at an optimal plan in terms of physical units. (This applies as well to foreign exchange, capital, and labor.) The dual solution reveals how an optimized plan can be realized through applying the law of value under the assumption of specified behavior.

Operations research, of which mathematical programming is a part, has time and again been shown to be highly useful to those handling a centrally-planned economy. By using mathematical programming to compare shadow prices and dual-channel prices, we can see just how inferior dual-channel pricing is, and how many mistakes it comes up with as a result.

Going from subjective goals to objective goals

The goals of a socialist economy are to satisfy the material and cultural needs of the people to the greatest degree possible. In the previous section, I attempted to express these goals in terms of mathematical modeling and object functions. I should clarify a few points here.

First, people need the products of both "labor" and "culture." The concept of GNP, which includes the value of tertiary industries, is therefore more in line with the needs of object functions than the concept of "national income" as we currently define it. Second, by using investment results and the discount rate, we can turn future personal consumption into an equivalent value of current consumption. We can use the monetary value of investment and turn it into an equivalent value of current consumption, if we assume that we keep investment results at a certain level. This helps us define "investment" in terms of "ultimate consumption."

Third (and this is the key point in this section), we should recognize that people's daily needs include housing, food, clothing, transport, entertainment and so on, all of which encompass different amounts of "labor" or different quantities of products. We must use some kind of price to do a weighted value of these different quantities, units, labor values, and so on. This is just as though we were computing GNP or the national income and coming up with an aggregate figure.

However, the moment we use this kind of aggregated value as our object function, we run into a bias in how we define the goals of our socialist production, given that the price system we use for the components of the aggregate is severely distorted. Prices that are artificially under-valued, such as grain and housing, lead to under-stating their importance in the material lives of people. The converse is true as well. This distortion then goes a step further in leading to a bias in allocation of resources. We should recognize that this is not a problem that has to do with mathematical programming. Instead, it has to do with the realities of economic life. People often criticize methods that aim for production output or for meeting aggregate indicators and that overlook actual results. The State Planning Commission, the Ministry of Finance, and other departments often make the same mistake. Prices have a great influence on policy making when they are used as parameters in decision-making.

The essence of the issue relates to figuring out what weighted value we should use in aggregating the needs of people. In the past, planning personnel simply used artificial (manmade) rules to mandate the structure of consumption. They set forth all kinds of economic indicators, among which were material-goods indicators. Clearly, this way of dealing with the issue is "subjective." Given that the purpose of production is to satisfy people's needs, we must respect the autonomy of individuals in deciding on what they want to consume. The public as consumer must give its own indication of the degree to which some needs are pressing and others are not. The answer, upon detailed reflection, is that we must use rational prices to aggregate the needs of people and put these into our object function. Such rational prices must reflect the scarcity of the labor or the product.

That is to say, we must shift the purpose of our economic planning from relying on a subjective structure to relying on an objective structure. (I make the assumption here that the purpose of our economic planning is equivalent to the purpose of socialist production.) Our planning must reflect the structure of what the public chooses for itself.

When actual prices are severely distorted, the shadow price as expressed in mathematical programming can better reflect the law of value. It can be demonstrated that shadow prices are a better indicator of the scarcity of goods and labor than our actual prices. Therefore, they better reflect the weighted value of the object function that defines the goals of society. The problem, however, is that there is no shadow price when the first mathematical programming calculation is done. Therefore, the modeling to resolve the first-time program must necessarily use prices that are not all that objective. These "manmade" prices are used as a weighted average in coming up with the object function. Using the shadow prices as a dual solution can only be expressed in the second programming calculation. Moreover, the shadow prices as derived by the second solution will not be the same as those derived by the first, but will incorporate improvements. Because of this, it would be best to carry out multiple calculations. If the solution process converges, in the end we will be using a reasonable "object."

This leads to a little known concept, namely the mathematical programming that ties together primitive and dual solutions. This concept is highly important not only in improving the planning process but in enabling greater competition in market systems. It also indirectly exposes the inadequacies of things like the Kantorowicz optimal planning theory.

At this point, at the very least we understand that the mathematical tools we should be using in our planning work include linear algebraic equilibrium equations, large-scale linear programming models, and, finally, what has now evolved: mathematical programming that ties together primitive and dual solutions.

Value human resources: recognize the need to use non-linear models

Economic growth around the world relies more and more on human resources and on motivating those resources. In many industries, the investment put into developing human resources is greater than that put into fixed assets. Many companies now make it part of their strategic plan to use competitive hiring of technical and scientific personnel and management personnel.

In contrast, traditional planning still mainly relies on investment in fixed assets as the sole engine that drives economic growth. The Harrod-Domar model in development economics is an example of this. One of the reasons for this is that using a single factor is much easier when doing planning calculations and modeling. One only needs to use linear equations or linear programming.

If you are using linear equations, the importance of developing human resources poses challenges however. It also presents much greater complexities when trying to do the work of resource allocation. Mathematically, the way you express production capacity must be through the use of non-linear functions, given the numbers of production factors involved. Only then can you truly reflect the purpose of combining factors, and show how substitutions of factors would work. At the same time, the appearance of this kind of non-linear function makes resource allocation extremely difficult. That applies to allocation by a plan as well as to allocation by a market. With respect to planning models, it means that the process of finding solutions relies on much higher technology and science.

Many important relationships in economic activity in fact exhibit non-linear qualities, not just production equations. For example, some demand equations and income distribution systems are of this nature. In the past, one way to deal technically with non-linearity was to convert the data into log-linear expressions and solve the equations via linear techniques. At this time, however, given our current modeling of the national economy and the way we do our planning, it is impossible for us to transform all data into linear equations.

What that means is that we must use a non-linear model that connects the primitive to a dual-price system if we want to improve the way in which we plan our national economy. In other words, the difficulty of even our improved planning process makes using this kind of non-linear model appropriate. We should take note of the fact that it is hard to derive solutions from such models, however, particularly when they are on a massive scale.

The fortunate thing is that modern technological advances provide us with tools and methods at the right time. The speed and size of computing power serves as the basis for computing these solutions. Non-linear programming that is based on computer technology has improved greatly in the past two decades. Meanwhile, a major discovery was made in the 1970s which plays an indirect role in all of this, and that is the way economists and mathematicians have been able to capitalize on the development of "topology and the fixed-point theorem" to work out effective solutions to general equilibrium. The following section will demonstrate that, in terms of their framework, the primitive-dual non-linear programming models and the "general equilibrium model that consists of non-linear functions" have an equivalent relationship. The two models can therefore serve as a reference for each other in terms of their solutions.

Moving from a closed economy to an open economy

In simple terms, in a traditional closed economy, imports and exports are used to make up for imbalances, both oversupply and undersupply. As much as possible, a country exports its surplus goods in order to earn hard currency and import things that it lacks. Meanwhile, it tries to maintain a balance of payments in foreign exchange. This process does not, however, do anything to explain why there are surpluses, shortages, and a structure that is oversupplied and undersupplied at the same time. It does not explain whether or not such a structure is rational and "optimum."

From the thought processes implied by how we formulated the plan for 2000, as part of China's 6th Five-Year Plan, I had the sense that our long-term plan is perpetually aimed at making up deficiencies in "short-line" production capacity. That is, the entire plan is aimed at reducing "undersupplies."

In contrast, the thought processes implied by an open economy include participating in the international division of labor in ways that focus on increasing the advantageous "oversupplies." Such an economy is not too worried about the "undersupplies." Put more rigorously, an open economy exports when it is more advantageous to do so than to sell the products domestically. It imports when it is better to import than to produce domestically. When prices are distorted, so-called "benefits" are not measured by the profit margin in current prices. Instead, they are measured by the degree to which they realize economic goals for the entire national economy. That is, they use a reasonable kind of shadow price.

This kind of improvement is extremely hard to incorporate into our current planning processes. It also is not easy, however, to determine how to handle imbalances through the use of imports and exports—which kinds of products to export, how much to export, and so on. Moreover, a glance at the process shows that decisions on what to export and so on are also distorted by the influence of current prices. Meanwhile, policy makers are trying to consider things from a comprehensive macroeconomic perspective, but the policy-making process and its methodology is a very mixed bag. It is impossible to ensure that "policy principles" are in fact strictly followed.

If we were to use modern mathematical programming to model an open economy, this would not present too many difficulties in terms of theory or methodology. The principles by which policy decisions are made would be clear and expressed in ways that give people confidence. Naturally, the scale of the model would be larger and calculations would take longer and be more complex.

The idea of moving toward an "open economy" has special significance for a centrally-planned economy. Small countries that are neighbors with western markets have an advantage in that their border price basically is a "reasonable shadow price." This makes it easier to use the law of value and computer modeling in calculations. For large countries, particularly those that require long-distance transport of goods, where transport and port facilities are limited and where exports consist mainly of primary goods, it can be demonstrated that the border price is not equivalent to the shadow price. Using outside prices is therefore not helpful in addressing the difficulties and complexity of domestic planning models and the law of value. Naturally, border prices can still provide highly important information that can be taken into reference.

Moving from static to dynamic

Any individual might tend to think that the words "dynamic" and "long-term" imply better things than "static" and "short-term," or even "annual." In fact, to a policy-planning person, these terms "dynamic" and "long-term" imply much more difficult and complex work and the need for deeper understanding.

Some people might say that the description of planning methods as described above overlooks the most important work of the State Planning Commission, namely decisions about projects that require major investment and guarantees for such projects. I would argue, however, that the balanced relationships and overall purpose of production are far more fundamental considerations.

So-called "dynamic" planning is an issue that must be considered over the cycles of many years. That is to say, investment in projects is done in order to realize better economic balance in the future. Either directly or indirectly, its purpose is to ensure a better material and cultural context for people's needs. For this reason, we must first answer a rather imprecise question: how much do we really know about balancing things in the future and about meeting future demand? Do we have any reliable forecasting methods? If we believe we do, and if our degree of error is not too great, then we should be able to use planning models as described in the above six sections to resolve dynamic and long-term planning issues.

Naturally, the task of such planning is much greater than that for static planning, as is its scale. The truly difficult problem comes when we have very little knowledge of future conditions. What we come up with for the future has a great deal of uncertainty. Assessing probabilities and dynamic plans are far more difficult. In theory, what we need to use then is random mathematical programming. Unfortunately, we do not yet have the tools to do that, whether they are mathematically based or computer based.

Another unfortunate thing is that it is increasingly difficult to forecast the future given the information explosion and the speed with which science and technology is developing. It would have been difficult for people to predict today's video cameras ten years ago, or what the cost of and demand for personal computers might be. Thirty or 40 years ago, Japanese people were lucky to be able to watch how the western European countries and the United States progressed in plotting out their own path of development. Japan then used industrial policy to guide its long-term development. When South Korea tried the same approach, though, the timing had changed and the results were "mixed" to the extent that industrial policy led that country into serious mistakes.

Another major challenge results from what the "Turnpike Theorem" has to tell us about economic growth. This can manifest itself in complex ways, but its overall implications are that balanced growth is the most efficient path to growth.

In short, traditional concepts are now being challenged. We can describe this in terms of an example from the field of nutrition. When a person knows for sure that he will get sick due to lacking some nutritional element right now, he should start supplementing his diet immediately with that element. If he does not know for sure what he needs, however, his best course of action is to maintain health every day, month, and year, and not consume things in any unusual way. That is, he should take a static approach to his nutrition. In this sense, "static" is not to be equated with being short-sighted. Only when we know about the future with great certainty should we deviate from the static equilibrium, and only then is the term "dynamic" more meaningful.

When dynamic programming is indeed a necessary step, it will be superior to "recurring formulas that apply to a static state" only when it is accompanied by effective methodologies. In light of our current methodologies and conclusions, neither of these approaches is very persuasive.

Proof of the equivalent price nature of modeling

This section focuses on comparing the economic performance of a market economy to an "improved" planned economy, after one makes the various assumptions described above and after a number of major improvements are made to our planning process. First, I must explain two preconditions necessary for the above analysis.

First, since a planned economy must respect the law of value, one can assume that all factors of production will be properly rewarded for their contribution to achieving the goals of the national economy. Because of this, the planned economy will not practice a system whereby everyone gets the same amount in the primary distribution of income. As for the policy role of redistribution of income, we assume that it does not fundamentally disturb or change the incentive system.

Second, according to many western microeconomic textbooks, a "market" leads to the optimum distribution of resources and this "optimum" is defined as satisfying the greatest amount of need for products and labor as defined by the after-tax purchasing power of citizens. This is the first theorem of welfare economics. It is the expression of computable general equilibrium. Other than differences in terminology and details, this goal of optimization is not fundamentally different from the goals of socialist production.

The above two points may seem to bear no direct relationship to what follows, but a close analysis will show that they are essential.

There is something called the Kahn-Tucker theorem in mathematical programming. In reality, this is a popularized and further developed expression of the Lagrange theorem. The Lagrange theorem deals with the issue of extreme values in calculus. Let us first take a fairly simplified form of an improved planned-economy model as our blueprint. I use the primitive-dual connection non-linear programming model. I use the Kahn-Tucker theorem to convert that in order to find the conditions for optimization. To our surprise, we find that the conditions are completely in accord with the conditions of the general equilibrium model. Going further, we can say that the two models are equivalent, or are the dual expression of one another.

If we use an open type of planned-economy model, in which imports and exports are carried out according to optimizing principles, then any work comparing the models is much more complex. However, if the import and export plan does indeed satisfy the optimized requirements of the target equation (object function), we still find that the optimized model of the primitive-dual connection non-linear model is equivalent to or has a dual relationship with the general equilibrium model.

This kind of "proof of equivalence" is significant. It shows that an improved form of planned economy can arrive at the optimization of resource allocation. That is, it can arrive at a Pareto optimum. In terms of resource allocation, therefore, it is not inferior to a market economy. Turning this around, however, under specified income redistribution structures, a market economy can also arrive at a situation that satisfies the goods and labor needs of the people to the greatest degree; that is, it can also satisfy social welfare objectives.

This serves to explain two different things. First, neither system can be described as superior or inferior merely through the use of abstract expressions. Second, it is vital that we address this question of how an improved planned-economy system is going to compete with a market system, through using analysis described in the six sections above.

Some people involved in the actual conduct of planning may criticize this as being intentionally abstruse. It does not address problems that our actual work urgently needs to address. The significance of proving equivalence lies in the following: if planners do not comprehend the meaning of improvements, they will find it hard to triumph over market economies in the course of competition.

This article is not yet able to compare the performance of medium- and long-term dynamic plans with the growth trajectory of the general equilibrium of a market economy. The reason is that the theory and practice behind a planned economy have not yet stipulated the principles and methodology that should be applied to medium- and long-term dynamic plans in any rigorous way.

Another key implication lies in the above proof of equivalence. That is, even after a planned economy is improved upon, and is able to take advantage of the latest technological tools, it still is not able to surpass the simplest market economy in terms of performance. Many examples in the world indicate that manmade systems are not as good as natural systems, and complex systems are not as good as simple ones. In philosophical terms, this presents a challenge to man's intelligence and desire to transform nature.

If we remove the two assumptions that are presented at the start of this article, namely, excellent information transmission and behavior of multiple levels of cadres that conforms to central government, the situation becomes more serious. Generally speaking, the information demands of a centrally-planned system are simply too great, while the costs of transmitting that information are extreme. What's more, it is not easy to make sure that all levels of cadres are totally aligned with the views of central planners.

What this means is that our centrally-planned economy is facing a monumental task if it wants to advance. Discussing that is outside the scope of this article.

Naturally, one could always come to a different conclusion. That is, that the theoretical model of a market economy has fundamental fallacies which tend to exaggerate its performance. This relates to the assumptions first presented in this article, as well as the research of a number of western economists over the past century or more.

A modest initial conclusion

This article looks at the directions and methods by which centrally-planned economies can be improved upon, within a certain scope of analysis. Within this limited scope, the article poses some useful assumptions. Exploratory results indicate that when improvements in the work of planning use non-linear optimized programming models that incorporate a primitive-dual connection type of open economy, the planned-economy system exhibits real improvement in many respects. Moreover, it can optimize the distribution of resources within a certain horizon. At the same time, we must admit that its performance after improvement does not yet surpass the performance of a Pareto optimum.

In the face of international competition, market economies are also improving themselves. One such improvement involves increased use of macroeconomic regulatory systems, and another is increased use of redistribution policies that are oriented toward a welfare society. Given international competition, centrally-planned economies cannot argue for their superiority purely in terms of abstract principles. They must specifically document the directions and principles by which they intend to improve. Ultimately, they must stand up to comparison in the real world.

As for the subject of integrating planned and market mechanisms, the ultimate issue is to clarify the advantages and shortcomings of each type of system after substantial improvements have been made. For now, at the very least it can be said that in the places where markets are ineffective, such as public finance, certain externalities, and in the context of natural monopolies, planned intervention is a more effective mechanism. In those areas in which markets can operate normally, the answer may well be determined by whether or not we find a better system. That possibility includes finding a kind of "mixed" system.

Among other things, this article attempts to point out that the competition among systems is intense on a global basis. We must absorb, and even go out to find, state-of-the-art knowledge and techniques that will allow us to design and improve our own system. A traditional way of thinking that is mainly character-ized by criticizing capitalism is not good enough. The many new developments in the world, including the information explosion, the diversification of demand, the uncertainties of the future, and the development of human resources, are all presenting new challenges to every system. It is imperative that we not overlook one crucial challenge, which is to recognize the important and formidable task of choosing the right system. This task must, moreover, pull together every bit of scientific effort that we can muster.

Note

1 This article was originally published in *Reform*, 1991, Vol. 1.

2   An economic analysis of housing reform[1]

(1991)

Housing reform and social security reform are two key elements of our overall reform in the near future. Many municipalities have already made housing reform their primary focus as they plan their economic structural reforms. Housing is a major supporting pillar in our strategy to increase and to restructure consumption. Increasing the size and quality of living quarters will also serve to increase the amounts of other types of products that are consumed. Having the public participate in funding the development of our housing industry is one path well worth considering.

At the same time, housing reform must take the issue of equity into consideration. If one portion of the population puts out a great deal of money to purchase what another part of the population is still getting for free, this particular reform policy will not be effective. In fact, housing reform can be regarded as the largest component of price reform. In what follows, I emphasize the economic aspect of the analysis. This is to ensure that our approach to housing reform is thorough, and has taken all things into consideration.

Principles of housing reform

Three principles characterize housing reform. The first is turning housing into a commodity (that is bought and sold). The second is ensuring that citizens all have their "rightful place to live." The third is transforming hidden subsidies into open subsidies, and then turning these into a component of wages.

These three principles are mutually interrelated. Turning housing into a commodity means handling the issue according to the law of value, and reforming the pricing system of housing. Ensuring that citizens have a place to live means enabling the great majority of municipal employees and their families to have the wherewithal to purchase their own home. It also means taking care of low-income people as appropriate and ensuring that they have basic housing.

This plan for housing reform starts out with housing rental and housing prices, which means that it also involves wage levels and propels further reform of our wage system. For this reason, after we have clearly understood the principles and significance of housing reform, we must set up the framework for analyzing a full set of economic and policy considerations. This will enable us to design policies correctly.

Considering housing reform from the aspect of reducing public spending by the State and reducing the subsidies that enterprises grant to employees

Our first priority is to get a clear idea of exactly how much in the way of subsidies our current system is providing. Our subsequent analysis will then be divided into several steps so that we can move fairly quickly from hidden subsidies to open subsidies, and then on to defining the subsidy amounts as wages.

For the great majority of production enterprises, in industrial or in the tertiary industries, labor costs include a portion that could be considered a normal housing rent. Naturally, in the future the State will continue to use two different methods to maintain certain subsidies. One is for low-income earners or one-career families, that is, single employees without families. (For the great majority of middle-income earners there will no longer be such a subsidy.) This policy-type of subsidy, in the category of redistribution of income, is in the interests of social fairness and is done to ensure the basic needs of all inhabitants. The second is for government employees. (This includes people working in the fields of medicine, education, and other public endeavors.) We may want to consider an exception for these people in order to stabilize our ranks of public workers (i.e. to retain people). We do that by not "realizing" wages in entirety (that is, we maintain a portion of wages as a housing subsidy).

Our methodology for analyzing housing policy has some problems

There are two main lines of thought with respect to housing reform right now. One feels that we should be thorough in straightening out the housing system. This takes into consideration the fact that both the State and enterprises cannot bear too great a burden at this initial stage of socialist development. The subsidies should be appropriate to our abilities. At the same time, we should undertake fundamental "commodification" of housing, so that housing too is in line with the law of value. This is a more holistic type of long-term thinking about reform altogether.

The second line of thought is more short-term in its thinking. It aims to generate funds in the near future by turning housing into a commodity. If that reduces the burden of subsidies, that also is fine, but the main point is to enliven the housing industry and create a market for the construction industry. This approach has not given much thought to other considerations. It does not include thorough preparation for fundamental change in the housing system.

There are two problems with the analytical approach of the second line of thought.

First, it does not take the time value of money into account in considering the whole issue of turning housing into a commodity. The result is that it underestimates housing prices and rent prices. Let us take an example. A 40 to 50 square meter apartment for two people is roughly in line with China's current level of economic development. If each square meter were priced at RMB 800–1,000, the couple buying this apartment should be able to pay for it in installments over a period of 30 years. On the surface of it, the apartment costs roughly RMB 40,000. This overlooks the whole issue of interest, however. RMB 40,000 is not the total sum paid out for the apartment. One has to consider the cash flow necessary to fund the payments, and this cash flow is generally underestimated.

Second, housing reform will lead to a change in the equilibrium point of three major markets. Because of this, housing must be considered in concert with other things. Housing reform is the largest type of price reform in terms of the total sum of money it affects. This total sum is quite sufficient to impact wage levels, for wages must increase to a degree before housing can in fact become a commodity, before people can purchase it. Wages are a labor cost. When this cost is entered into the prices of all kinds of produced goods, the market for all those goods is affected. The price equilibrium of markets for those goods must necessarily change. As housing reform takes hold, the production costs will be "realized" or expressed in ongoing price increases. Wages will be "realized," costs will be "realized," depreciation will be "realized," interest rates will be "realized." The equilibrium prices of many goods will be affected and will change. For a very considerable number of our companies that are either making a loss, or close to making a loss, and particularly for our enterprises that produce primary goods which we have priced at very low levels, pressures to increase wage levels will have a considerable impact on the prices of goods that they produce.

This will then cause a chain reaction due to the input–output nature of goods production. It will generate a comprehensive shift in equilibrium. Meanwhile, it is unclear whether or not wage increases will respond completely to increases in the level of overall prices. In addition to impacting product markets and labor costs, this chain reaction will have an impact on the cost of money. Housing reform should therefore be seen as involving changes in the equilibrium of the entire economy. We might decide to take too small a step at the outset, however, thinking to limit the impact on commodity prices. That is, we might use a different kind of subsidy to maintain original prices, but we are then simply replacing one kind of price distortion with another. We are shifting the distortion and not resolving the issue in any fundamental way.

A few municipalities are leading the way in housing reform as pilot projects. These will be affected by changes in price equilibrium. As the commodity prices of goods produced in their factories rise, these factories will be in an unfavorable competitive position relative to cities that have not instituted housing reform. There will then be pressure to avoid "realization" of wages. Some units in pilot areas have tried to turn "hidden subsidies" into "housing certificates" as a first stage in turning subsidized housing into wages. Although the first step has been quite small, it implies that there will be a second, third, fourth, and fifth step until housing is truly turned into a commodity.

The methodology being used to date suffers from being over-simplified and short-sighted. It does not take the full scope of ramifications into consideration. Once the second step runs into problems, it will be hard to muster the determination to carry on.

Accounting problems that relate to housing reform

Again, let us take an example. A couple decides to purchase an apartment that has a current price of RMB 40,000, and they pay for this in installments over 30 years. These installments should be entered into the amount they are paid as wages. In doing so, one has to take account of the time value of money. If there is no advance payment, and the interest rate is roughly 8 percent, then the couple needs to pay RMB 292 per month. Each pays one-half, so each pays RMB 146 per month. At the end of 30 years, they own the apartment and, in current terms, they have paid out RMB 105,000. This sum should not be overlooked when an enterprise is allocating monthly wage amounts that incorporate "realized" housing.

Some people may use a low interest rate to figure the total. For example, they lower the 8 percent to 5.3 percent, so that the total monthly payment is around RMB 222 and each person pays roughly RMB 111. The total paid out after 30 years then becomes RMB 80,000, but that is still twice the original RMB 40,000.

Naturally, there will be those who want to use an even lower interest rate, or some other method of accounting. Some people will say that we should not allocate this entire amount into the accounting for wages, that during this transition period in China we should perhaps maintain a certain level of subsidy. Whether it is the government or the enterprise paying out this subsidy, however, in the end we have to figure out exactly how much it is. We need a calculation in mind. What's more, we will need to think about what kind of welfare policies we should plan for over a certain number of years into the future so as to cover these subsidies (that is, should we reduce subsidies, or should we institute taxation policies to ensure that we cover the subsidies?).

If we use an interest rate that is lower than 5 percent, this implies that we are simply shifting the subsidy to another form of payment. Interest rates reflect the opportunity cost of money and the discount rate that society places on money. When GNP grows at an annual rate of around 6 percent, most investments in production industries can return that or more. Naturally, we can use a variety of financial measures to realize low interest rates, but artificially low interest rates can only be realized by subsidizing the rates in other areas, or making up the gap between the interest rates and the actual discount rate in society. Meanwhile, the actual discount rate in society is to a certain degree determined by objective laws.

One way of subsidizing interest rates is for the government to provide subsidies to banks as they in turn provide mortgages to people. (Or the government can set up "policy-type lenders" itself.) If the government takes interest rates down to zero, then the couple as described above pays only RMB 40,000 and that's it. If the real interest rate at equilibrium is 8 percent, however, this implies that the government is subsidizing the buyers to the tune of around RMB 65,000. It is, moreover, handing over all property rights to the apartment to individuals.

We cannot use a new price distortion to substitute for an old price distortion. What that means is that we cannot artificially put our subsidized interest rate for housing purchases at too low a level. Another method is for the buyer to deposit his purchase funds into a bank, which provides him with a low interest rate in return. This is a contractual method by which he receives preferential rights to housing in return for low rates. In fact, this is like the realization that wool comes off the back of a sheep that you've got to care for—that is, you get what you pay for in the end. You are getting preferential rights to housing by paying a high price.

This method also relates to two other questions that must be addressed. First, when does ownership of the apartment actually begin? Does this constitute preferential treatment? Second, can younger people rely on the income of their parents for purchasing housing, and is this a reasonable outcome in terms of equitable distribution?

Even if we subsidize interest rates as a way to maintain a certain subsidy for housing, all of the above methods will still have to deal with the issue of "realizing" wages. At the low rate of 5.3 percent, the couple as described above each pays out RMB 111 per month and only gets property rights to the apartment after 30 years of paying in installments. If wages double over that time, so that they come to around RMB 300–400, then the monthly installments are roughly one-third of income. International comparisons indicate that this is a reasonable level. If we use existing low wage rates, however, the couple will almost certainly not be able to make the payments.

Our current wage rates were never intended to cover a normal fee for housing. At the same time, we never thought that the cost of building housing would be distributed over the costs of all goods produced in the economy. The extent of wage reform is so great, however, that it has a major impact on price stability and equilibrium. It is very helpful, therefore, to look at the entire aspect of housing reform when we design policy and come up with steps for implementation.

Turning housing into a commodity has very clear implications for tax revenues

"Realizing" the actual cost of wages will be a major quantitative event, so we must take the taxes that the enterprise pays into account. Housing reform places new demands on our tax system. We must consider how the tax base of the enterprise will be reduced, and how the tax base of indirect taxes will be increased.

First the realization of wages will increase the cost of labor. This will lead to a clear increase in the tax base of value-added tax. As the enterprise's profits are reduced, this will lead to a smaller tax base for direct taxes. If we do not institute coordinated policies that go along with tax revenue changes and the new tax base structure, our aggregate tax revenues may drop precipitously. We must therefore take into consideration the comparative relationship between direct and indirect taxes, and the relationship among different kinds of taxes and tax rates. Once our housing reform takes a larger step, or once we finish the first step and get ready for the second and third, we must carefully consider the whole issue of our tax base. If we take very small steps, we still have the problem of not knowing exactly how much in the way of subsidies we are providing. The accounting is unclear. After the fact, we may discover tax implications that we did not anticipate early on due to this lack of clarity.

Housing reform is the largest component of price reform

The nation's price index will be far more impacted by turning housing into a commodity than by any other reform. The impact of housing reform will far surpass the impact of price reform on the means of production. It will have a greater impact than reform of exchange rates and the liberalization of prices on all goods and services.

In the course of doing preparatory work for price reform in recent years, we have done fairly detailed analysis of the situation as it relates to the means of production. We have measured the extent to which hidden subsidies will become "open" subsidies as we turn State-mandated prices into prices set by the market. We have felt that we should turn essentially all, or the greater part of, hidden subsidies into "open subsidies," and then allocate "open subsidies" by head count in any given enterprise. If that is not reasonable, we then go a step further in reforming the wages of the enterprise. All of these price reforms should create a synchronized process that includes market prices of goods and costs of wages. That is, if changes in price levels lead to more reasonable prices, we can, to a greater or lesser extent, allow wages to rise in order not to lower standards of living.

Rising wages will create changes in production costs. Changes in costs will again lead to price hikes for some goods. For enterprises that are either making a loss already or making very little profit, we should either allow them to raise prices on goods or we should ask them to get out of the market and find other ways to survive. Changes in this synchronized process are a stepped or phased process that yields results at each stage. The idea is to eventually approach a new equilibrium.

It is precisely because price reform is necessarily linked to wages and impacts the entire society that it has faced such setbacks. At a certain stage, people begin to equivocate and lose their determination. They are concerned about the capacity of people to bear the results. For this reason, it may be that we have done inadequate preparation if we intend to put housing reform at the forefront of our price reform. We have not demonstrated the sequential nature of this reform, or prepared for coordinating policies that must accompany it. These things deserve some balanced reflection.

Housing prices are seriously distorted with regard to the extent to which prices are distorted throughout the entire economy. Our housing system has very major problems. In terms of our subsidies to society overall, those for housing stand out as foremost—they constitute the largest subsidy. (We must remember that we have never done any real accounting to calculate housing as a commodity. This has allowed us to be rather unclear about the difficulties involved in housing reform.) In terms of "shock value," that is, in terms of the ability of people to tolerate the effects of housing reform, this reform will be more severe than any other as well.

The influence of housing reform on income distribution results

At present, the way some areas are handling housing reform is a cause for concern in terms of the equity of income distribution. They are using a "two-track" pricing method. In Step One of the sale of "commodity housing," each of three parties bears the burden of paying one-third of the price. That is, the State, the enterprise, and the individual each cover one-third. These areas, however, are allowing the individual to pay his one-third of the price in installments. If the installments are spread out over 30 years, the individual can buy the flat by paying only one-sixth of the total price.

Once the flat is bought, a number of questions remain about the subsidy and actual property rights to the flat. "Transferring" (or selling) the flat is currently not allowed. If this becomes allowed in the future, however, then the question becomes whether or not the owner also has to pay back the subsidy.

This kind of pilot program has a great many loopholes in it. It is very hard to keep the new owner from "renting out" his flat, or selling it in actuality by using an alias or through a front. Since China's entire economy is in the process of correcting distortions, and reducing subsidies, the second stage of housing reform may not be the same as the first. The second stage may have less favorable conditions. By that time, the State and the enterprise may well not be able to cover one-third each of the price, which means the individual will have to cover more. Instead of paying one-sixth of the total, he now may have to pay one-third. The final group of people who participate in housing reform may actually have to pay one-half the price.

As time goes on, the percentage that an individual has to pay out will definitely increase. The question for policy makers is whether or not this is an acceptable kind of income distribution policy. Right now, the average wage-earner cannot afford to purchase his home. People who are better off are able to seize the opportunity to buy now, and they are able to buy at the lower prices. Average wage-earners will buy at a higher price, while low-income people are even less able to pay right now and will only come at the end of the line, if ever. This end-result is not in line with socialist principles of equity. Not only is the distribution of subsidies unequal, but it actually favors those with a higher income.

The positive side of housing reform is that it provides the opportunity for people to buy housing at all. Often, however, it is the elderly in a household that help their son or daughter buy a home. This too has implications for income distribution. When generations are living together in one home, the son or daughter may just have started work and may not have sufficient income to purchase a home. As a result, the parents put up hard-earned money that they have saved for years. They then are not able to enjoy that money in later life. This in fact exploits a percentage of the retirement funds of the older generation. The distribution in terms of age cohort is not equitable. If, on the other hand, our overall reform is undertaken in a thorough way, we hope to enable younger people to have enough in wages to pay for themselves. They should be able to pay either higher rents or pay for ownership through installments.

Meanwhile, the allocation of housing as performed by units was never even-handed. Some industries had housing and others did not. Some units had neither housing nor the money to build or buy. Each one has therefore adopted its own ways and means for its employees as it undertakes reform, and this has led to a disparity in the selling price of housing. Price disparities are another issue when it comes to evaluating the reasonableness of income distribution policies.

One way to overcome unequal income distribution as we undertake housing reform is to require that those who have more space pay more in rent. As an income distribution policy measure, this should be done over a broad area, how-ever. Other considerations should be taken into account. For example, in the past, different grade levels of cadres were allowed different levels of compensation but these were generally not in the form of salary. Other means were used. For exam-ple, the salary difference between a department head and a section head might not be that great, but the department head received more in the way of medical care, housing, assistance with transportation, and so on. All of these material forms of compensation made the difference in grade levels quite substantial. How does housing reform intend to deal with these issues? Does it intend to increase the degree of egalitarian treatment, or does it intend to incorporate all of the major compensation differentials into differences in wages? If we adopt the latter course of action, it will still be hard to resolve the legacy of non-monetary assets that were a part of our earlier days. I am referring here to the distorting effect of the already existing "inventory." If we do not admit that disparities in compensation already exist, not only will this conflict with our income distribution principles, it will also make housing reform all that much harder.

Note

1   This article was originally published in the third issue of *Comprehensive Economic and Social Systems* in 1991.

3 Moving toward an open economy[1]
(1992)

A socialist market economy should be an open economy

The Third Plenary Session of the 11th Central Committee of the Communist Party of China confirmed the overall policy line with respect to structural reform of China's economy and its "opening up." The term "opening up" was used with respect to China's comparatively closed economic system of the past. In English, the term is described as an "open door policy." In a metaphorical way, this describes a door that is in the process of opening from having been basically shut. At the beginning, it opens a little, then gradually a little more. But exactly how far it opens, to what degree, is something that has not to date been answered in any clear way. The reason is that "opening up" is a dynamic process. It is not demarcated by any explicitly defined goal that will serve as the "model" in the end.

We should in fact be more explicit about what kind of economic model we want to achieve in the end by "opening up to the outside." In the same way, "reform" as a term has the problem of no clearly defined end result. From the time when it first began, reform has gone through a process. Economic structural reform began with importing market mechanisms as a regulatory means, it confirmed "socialist production" goals, it allowed the use of material incentives, and it was gradually extended to enterprises, prices, public finance, taxation, banking and finance, domestic and international trade, and so on. The Third Plenary Session of the 12th Central Committee of the Communist Party of China (1984) then confirmed a "socialist commodity economy." By the time of the 13th National Party Congress (1987), the mutual interconnectedness of government, market, and enterprises was confirmed. By now, everyone has reached a consensus which is that China should establish a socialist market economy. Now, a better understanding of the ultimate "target model" of reform will have a profound influence on realizing and furthering reform.

In similar fashion, the question could be asked about what kind of model should correspond to the process of "opening up." I personally feel that the model corresponding to a socialist market economy should be one that is an "open economy." There are certain distinctions between an open economy and "opening up to the outside." From the perspective of economic concepts and models, "opening up to the outside" is a process and an orientation. One could apply it to almost anything.

An open economy, in contrast, is specifically used to contrast a system with a "closed economy." An open economy places emphasis on the way that the domestic economy is linked in to the overall international market. It seeks to participate in the international division of labor as much as possible. At the same time, it seeks to make use of its comparative advantage in the international division of labor.

An open economy is one in which businesses are responsible for their own profits and losses in international markets. They operate autonomously, with "open" operations and in the context of systems that allow for entry into businesses and markets. Not only are they distinct from the traditional State trading system of the centrally-planned economy, but they should be differentiated from excessive protectionism, that is, from any system that uses tariffs and non-tariff barriers to entry to cut off economic systems from a country's domestic markets as well as international markets.

Although international markets also have many unsound aspects, and certain developed countries also carry on a degree of protectionism, an "open economy" operates in ways that makes these the exception. Speaking in overall terms, an open economy signifies a fairly high degree of participation in international markets and the international division of labor. Moreover, it espouses liberalized trade systems.

One point should be noted here, which is that the concept of an open economy is somewhat different from what people usually think of as an "export-oriented economy." Many people believe that the definition of an "open economy" is determined by the percentage of foreign trade in GNP. If the percentage is high, the country is relatively "export-oriented." In fact, this depends to a large extent on the size of the country. Small countries might have foreign trade volume that exceeds their GNP, while the trade volume percentage of a large economy with a large domestic market may be small. An open economy mainly focuses on the extent to which a country's domestic economy is linked up with the international economy.

Of course we should note that the World Bank has come to redefine the term "export-oriented economy." By now, its definition relates mainly to an even-handed policy approach of encouraging exports while practicing import substitution. It refers to policies that are more neutral in this regard and that do not have a bias toward either one. In this sense, an export-oriented economy is no different from an open economy.

In the past dozen or so years, as China was becoming "market-oriented," the country had already moved considerably in opening up to the outside. In the past, when we talked about opening up as a concept, we mainly meant things like exchanging people and technologies, importing foreign investment, opening up special trade zones, and developing cities along the coast. Special Economic Zones, for example, fall under the jurisdiction of the Office of Special Economic Zones under the State Council. In fact, however, the extent to which a country is "open" depends mainly on its trade system. This holds for all countries in the world, on an international basis.

Making foreign trade "market-oriented" is a prerequisite for achieving a degree of openness in trade. Attracting in foreign investment and technological exchange can only result if the international flow of production factors is liberalized and facilitated. The more we place controls on trade, the more this limits the extent to which we can open up or liberalize in other areas. China has first-hand experience of this. This article therefore looks at how to move toward an open economy from the specific perspective of our trading system. It seeks to improve our conceptual understanding of "opening to the outside" by looking at the fundamentals of the issue.

First, let us evaluate how far we have come in opening up our trade system to date.

1 In terms of product markets, economists estimate that some 60 to 70 percent of China's product prices are currently determined by market supply and demand relationships. Naturally, the forces of supply and demand are not necessarily at a point of general equilibrium and prices have not necessarily reached equilibrium as a result. The prices of certain very important raw materials are not determined by the market. At the same time, we have such things as intervention and imperfect market behavior such that pricing is not able to reach an ideal Pareto optimum. As compared to our previous system, however, the traditional system by which the government set prices, the country's prices are basically now determined by supply and demand.

2 In terms of economic structure, the total volume of imports and exports has increased dramatically. In 1991, the aggregate volume of foreign trade reached over USD 130 billion. China is moving toward the front ranks of foreign trade in the world in terms of total trade volume. The structure of our imports and exports is also getting better. The structure of exports in particular shows that manufactured goods are increasing and are by now around 75 percent of the total.

3 In terms of trade policies, we have made good progress. We are gradually achieving a situation in which foreign trade enterprises are responsible for their own profits and losses. We are eliminating export subsidies. While granting autonomy in operations to trade enterprises, we are integrating the two functions of "industry" and "trade," and "technology" and "trade" in opening up various sectors of imports and exports. What that means is that a number of industrial enterprises are now able to handle their own foreign trade directly. They can develop international markets themselves, as well as work through agents.

On the import side, we are increasingly lowering non-tariff trade barriers and administrative interference. The percentage of importing done by autonomous decision-making on the part of microeconomic entities is growing. We have basically eliminated import subsidies. The degree to which enterprises have the freedom to make their own purchases on international markets is growing. At the same time, we are opening up the foreign exchange "adjustment" market. We have adjusted the exchange rate a number of times so that the RMB is more in line with convertibility, that is, with a real currency exchange value, in how we manage foreign exchange.

4 While transforming the model by which we conduct foreign trade, we have already made progress in terms of the flow of capital, particularly with respect to attracting in foreign investment. Some of our own enterprises are also already investing overseas. We have made enormous progress in terms of commercial law and the protection of intellectual property.

Despite this progress, for the past three years the World Bank has continued to classify China as a "generally inward-looking country" in its classification of economies into four types. (Those are inward-looking, generally inward-looking, outward-looking, and generally outward-looking.) What this means is that we have made some progress in opening up to the outside but we have not reached a level of being "outward-looking." Our own self-evaluation might be more optimistic, but this is what the World Bank says. In short, we still have a long road ahead of us. To start with, we need to specify the direction we will be taking, which is towards an "open economy."

A "socialist market economy" includes recognizing the positive role played by the market in allocating resources

The Stalinist model of economics, that is, the traditional form of the study of centrally-planned economies, views a market economy as being both "blind" and a form of "anarchism" (literally "without government" in the Chinese term). In contrast, a planned economy alone can function with the help of a plan. It "develops" the economy of the country according to proportions. (The author uses the active form of the verb. That is, the economy is something that is done by the government.)

Traditional classical economics and neo-classical economics have, instead, demonstrated that the market is an effective way to allocate resources. It assumes that general equilibrium will be reached if the three major markets are sound and complete, namely the markets for products, labor, and capital. Such equilibrium is defined as the Pareto optimum. That is, resources have been allocated in the optimum way. Naturally, economics in our modern age has built upon that foundation and generated a number of schools of thought. All of these admit that the market is not effective in certain specific aspects. New theoretical ideas crop up all the time that explore how to supplement the market when it fails, so as to achieve better allocation of resources.

Our actual reform experience over all these years has, in fact, been an exercise in introducing market mechanisms. At the same time, it has been a process of enabling these market mechanisms to play a larger role. In both theoretical and conceptual terms, however, we have not explicitly come up with a definition of the benefits of a market economy. In the past, our understanding was that these benefits included mobilizing the enthusiasm of people and thereby generating competitive pressures so that we could revitalize the economy. The idea was to get rid of things that did not work and support those that did. Our ongoing understanding was also, however, that a market was not efficient in allocating resources and that it would lead to tremendous waste. In our formal discussions, therefore, we continued to criticize the market as being "blind," and as being anarchistic. We continued to think that only planned measures would be effective in allocating resources.

Some cadres among us gradually began to realize that more efficient allocation of resources and motivating people were two sides to the same thing. If improper mechanisms are used to try to allocate resources, then you can't generate effective incentive mechanisms. If incentive mechanisms are sound, that will definitely help in optimizing resource allocation. These necessarily are two aspects of the same concept. From the perspective of mathematical modeling, the two bear a thesis and antithesis relationship to one another.

We have begun to reach consensus about the idea that the "target mode" of China's economic reform should be "a socialist market economy." This dates from the time of the 14th National Congress of the Communist Party of China. The question then is, "what exactly is a socialist market economy?" What are its core features?

I believe that we need to be clear about the fact that a market economy is an effective means of allocating resources. Transforming our old way of thinking about it is profoundly significant in terms of economic theory. If we recognize that a market is effective in allocating resources, this cuts through a whole series of other theoretical questions like a sharp knife. Since domestic markets are highly imperfect, reforming our pricing system and cultivating markets will become a major goal of reform. If we admit that international markets are an effective way to allocate resources, it will become simply apparent that we must participate in the international division of labor. Participating in international competition, having resources allocated by the way they respond to price signals in international markets, will in turn determine the structure of our trade. It will determine the directions in which capital flows. This will in turn be a kind of optimized allocation. As division of labor occurs in the process, division of labor itself will be optimized. This must be the fundamental standpoint from which we evaluate an open economy.

Other characteristics can be inferred from this standpoint. Meanwhile, the theory of comparative advantage in trade is also based on this understanding of resource allocation. Various resources have differing degrees of liquidity (or mobility) in international markets. Capital and technology flow somewhat more easily. The mobility of labor is less, but is instead realized in the course of international trade through being incorporated in products. Because of this, price signals in international markets help allocate resources and determine trade quantities and the structure of trade.

Naturally, international markets are not complete and ideal in themselves. They too have shortcomings, including protectionism, regional consolidations (groupings), and either bilateral or multilateral relations among regions. However, in terms of both theory and practice, international free trade markets as defined by the GATT (the General Agreement on Tariffs and Trade, which is now the World

Trade Organization (WTO)) are able to allocate resources in better fashion. By admitting that a socialist market economy and the market itself play a role in allocating resources effectively, we can indirectly infer that international markets play a positive role in optimizing the allocation of resources. We can realize that we should accelerate the process of having our "opening up" be oriented in the direction of an "open economy."

Liberalizing trade operations

Looking back to the time before reform, China was a relatively closed economy. It had only around ten "Foreign Trade Corporations" that were under the direct jurisdiction of the Ministry of Foreign Trade. Each of these was oriented to a specific line of business. Any overlapping of authority was not permitted. At the same time, these enterprises were not responsible for their own budgets. They operated strictly according to the plan. The whole system was what western countries call a classic form of State Trading.

By now, the situation has fundamentally changed. Not only have many different kinds of foreign trade companies been established but controls over trade in many products have been eliminated. The role of the "import and export plan" is already greatly diminished. It could be said that the great majority of products are already dealt with in a liberalized or open way.

In the early period of reform, we began to set up companies that dealt in both industry and trade. Later, we also established many local (provincial-level) trade companies. After that, we extended import and export privileges to quite a few industrial enterprises. We allowed different trading companies to compete among themselves as they imported and exported products. By the end of 1987, we had instituted a system whereby trade in light industry, handicrafts, and garments could be carried out in a liberalized way by entities that had to bear the responsibility for their own profits and losses. At the end of 1990, we formally adopted a system of full responsibility for profits and losses. In fact, the results of the reform process in China's foreign trade sphere have witnessed an incremental expansion of the open nature of operations.

One of the standards by which we measure an open economy is the ease of market entry, that is, whether or not entities are allowed to participate in foreign trade, and the degree to which operations are "open." So-called "free market entry" means each enterprise has the right to decide by itself whether or not to engage in foreign trade, depending on its capacities and business results. Controls do not restrict market entry. The term "open operations" means that there are basically no controls on the range of products in which a company or enterprise wishes to trade.

Naturally, some products that are of a sensitive nature, such as drugs, certain pharmaceuticals, and weapons, are an exception to this and cannot be uncontrolled. The great majority of normal trade goods (some 90 percent of all goods traded in international markets) should be "opened" or not controlled. At the same time, the spirit of the GATT requires that a country have "open operations." At the 13th National Congress, the Communist Party of China formally set forth a guiding principle that called for, "responsibility for profits and losses [which means self-financing, no covering of losses by the government], liberalized operations, an integration of industry and trading functions, and the promoting of an agency system." This policy line was correct. We should continue to adhere to this by undertaking ongoing reform

However, in 1988, fairly high inflation made an appearance in China. At the time, some cadres believed that this was related to having too many companies involved in the process of circulating goods. In order to limit the problem, they felt that we should cut down on the number of such companies and also limit and strictly control their scope of operations. Given this situation, after 1989, China revised the provisions that applied to the trading companies outside of the 13 large trading corporations as noted above. We removed two phrases about allowing "liberalization of operations [or open operations]" and "promoting an agency system."

Given the context of the time, such revisions were perhaps understandable. As we revisit the subject today, however, we can recognize that such revisions were not helpful in accelerating reform and opening up. They were not in line with the reform orientation of a socialist market economy. I feel that we should now reinstitute these two phrases, "liberalization of operations" and "promoting an agency system." We need to do this in order to optimize the way we allocate resources. Since we already accept that a market in and of itself has the ability to optimize resource allocation, if we control what entities in that market do, this damages our cause. If we place this or that restriction on them, it will impact resource allocation and also not be in line with our principles of a socialist market economy. Moreover, it will hurt our desire to enter the GATT. Foreigners are paying great attention to whether or not we make these revisions. Our removal of the term "liberalized operations" has had a negative effect on being able to restore our standing as a signatory to GATT. It has hurt our desire for further participation in the international economic system.

"Promoting an agency system" as our development orientation is also correct. Nevertheless, some cadres have interpreted this to mean we should have a 100 percent agency system. I take this hyperbole as a way to impose their views on others. We see the same in academic circles. For example, when someone says we should "marketize," others say that the speaker is in favor of "100 percent marketization," without any planning at all. Misinterpreting a person's ideas in order to set up something to criticize is not uncommon. Another example would be the mechanization of agriculture—wanting to mechanize does not mean that all agricultural operations are mechanized and that no physical labor is involved at all. When we say that we should "reduce the age of cadres," that does not mean across the board—nobody would go to that extreme.

Why is it that some reform ideas are being distorted in this way, in order to try to make them indefensible? It makes one wonder exactly what is going on. Promoting an agency system simply means that production companies are allowed greater autonomy in their own operations. It means that industrial enterprises and trading enterprises can form a new kind of relationship, one that is in the mutual interests of both. "Promoting an agency system" as one of the orientations of our reform should not be swayed by the will of a minority.

Our theory with respect to foreign trade calls for new progress

Before reform and opening up, as well as in the early days of the process, we criticized the basic precepts of western trade economics as "vulgar bourgeois economics." We opposed them. We criticized the theory of comparative advantage as proposed by David Ricardo and Adam Smith. Many of our old textbooks said that imperialist monopoly capital manipulated international markets. Through this manipulation, imperialists set up unequal price relationships that exploited the interests of developing nations. Under such circumstances, it was impossible for the laws of comparative advantage to be accurately reflected. The entire theoretical underpinning of a centrally-planned economy was entirely different from that of a market economy. Many of the fundamental conditions and assumptions were different.

As a result, our theory back then criticized and rejected the laws of market economics. It was understandable therefore that we also had a certain point of view on foreign trade. As our opening to the outside proceeded, however, it became more obvious that our theory could not fall too far behind actual reality. By now, more and more people agree that the theory of comparative advantage is fundamental to international trade.

This was made even more apparent as the Japanese yen appreciated in 1986 and many Japanese processing industries moved to newly-industrialized nations. China also hopes to participate in and indeed seize the industrial restructuring opportunities created by trade shifts. After some processing industries shifted from Japan to the "four little dragons," a great number of their low-level processing industries in turn shifted to China. They came to Guangdong, Fujian, and other regions. Given this extremely fine moment, many cadres now made use of the times to propose certain policies. They used the theory of comparative advantage and the theories of shifting those comparative advantages to say that China should participate actively in the process of structural shifts. We should conduct thorough research into how we ourselves took advantage of comparative advantages. We should develop our own form of export-oriented economy.

Our traditional economic theory relegated foreign trade to a position that merely "made up for what we lacked and got rid of our surplus." In contrast to this, Ricardo's comparative advantage theory was now more suited to a country that was already implementing reform. Meanwhile, some comrades now pointed out that Ricardo's economic analysis was actually in line with that of Marx. Both made use of the labor theory of value. Because of this, it was now acceptable for China to look on Ricardo's theories with favor. What they meant by this, and even said explicitly, was that anything not actually based on the labor theory of value was still a form of "vulgar bourgeois economics." For example, they continued to be critical of the Heckscher-Ohlin (H-O) theory. This had grown out of the general theory of equilibrium and appeared some 30 years ago. Among other things, it pointed out that a country's international trade structure and behavior was directly guided by prices in the international market. In contrast to the cost of labor in a country and division of labor skills, prices were a more direct determining factor in the process of resource allocation.

Some comrades attempted to say that Ricardo's theory of competitive advantage stood in opposition to the H-O theory. Therefore the former was acceptable while the latter was "vulgar economics." In the international community of economists, few regard the two as being in opposition. It may be that perceptions that were formed years ago influence the traditional view of foreign trade theory as within traditional socialism. This approach says that the idea of comparative advantage is based on a labor theory of value, and is close to analytical methods used by Marx. That is, analyzing a country's comparative advantage can be done by looking at its specific qualities and endowments. In contrast, the H-O theory is based on the general theory of equilibrium. It is completely within the sphere of neo-classical economics with its idea that resources are allocated by the market.

This then leads to the core issue of China's economic reform: what kind of economic model are we going to use to allocate resources? How logical is it if we choose to have market forces allocate resources yet do not accept the general theory of equilibrium, a theory that believes in market allocation of resources? How logical is it to try to create a socialist market economy and yet utterly reject the basis of neo-classical economics? And how logical is it to encourage enterprises to engage actively in foreign trade yet still deny that international market prices play a direct role in the structure of trade? I personally think people need to think more seriously about these things.

Modern economics has advanced considerably in the sphere of international trade. If we deny the theoretical basis of the H-O theory, however, and the basic framework of market-economy analysis that goes along with the general theory of equilibrium, we also cannot make use of many of these newer theories, in addition to the older ones. Or, if we do use them, we will be hypocritical in our approach. We will not be able to adopt a great deal of research in any proper way, and put it to work on our behalf. This includes such things as the development model used by the four small dragons that has attracted such attention since the late 1970s. It includes the views of Kruger and Bhawati on how to move from a controlled economy towards a free-trade system, and it includes the outward-looking model as proposed by the World Bank for developing countries.

At present, the goal of our reform is to set up a socialist market economy, and to use the market as an effective means in optimizing resource allocation. This implies that we must research the theory behind this, and its inherent relationship to Marxist economic theory. In terms of the theory behind foreign trade, we must revisit the question of whether or not this theory is applicable to China's socialist market economy as it "opens up to the outside." Right now, more and more people are recognizing that Stalinist economics, with its centrally-planned economic theory, may have good intentions and many fine assumptions but cannot in fact reach a Pareto optimum. Stalinist economics is unable to arrive at an optimum allocation of resources. Given this realization, we now have an enormous amount of work to do in creating the theoretical basis for moving as fast as possible toward an open-style economy.

Convertibility of the currency

One major step forward in expanding China's "openness" will be to realize convertibility of our currency. To conform to an "open-style economy," our currency should be convertible. Naturally, the process of transitioning from a closed to an open economy must be done in stages, and convertibility should happen at the appropriate stage. Conceptually, however, we should be clear that the orientation of reform and opening up requires that we realize convertibility. We will only be able to participate in the international division of labor if our currency is convertible.

First, let us look at it from the perspective of the market in goods. Over-valuing a currency is fundamentally a way to protect the nation's own industries. It is done to serve the traditional centrally-planned system. It is an import-substitution strategy of development. It requires a corresponding set of policies that subject imports to administrative intervention. On the one hand, this means that the use of foreign exchange is concentrated on things that serve the national economy as organized by the plan. On the other hand, this means that the nation's industries are protected. An over-valued currency discriminates financially against exports. It prevents exports from growing to the fullest extent and thereby prevents the country from full participation in the international division of labor.

Second, let us look at it from the perspective of capital flows. An inconvertible currency prevents capital from flowing freely. For example, China started allowing Sino-foreign joint ventures in 1979, but still required a balance in the foreign exchange of the three types of enterprises carrying on such joint ventures. This limited the way in which the market was allowed to allocate resources, both domestic resources and those coming from abroad. Of course, in the past couple of years, the official rate and the market rate are getting closer. At the same time, the percentage of foreign exchange built up by exporting enterprises is fairly high. Meanwhile we have completely opened up the foreign-exchange adjustment market (the "swap" market), and allow foreign-invested enterprises to use this market to resolve their foreign-exchange balancing issues. This has alleviated the problems somewhat and is a step in the right direction of realizing convertibility. Sooner or later, however, we must resolve to make the currency convertible. We must seize the opportune time to do this. Addressing this problem as soon as possible will be advantageous to the growth of our socialist market economy.

Right now, though, the fact is that quite a few people still have grave doubts about this. First, they think that making our currency convertible will require "reasonable" adjustments to the exchange rate and that this then will impact the overall price level of goods within the country. After so many years of reform, this concern should, by all rights, have diminished somewhat. Adjusting exchange rates will indeed have a certain impact on the price of imported goods, but a more critical issue is controlling aggregate demand. If aggregate demand is strongly controlled, the prices of some imported goods will rise and will absorb more purchasing power, forcing the prices of other goods to fall. The aggregate level of prices will not necessarily respond to the "push" of exchange rates with an overall rise.

During the period in which we were combating inflation, we made two adjustments to exchange rates at the end of 1989 and the end of 1990. At that time, we were controlling aggregate demand in a fairly stringent way. It is fair to say that there is no clear evidence to prove that our exchange-rate adjustments really had any major effect on inflation.

People also believe that we can achieve convertibility only when we have large reserves of foreign exchange, when exports are extremely strong, and foreign trade is well developed. Only then will we be able to cope with the people's desire to convert our currency into foreign exchange. In superficial terms, this has some logic to it. A deeper analysis shows that it is not necessarily correct.

International experience indicates that some countries undertook a forced conversion of their currencies precisely when they were in the worst straits, when their foreign exchange reserves were near zero and they shouldered enormous debt. In such cases, the question was whether or not the people believed the government when it said that the domestic currency would be convertible on the basis of equivalent value. They had to believe that the money in their hands would be valued at a rate equivalent to the hard currency of other countries. They had to believe that they could convert it any time they wished so that they would not rush to convert massive amounts all at once, or would not try to shift their money overseas. In economic terms, this is known as the commitment effect. This principle of economics has been widely accepted in the field. We say that the government is committing to convertibility of the currency under reasonable exchange-rate mechanisms (that is, equilibrium rates). This commitment also has specific functions and results when it comes to fighting inflation. Under conditions of severe inflation, implementing convertibility of the currency will in fact rebuild people's confidence in their own currency and hold down inflation.

On protectionism

One point of view in China holds that the country should implement policies that protect its national industries when it comes to foreign trade. I feel we should give this suggestion very serious reflection. Inappropriate trade protectionism and refusing to allow competitive pressures into the country will not only lead to equivalent retaliation by other countries, but it will hurt our own domestic enterprises. Over time, it will lead to their lowered efficiency and material losses.

People often treat import policies and export policies as two different subjects. They feel that the easiest and most effective way to conserve foreign exchange receipts is to limit imports (that is, to encourage import substitution), and to encourage exports. Economic analysis makes it clear, however, that these two things cannot be strictly segregated. Excessive limits on imports, particularly via administrative means, will attack our export industries in three specific ways. First, it will guide production factors in the direction of import substitution industries as opposed to export industries. Second, it will prevent export industries from being able to select and purchase inputs at the appropriate times, via the right channels, and at good prices. Third, import restrictions generally will put artificial pressure on the exchange rate (including market rates). As a result, there will be across-the-board discrimination against export industries. This will be equivalent to an extra tax on exporting industries that serves to limit their development.

Restrictions on imports can not only create artificial pressures on the price of foreign exchange in the market, but they can create certain conditions the government must deal with in maintaining the value of our own currency. This kind of pressure on the exchange rate discriminates against all exporters on a universal basis. Due to unfavorable financial considerations, this means that exports do not reach their full potential. This in turn prevents the country from achieving the ideal state in terms of the international division of labor. Import restrictions are often expressed in the form of mandated controls on the channels for getting foreign exchange. On the surface of things, it may appear as though intervention with respect to those importers who already have foreign exchange is not so bad. In reality, there are huge potential numbers of importers who have no ability at all to go through normal channels to get foreign exchange.

Trade protectionism comes at a variety of costs to our society at large. Economists generally divide the losses in efficiency into damage to consumers and damage to production. Damage to consumers comes about because trade protectionism generally makes consumers pay higher prices for their purchases. This then reduces their purchases of the goods being protected. Producers benefit from relatively high prices and therefore increase their output of low-efficiency production.

Damage to producers comes about because of the opportunity cost of using inputs in one way as opposed to another. They put resources that might have gone into other economic activity (including producing for export) into production of import-substitution items. Research into the real costs of protectionism has attempted to quantify the production losses to both consumers and producers. It has shown that the losses in any one year might not be so large, but when the losses are repeated year after year, they add up. So long as you have protectionism, you pay the price.

Another aspect of this is domestic monopolies. When trade protection is directed toward protecting such industries, it can exacerbate low efficiencies. (Damage then results from low efficiency that derives from even less competitive pressure and even more desire to maintain the status quo.) Moreover, protectionism provides an incentive for importers to seek to obtain import licenses and permits. A trade in such licenses is the result. Profits come from activities that are not related to production at all. This then results in a waste of financial resources.

We should recognize that the role that international markets play in allocating resources is fundamentally positive. Even if some developed countries do follow some protectionist policies, this is not so much out of economic imperatives as it is out of political considerations. In such instances, the economic goals of the country are subordinated to the political goals of some politicians. In order to win elections, they wave the banner of protectionism and make promises to protect the jobs of a certain segment of the country's citizens. Such political methods are severely criticized by economists. The methods expose the fact that protectionism is not in fact helping employment of the country overall but instead is putting a heavy burden on consumers and leading to misallocation of resources.

One more point should be made clear. In overall terms, the economic systems of developed countries are "free-trade" systems. Protectionism and trade controls are the exception, not the rule. We cannot use the excuse of saying that "other people are protectionist, so why not us?" as a way to think that protectionism will be in our country's economic interests.

As a country, China encompasses the needs of many different types of interests. These include political interests, local interests, the interests of different sectors or departments, and the interests of the public at all levels of employment and all kinds of industries. Overall, however, China is still a country with a low per capita income. All considerations must center on economic construction and economic interests as a whole. We should therefore examine and discuss foreign trade policies one by one. Other than a small number of protectionist measures that may need to be kept during a transition period, we should seriously reconsider and change the majority of import substitution policies that we implemented in the past. We should be courageous as we decide which to keep and which to discard. This is the only way we will be able to participate in international competition and the international division of labor. It is the only way we will be able to optimize allocation of resources via the mechanism of international competition and move, as soon as possible, in the direction of an open economy.

One interesting phenomenon should be noted here. As China eliminated or reduced protectionist policies, those industries that were affected opposed this on all fronts and acted as though the sky was falling. A few years later, though, one finds that those industries actually benefited from the new competitive environment. Not only are they still alive, but they are competitive and now motivated to export. Our tape recorder business is one example. Naturally, people who preferred a closed economy will feel differently. They will continue to declare that these sectors are vulnerable and need help. Even though their previous production levels were very low, they at least were able to fend for themselves.

International experience shows that the job losses and production losses brought on by reducing protectionism are actually less than anticipated over the transition period.

Thoughts on the new international economic order

This term, a "new international economic order," has been talked about for years, but it means different things to different countries, depending on where they stand. For a long time, to the group of developing countries it meant having developed countries provide them with assistance, through governmental intervention and political means. It meant setting up a new order that benefited the growth of developing countries.

Related to this is the idea that protecting the interests of developing countries means protecting (or supporting) the price of primary commodities. If the price of primary commodities falls, this is seen as unfavorable to the development of developing countries. At the same time, it means lowering the prices of manufactured products which helps enable developing countries to import.

In the late 1970s and the 1980s, however, people began to reconsider this idea. They began to recognize on a more widespread basis that the success of the four little dragons did not follow this logic. Not only were the requirements of the new international economic order difficult to implement but they did not necessarily create real wealth for developing countries. People began to lean in the direction of a free-trade type of open economy model and to feel that this was instead a better path.

Given this international climate of opinion, the policy recommendations that had served as the core of a previous attempt to readjust north–south relations by the United Nations Conference on Trade and Development (UNCTAD) were somewhat weakened. Fewer people now paid much attention to them. By now, people are still talking about the new international economic order, and promoting it, but the message of each country has slightly different implications. Those countries that conduct an "open-style economy" are mainly ones that have few natural resources but large populations. They are unable to export large quantities of primary goods but they have analyzed their human assets quite effectively. Their labor costs are low and their workforce is well qualified. Given such advantages, they have chosen to put major effort into developing processing industries. They are aiming at exporting manufactured goods as a development strategy. The policies supported by these countries in the past no longer apply. Protect the prices of primary goods and keep manufactured prices low is no longer favorable to the new development strategy.

So far as China is concerned, the economic situation was always said to include "a large land mass and plenty of resources." In fact, more and more people are coming to realize that China is a country with very few natural resources per capita. As its economy develops, and as living standards improve, the scarcity of the country's natural resources becomes ever more apparent. Given this, it is fair to say that China does not in fact have plentiful primary resources that can be exported to earn the country foreign exchange over the long run. In recent years, China's coastal areas have gradually transformed themselves into outward-looking economies. China's exports of manufactured goods have gone from around 50 percent of total exports to something approaching 80 percent.

Given this situation, we should now be more precise in defining what we consider to be the "new international economic order." Would a free-trade international economic order be more beneficial to China, or would more government intervention be better, with controls on foreign trade? We should look at exactly what benefits we could derive from protecting the prices of primary goods. What would the effect of lowering the prices of manufactured goods be on our large quantity of exported manufactured goods? (The volume of such exports continues to grow but also the diversity of manufactured goods.)

Policy leanings of the traditional "north–south" dialogue include many that are no longer aligned with China's economic interests. We should probe the sources of these policy inclinations. To a degree, we may well find that they are derived from the influence of the economic thinking that came out of the former Soviet Union. Such thinking is not necessarily beneficial to developing countries.

It is in the interests of a few developing countries, such as those with oil or other natural resources, to maintain the price levels of primary products. Other than these, however, most outward-oriented developing countries may find it more in their interests to support the free-trade system of GATT. Indeed, some are even more determined to do this than developed countries. Given that China is now reevaluating the traditional view of north–south economic relations, the process of "moving toward an open economy" is a highly significant topic.

Note

1 This was originally published in *Comparative Economic and Social Systems*, Issue 5th, 1992.

4 Fiscal and tax reform, and an overall economic analysis[1]

(1992)

Three major distortions in the Chinese economy

Price distortions

1 Price distortions in China are structural. Under China's traditional centrally-planned economy, the structural nature of these distortions is quite clear. First, prices that we set for primary products are too low. Second, there is a scissor-price differential between industrial and agricultural products. Third, prices of manufactured goods are generally too high (with some exceptions). Fourth, there is an arbitrary nature to the relative pricing of manufactured goods, while pricing of new products is relatively high, while that of old products is relatively low.

In terms of how to reform the system, there are advantages to having such clearly defined structural price distortions. First, it is easier to discern the rules that are causing distortions and to measure them overall. Second, until such time as prices are corrected, we can apply taxes to remedy unreasonable prices in certain products. We can use product taxes, resource taxes, and land-use taxes to resolve quite a few of the differentials among different categories, lessening the pain that some are feeling and the pleasure that some are enjoying with the current price structure. However, until there is a fairly systematic understanding of the situation, people will not be firmly resolved to carry out reform.

In the early period of reform, we first released price controls on the production of an enterprise that exceeded the output required by the plan. That amount could be sold by the producer at non-controlled prices. That was the start of a "dual track" pricing system. Since we began reform of enterprises fairly early, it was understandable that this phenomenon might occur naturally when price distortions had not yet been eliminated. However, at the end of 1984 we took the initiative in formally implementing a two-track pricing system. We said that it was a transitional method, but in fact it was done to avoid price reform. Not only did it then lead to tremendous changes and differences of opinion within government but it brought new distortions into our economic structure. They were so extreme that it became hard to use any systematic measures to address the conflicts.

The two-track pricing system is a mortal threat to our taxation system. It requires that we implement an indirect form of taxation. That is, different tax rates are applied to economic activity that is "within the plan" and "outside the plan." Not only are there tremendous technical problems to this approach, but it is hard to differentiate between the two tracks. The percentages of products being priced at inside- and outside-the-plan prices change at any time, making it almost impossible to implement two tiers of taxes for the two different pricing systems. Meanwhile, a unitary tax rate leads to the inability to regulate the colossal inequalities caused by the two-track system.

In this most recent period, the government has adopted a number of measures to address the unreasonable pricing phenomena. Between 1985 and 1988, for example, it adopted various regulatory methods to try to alleviate structural problems to a degree. In overall terms, however, while price distortions are structural, that structure is also chaotic and does not conform to any rules. It therefore becomes hard to use any standardized system to make sure that enterprises are able to compete on an equal basis. The only solution really is to firmly resolve to push forward price reform.

2　Prices evolve in an involuntary manner. Price reform can result from proactive measures and voluntary efforts, but prices can also change as the result of a passive response to various kinds of pressures. The fact that China's price distortions have moderated to a considerable degree is mainly the result of such involuntary or passive responses. One could call this process "price evolution of an involuntary nature."

Proactive price reform means taking the initiative in designing ways to reduce price distortions, including ways to make sure plan prices approach those set by the market and "released" prices. Proactive price reform also means taking supply and demand into consideration as much as possible in those circumstances in which the market is not effective in setting prices, and when administrative price-setting is necessary. The term "voluntary" or "taking the initiative" as used here means that the government recognizes the negative effect that price distortions are having on resource allocation as well as on income distribution, and that the government then seeks to correct these distortions. "Involuntary" price evolution refers to situations in which economic reform is already moving forward in other aspects, and reform measures unavoidably are transmitted to pricing as well. Unable to control such transmitted effects, we gradually see prices change.

Another problem arises when public finance lacks the capacity to provide subsidies and these are therefore unavoidably reduced. The third kind is when local governments and enterprises violate the rules as set by the central government and its pricing departments. They take it on themselves to revise price controls. This leads to further changes in price structures.

The above three types of involuntary price change mainly show up in the following ways.

First, "opening up to the outside" has had a massive impact on domestic price systems within China. By now, domestic prices are in the process of moving toward international market prices. This has catalyzed a change in price structures altogether, building up a cumulative total change that is extremely influential.

Second, the government has unavoidably had to reduce subsidies due to scarcity of public funds. This has led to successful correction of price distortions in specific areas. In July of 1986, for example, China adjusted the exchange rate to a level of RMB 3.7 to USD 1. In order to prevent too much impact on domestic prices at the time (in 1985, prices had risen substantially and the price index was rising at a rate of 8.8 percent), the government decided to maintain the previous exchange rate of RMB 3.2 to USD 1 for certain imported products when it calculated the customs duty. At the same time, it provided price subsidies for 28 kinds of imported products. Seen from today, these actions seem amusing. At the time, however, there were different opinions on them among economic circles and people in the Ministry of Foreign economic relations and trade. Some proposed eliminating these subsidies, while the departments in charge of product pricing wanted to keep them. The result was that subsidies continued for many years. When it became harder and harder to balance the national budget, and reducing spending became a highly prominent issue, only then did we start to reduce the import subsidies. Now, only a few of the subsidies for 28 categories of imports remain. From the perspective of evaluating how policy is made, these changes were mainly forced on the country by a tight fiscal situation. They were not a matter of voluntarily choosing to reduce distortions.

3 Changes occur on their own after tightening measures are taken. After inflation became apparent in 1988, we adopted extremely stringent tightening policies and basically froze prices to a large extent. As these policies of tightening aggregate demand began to take effect, the market went from a flourishing situation to a more balanced level and then softened. Some prices fell to levels that were below the mandated prices set by the commodity pricing authorities. (One example would be color television sets.)

Many local level governments adopted a "one eye open one eye shut" attitude to this. They wanted to keep their economies moving and invigorate marketing channels, plus they wanted to increase the variety of goods that were available. Meanwhile, the State pricing authorities also gradually relaxed controls. The result was an automatic process.

4 Local governments and enterprises did what they wanted to do in terms of price controls. To a certain degree, they violated the pricing policy rules of the State. After the intense inflation of 1988, the central government required all provincial governments to take responsibility for keeping down their own prices and making sure the overall index stayed below a certain threshold. Some provinces recognized that strengthening price controls too much would make it hard

for enterprises to survive. This would add to the burden on local government finances and increase loopholes in income distribution even more. They therefore did not carry out excessively restrictive price controls. Other provinces did indeed institute strict controls on prices and used large sums to pay for subsidies to cover. One year later, people began to recognize the differences among regions. Those provinces that had not instituted new price controls had prices that were not in fact all that higher, if higher at all, than others. Some of the figures were in fact lower than other provinces. Those provinces that had given substantial price subsidies began to have obvious problems in meeting their budgets. Meanwhile, their price levels were not outstandingly better than anyone else's. Starting in 1990, there was a distinct increase in the number of local governments who took the liberty of relaxing price controls on their own.

Summing up the above, and the resulting changes, we can see that the passive form of price reform was able to correct distortions in prices to a large degree. In quantitative terms, "opening up to the outside" played a role that was particularly apparent.

The main difficulty with a voluntary or self-initiated approach to price reform is that it is hard for policy-making levels (of the government) to muster the determination to do something. The result is a prolonged period of price "evolution" that is passive. If we were to compare the two options, again in quantitative terms we find a remarkable difference. It comes from the so-called Pareto differential. In the process of dynamic growth this is reflected in a differential in growth rates.

In terms of income distribution, if the government takes the initiative in carrying out price reform, it can have some influence over the results. A passive approach to price reform also gradually leads to more rational prices, but inequalities in income distribution have already become an established fact over the course of the process. The loss of control over income distribution lowers the confidence of people in their government.

If a passive approach to price reform is allowed to go on for a long time, substantial distortions can form in the whole pricing system. All levels of government cadres who are in positions of authority can then take advantage of the price differentials. It is very easy for personal interests to get the upper hand through the use of "administrative intervention" in business. This makes it hard to carry out clean government. We should take this into serious consideration as we think over the options for price reform, and the costs we have to pay

China's price-system reform contains both voluntary or initiated price reforms, and involuntary or passive price reforms. Reform of agricultural prices in the early part of the reform, as well as textile prices, prices on small items, light industry, electronics, were all of the voluntary or initiated type. This included implementing the "four differentials" policy as well as various price adjustments carried out just recently. Meanwhile, involuntary reforms generally occurred when unfavorable factors became so bad they could not be accommodated any longer. The adjustments to our exchange rates at the end of 1989 were the most prominent example.

In 1988, after the high point of inflation, if we did not adjust the exchange rate then exports would not go up and enterprises would begin to suffer losses. Budgetary discipline would be hard to maintain. The international experience has taught us repeatedly that during years of inflation a country should maintain an exchange rate that is aligned with reality. Nevertheless, the policy to adjust exchange rates was not decided upon until December 1989. What's more, even then the adjustment was fairly modest. The financial problems that built up over the course of 1989 are still being felt today.

In today's pricing system, a considerable percentage of prices are determined by the market. According to the estimates of many economists, as well as to the tenor of foreign news on the subject, some 70 percent of commodity prices are determined by the market. When we say, "determined by the market," this does not mean that the prices as arrived at are reasonable. The overlapping influence of price distortions and blockaded local markets still influence the final price levels in the market.

The early period of "commodity" prices were affected by the influence of administrative setting of prices to a large extent. They could also be adjusted by tax revenue. By today, though, around 70 percent of commodity prices are already determined by the market, but differentiated tax treatment can cause considerable differences among commodity prices. There is already no sound basis for this continuing to be the case.

Final price levels are now formed after the influence of taxes. These taxes affect the equilibrium point of supply and demand. No administrative pricing in fact needs to be complemented by differentiated tax rates. Under such circumstances, there is considerable doubt as to whether or not the indirect tax system still needs such differentiated tax rates. The added-value tax differentials that lead to artificial changes in supply and demand equilibrium are also unreasonable. By now, we no longer need tax policies to play a role in shifting price equilibrium one way or another.

A distorted relationship between costs and profits

A distorted relationship between costs and profits is only one of the many distortions that currently exist in Chinese economic activity, but this one has a very broad impact. The distortion is mainly characterized by overly low costs that create profits that are unusually large. Not only does this create obstacles to China's reform orientation, namely a "commodity economy with a plan," but it also makes it harder to figure out the proper income distribution between the State and enterprises. Only if we eliminate this distortion as soon as possible will we be able to establish market mechanisms that allow for fair competition. Only then can we speed up the pace of our overall reform.

The causes of this distortion in China's past.

Under the traditional form of a centrally-planned economy, enterprises were not independent entities with autonomous decision-making authority and they did not bear responsibility for their own profits and losses. Instead, they were cost management centers. Production plans were determined by "upper levels" of authority. Raw materials were allocated on a uniform basis by those upper levels. Sales of the products were arranged through the State plan. Prices too were set by the plan. Decisions to develop new products, or to renovate equipment, were made by submitting requests to upper levels for permission. This system made cost accounting severely deficient in two respects. In order to make it easier for the factory to control costs, the upper level authorities did their best to define things that were easy to account for and supervise as "costs." Other items that were less flexible and less easy to organize were handled through "planned appropriations" from upper level authorities.

This led to a shrinking of the whole concept of "costs." According to the *"Cost management regulations of State-Owned Enterprises"* put out by the State Council in 1984, as well as the *"Methods of accounting for costs in State-owned industrial enterprises"* put out by the Ministry of Finance in 1986, the categories that could be included in cost expenditures included mainly: "raw materials," "fuel and power," "wages and welfare expenses," "factory expenses," "enterprise management [administration] fees," and "administrative expenses." Specified items were not included. Instead, many current actual cost items are left unaccounted for—for example, depreciation rates that are too low, not enough to sustain the original productivity of an operation, wages that include only part of the actual remuneration to workers, and so on. Since costs are not completely accounted for, the resulting profit calculations are invalid.

Cost–profit distortions in reality

1   We have long used a system that pays low wages (while also paying in other benefits). All entities that use this low-wage system should incorporate those items that are not included into their wages as "costs." Such things would include housing, a portion of welfare benefits, pensions, and a portion of social security. In some enterprises that pay very low wages, far lower than compensation should be for labor, wages are often supplemented by payments made out of profits in the form of various types of bonuses. Such bonuses can even be larger than the total amount paid out in wages. Some enterprises have no profits but yet are able to pay out bonuses, even though they owe money on loans and "suspend" the repayment of those loans. What's more, these bonuses are rigid in that they only go up and never go down.

2   Under a depreciation system that is too low, some enterprises have inadequate funds to carry on simple re-production. The enterprise does not have the authority to make the determination on this, since a large part of depreciation is pooled for centralized use by higher authorities. This then creates two different distortions. On the one hand, lowered depreciation makes accounting for costs too low. On the other hand, that part that is pooled for centralized use by higher authorities lowers the capacity of the enterprise to carry out

self-improvements. Some enterprises do technological renovation with bank loans but then are unable to use depreciation allowances to pay them back.
3   Some people push down costs through various means, such as by intentionally lowering interest rates, taking in raw materials at artificially low prices, restricting new product research, and so on. All of these create a bias in the real costs of production and fees.

Inaccurate accounting of costs exaggerates the size of profits. The share of net profits in total output value of all kinds of enterprises in China is therefore quite a bit higher than it is in other countries. If you look only at those industrial enterprises that have independent accounting for profits, in 1989 alone aggregate profits came to RMB 220 billion, which was 14.4 percent of GNP in that year.[2] Within this figure, certain things have already been deducted out such as distorting price factors which cause a loss to enterprises and industries. Otherwise the profitability of enterprises would be even more impressive.

A distorted structure of costs and profits must inevitably bring on a distorted structure of tax revenues. Since cost accounting is inadequate, and the apparent level of enterprise profits is higher than the actual level, and since income tax has to be paid on an exaggerated tax base, the tax rate on enterprises is high. For large- and medium-sized State-Owned Enterprises it comes to as high as 55 percent. On top of this are the various funds required for energy and transport, and the "State budget adjustments," and so on. The burden on enterprises ends up being extremely heavy. The remaining profits must, to a large extent, be paid out in real costs. As a result, both State and enterprise are in difficult territory when it comes to "distribution," deciding which party is to get how much of the results.

The State feels that the enterprise is already making plenty of profits. The State budget meanwhile is in serious trouble and the State wants to "centralize control" as a result. That is, it wants to pool the resulting profits to help with State finances. The enterprise, on the other hand, feels a very heavy burden. It has little autonomy to do what it needs to do. The reasons include the tax distortion caused by a distorted cost–profit structure and the distortion of the tax base itself.

The negative consequences of the distorted cost–profit structure

The result of controlling costs at the factory level, as well as the ex-factory price and retail prices, has led to high profits at the "circulation system" level. The State has then retrieved this extra benefit and drawn it into its own coffers by using a "circulation tax." After reform, non-State-owned entities entered into business operations and the result has been that the circulation sector became less easy to supervise and control. This sector has been particularly profitable and "hot," given that its profits increase even more during times of inflation. This has come to the notice of all levels of government. Some people feel there are too many companies in this sector, while every time a product goes from one hand to another it extracts a layer of profits. The end result is higher prices. People in leadership positions are therefore considering "rectifying" the sector and limiting market entry. Since 1988, they have declared that restrictions on the number of companies in the circulation sector are in the "important policy" category.

In fact, the tertiary industries in China have not developed to their full potential at all. Looking at other international comparisons, whether you are talking about developed market-economy countries or developing countries, China's output and employment in tertiary industries is quite low. In many developed countries, tertiary industry production value comes to around 70 percent of GNP. Within this, a considerable portion can be attributed to "circulation" and services. Tertiary industries in developing countries are also more highly developed than in China. In Brazil, tertiary-industry output stood at 50 percent of GNP in the 1980s. In India, it reached 46 percent. In China, the amount was only 20 percent until three years ago and now it still comes to only around 23 to 27 percent.

Meanwhile, the number of people employed in our tertiary industries is low. The network of operational outlets is inadequate and should be expanded considerably. However, since the per capita profit of our circulation sector is much higher than normal, whether you compare it to other industries in China or to those of other commodity-economy countries, it has brought on the restrictions noted above. The distorted "distribution structure" has been created by distorted cost–profit structures and also by distorted ways of thinking.

Universally competitive mechanisms can bring about relatively quick results, which is one of the important long-term motivations for our reform. Meanwhile, setting up competitive mechanisms requires costs that are "real." Costs that are not real, and ex-factory prices that are not real, will lead to "bargaining" practices, which undermine competition. The problem right now is that when an enterprise has prices that are too high, it becomes less competitive. Instead of figuring out ways to lower its costs and raise its quality, however, so that its products become more competitive, it tries to figure out ways to get officials to bargain on its behalf. It looks at the treatment that other entities are getting and then asks for more favorable preferential policies. Taxes are one such policy. Bargaining is done by using the contract system for the State component of production (*cheng-bao*). As for newly established enterprises (that have no State component of production), different industries have different rules with respect to reducing or exempting taxes. Meanwhile, the lines between "industries" are unclear. An excessive amount of preferential policy treatment has greatly reduced the standardization of our taxation system.

A distorted relationship between central and local in terms of government functions

1 The distortions in the functions of central and local government are an expression of the classic thinking behind an administrative kind of separation of authorities. Local governments are a level of administrative authority in China's tiered structure of management. They are an indispensable part of the government's public finance system. That we must recognize the important role of local governments in this process and give them a degree

of self-autonomy is not in question. This has always been part of the original intention of our reform. The question comes when we try to decide exactly what kinds of autonomy local governments should have, and how the central government goes about extending that autonomy.

The relationship between China's central and local governments has never been clearly defined. This has been manifested in the following ways. First, reform intended to "release authority down to lower levels and allow profits to stay at lower levels" but what we have done in fact is use administrative means to create a simplification of "division of authority." Second, we thought that macroeconomic measures too could be split up among different levels of government, that each level of authority could handle its own. Third, we have discovered that the central government is in fact reluctant to give up control over things that should be handled by local levels. Fourth, we have felt that enterprises should in fact be "managed" to a degree, and by someone, and that they are most appropriately managed by local governments. Fifth, we have treated local governments as economic entities in their own right, as similar to enterprises, and we have asked that they be "responsible for their own profits and losses" in terms of public finance expenditures and revenues.

The result of the above ways of thinking and handling things has been the loss of control over macroeconomic measures and an intensification of "administrative" separation of authority. Meanwhile, the relationship between central and local governments has become a cyclical process of centralization and then decentralization of authority.

2   The distortion of the functions of local government has been reflected in how local governments interfere in enterprises and the market.

Local governments now do their best to increase tax revenues. That is the chief object of their behavior. What this has done is to create a great deal of behavior that is not in fact aligned with the best interests of the entire body. Our traditional planned-economy system never had explicit rules about the functions of local governments. We simply felt that local governments were a branch of the central government. Local governments therefore had the mission to carry out on a local level whatever it was that the central government should be doing. Since a great deal of things had to be done, it was natural that there had to be funding for these things and increasing tax revenues has become of paramount importance as a result. Especially given that we specified our system would now be one of "each eating at his own hearth" (and therefore providing his own food), with each level of public finance providing for itself, it has become quite clear that the more one can garner in tax revenues, the more one can spend and the better the outcome will be.

In order to increase tax revenues, local governments have been very actively engaged in "getting on the horse" of any enterprises that were profitable. After mounting up on such horses, local governments have then used any means possible to protect their local markets. They have prevented similar products from "outside" from coming into their markets in order to maintain high production levels of their own industries. The aim has been to increase local tax revenues. This whole way of doing things has prevented the establishment of competitive mechanisms and it has reduced the scale of economic operations. The problem is getting worse all the time. It has led to a fragmentation of local markets.

The interference of local governments in the operations of profitable enterprises has shifted the attention of local governments away from a number of things they should have been doing. The primary responsibility of local governments is in fact to improve the basic infrastructure of the area and manage the overall socio-economic environment. It is to attract in more investment, and ensure the economic soundness of the region. At the same time, local governments should put major effort into improving education and cultivating better human resources. They should improve the employment levels of their region, but not personally intervene in the operating of enterprises.

Under our current system, however, these functions have become relatively unimportant compared to the goal of increasing financial revenues.

Different critiques of our reform policies with respect to public finance and taxation

China's tax reform has accomplished a number of good results since the first reform of 1983, which was called "changing profits into taxes." Reforming the tax system involves a very broad range of issues, however. Many things have not been well coordinated with other reforms and particularly with price reforms. Moreover, there have been problems in the design of tax reform so that the initial aim of reform has not in fact been achieved. This has led to some controversy about tax reform issues that include the orientation of ongoing reforms, the magnitude of reforms, and even reform itself. In what follows, I present some of the views on this.

Criticism of the two-step process of changing profits into taxes

In overall terms, the first step in the process of changing profits into taxes was successful. As a transitional measure, the second step used tax revenues to try to moderate the unreasonable parts of prices and this was defensible.

However, we have not been able to achieve complete results as expected. Problems included the fact that the people designing the process were unclear in their own thinking about guidelines and technical methodologies. A number of loopholes were allowed to remain that enabled ongoing inequality in how enterprises were treated. These came about because of the varying degrees of implementation of the product tax, the resource tax, the fixed asset fees, and so on. Because of this, there was no alternative but to set up a great number of "adjustment" taxes as a part of the second step in the process of changing profits into taxes. This led to "fumbles" on a number of counts.

One thing deserves special mention. As we summarized our experience and designed the whole process, we did not focus on the root cause of why we needed to set up adjustment taxes. Some cadres simply attributed the problems to the idea that the functions of taxes and prices are different. These two systems should not be engaged in trying to support one another. Or cadres rejected the possibility of unifying the income tax for enterprises altogether. Because they did not understand it thoroughly, they were not able to resolve the problem.

The most severe criticism of the two-step process of changing profits into taxes came from the idea that China simply cannot carry out a standardized tax revenue system. As a result, China should conduct different *cheng-bao* or contract systems based on specific circumstances. These people felt that although the overall idea of changing profits into taxes was good, actual implementation was necessarily going to fail. We were not going to be able to create equal conditions by using a standardized tax. Evidence of this failure, they felt, was the launch of the *cheng-bao* system in 1987.[3]

I feel there are major problems with these kinds of thinking. First, it is quite true that the two-step process has been inadequate in certain ways. It has not achieved the desired results. This is unavoidably linked to the capacities and level of understanding of those who designed the process, people in our economic theory circles and policy-making departments. However, this does not mean that we should reject the whole orientation of standardizing our management of the issue. We should not say that this problem implicates the entire orientation of reform.

The goal of reform is to optimize resource allocation, and to set up new incentive systems. Our theoretical analysis makes it clear that market mechanisms that operate through fair competition can indeed use standardized measures to achieve the desired results. Meanwhile, special circumstances often contain their own inherent laws. The unequal factors that are the legacy of the centrally-planned system also abide by certain rules. Through a series of policy measures, therefore, we can arrive at competitive conditions by balancing things out. We can realize a standardized system of tax revenue administration. As for those enterprises that do indeed have different levels of efficiency, we should adopt measures to encourage improvement by various means, including putting pressure on inefficient enterprises. We gradually move in the direction of relatively improved performance overall. We have been left with a legacy of unreasonable factors but this does not mean that we should allow this to block our efforts to achieve a standardized system overall.

Some people feel that there should be no coordinated link between our tax-revenue policies and our pricing policies. Irrational pricing should be dealt with by price reforms, while tax revenue problems should be handled on their own. This way of looking at things is also incorrect. Indirect taxes have always been closely tied to the pricing system.

Take products subject to the commodity tax as an example. In addition to having different tax rates on different products, we also have the phenomenon of redundant taxation on certain products (since constituent products are taxed as the final product is produced). This has a very obvious effect on the price structure of the ultimate product. Moreover, given that the overall level of our current customs duties is relatively high, and there are major differences among rates, the impact of customs duties on price structures is also quite apparent. Meanwhile, the consumption tax has the effect of directly increasing the retail price of some specific products. It is clear that these various tax considerations have a major impact on prices.

Two kinds of influences are brought to bear on prices. One is that tax revenues are used proactively to adjust the domestic price of certain products, which causes them to deviate from a neutral equilibrium point so as to modify the supply and demand relationship. Another is the irrational nature of the old pricing system. This created an unequal situation among enterprises in terms of those that benefited and those that suffered. As we transition to a system in which each enterprise is responsible for its own profits and losses, we need to use taxation as a means to moderate the process and alleviate these contradictions.

When we first undertook the design of a tax system on products, our work was fairly rough hewn. The result was that we did not achieve the ideal situation in enabling taxes to moderate irrational pricing structures. As time went on, we had to adopt a large number of "adjustment" taxes. This kind of targeted tax, with different rates for different entities, was in fact like whipping just one cow to make the team go faster, which led to enormous criticism. We should, however, be clear about just where the problem lies. Is it in the defects of our design work in terms of our understanding and adjustment taxes (including our policies with respect to less advanced enterprises), or is it that the tax system fundamentally should have no role in trying to moderate the irrational nature of our prices?

Another aspect to consider is that distortions in the economy are not all the result of prices. From the outset, we should not expect product taxes to resolve all issues. Our use of adjustment taxes is also helpful in addressing other problems in the system.

The contract system (cheng-bao system), and integrated sets of reforms that go along with it

In looking at progress made on our tax reform, it is worth mentioning the overall design thinking that envisaged coordinated reforms in 1986. Those integrated reforms involved prices, taxation, and public finance. The hope was to accelerate our movement toward a commodity economy with a unified market and fair competition. This included changing the system that allowed for central government as well as local government to interference in enterprises. Since our policy options generally involved interlocking factors, we had to maintain a certain degree of flexibility and opportunism. In the end, the overall design thinking was not adopted. Starting at the end of 1986, China's economy moved more clearly in the direction of administrative decentralization with a stronger tint of bargaining.

Since the end of 1987, State-Owned Enterprises have strongly promoted the enterprise contract system. The main feature of this system is the "handing up" of taxes to higher levels of authority. This has complicated the relationship between the State and enterprises. Meanwhile, the instability of the external environment has meant that the contractual targets have not been met and have stayed "rigid" for a number of years. Some enterprises have been able to accomplish their objectives quite easily in "handing up" the target amount. Others have not, despite major efforts.

In 1988, China began implementing a system of public finance that was based on the original public-finance system of the country. Each administrative unit was required to "take responsibility" for fulfilling its own duties. These were defined in many different ways, however, for all the 37 provinces and autonomous regions, and the municipalities under the direct jurisdiction of the central government. Meanwhile, each of these provincial and municipal jurisdictions also started implementing even more complicated "responsibility systems" with the levels of government under them.

These public-finance "responsibility systems" had a highly arbitrary nature to them. The result was a weakening of budgeting constraints. The most obvious indication of this was the mutual encroachment of the central government and local (provincial) governments on each other's authorities. In order for local governments to maximize benefits to their own turf, each went into a one-on-one negotiation with the central government and asked for concessions. The result was that central-government revenues declined every year. Meanwhile, the central government used hardcore commands that came under a variety of names as well as "apportioning measures" in order to retrieve some of the lost revenues. They even went so far as to "borrow funds" from local governments. This made it hard to carry through with reforms that were meant to "devolve authority down to lower levels." The mutual erosion of authorities and mutual squeezing of each other was extended to each level of government down the line. The general practice in this "*bao-gan*" system was to "*bao*" but not to "*gan*."

Different kinds of defective thinking that condone ongoing distortions in the system

Three different approaches allowed for ongoing distortions. Those were "separation of tax from profit," "repayment of loans after tax," and "contracting after tax."

THE PROPOSAL TO SEPARATE TAX FROM PROFIT, TO REPAY LOANS AFTER TAX, AND TO CONTRACT AFTER TAX

After the *cheng-bao* system was instituted, three different approaches were proposed as part of the thinking behind how to handle the *cheng-bao* system. (The *cheng-bao* system involved having an enterprise meet its target quotas for the government plan under a contracted responsibility system, after which it could sell the rest of its production on the market.)

These three were "separating out the stream of profits from the stream of taxes," "repaying or amortizing loans after taxes had been paid," and "meeting contractual obligations after taxes had been paid."

It may be that the whole *cheng-bao* system provides certain improvements over our existing system but it also presents major problems when it comes to furthering reform. It generates a number of new issues for a system that is already highly distorted. People who approve of the *cheng-bao* system for enterprises, and who think that this is the right way to go about reform overall, have now put forth these three new approaches as a way to improve the *cheng-bao* system itself in fundamental ways.

As pointed out by the World Bank and other experts, there are major problems with the *cheng-bao* system and one of these is the idea of "separating out" profit streams from tax streams. That is, to a large extent, the *cheng-bao* system encompasses all taxes, including the indirect tax. Some people have therefore suggested the idea of lowering the income tax rate to the proper degree. After that tax is paid, we then go about separating profits from taxes. Indirect taxes would still need to be paid in full, and the income tax would need to be paid according to the lowered rate. As for that portion of profits that are left over, once the standardized tax payment has been paid, we would use the *cheng-bao* method to (again) "hand up" to the State Asset Commission or relevant financial departments a portion of those profits as a dividend on fixed assets. By this line of thinking, tax and profit would in the future move toward public coffers in two different and distinct lines of income.

Many people both inside and outside China have misconceptions about this idea of a separation of taxes and profits. Foreigners think of it in simplistic terms as per the direct translation, dividing out or separating tax revenues and profits. They have not taken note of the fact that the contractual system incorporates a negotiation of how much to "hand up" to central government and how much remains in profit, and that after that division is made, there is another negotiation on how much goes to State coffers through a different channel. Many people within China feel that these two different streams of money can be separated out since they are in different categories. The key to the issue, however, lies in how much profit is left over after paying the income tax and how much of that in turn has to be "handed over" to the State-owned Assets Supervision and Administration Commission of the State Council (SASAC). This is still a matter of bargaining, that is, of negotiating the contract. The idea of separating out taxes from profits simply continues the basic idea behind the *cheng-bao* system. It does not in fact resolve the problem.

Let's take this a step further. One thought is to figure out in advance how much after-tax profit there will be, and then how much has to "be handed up" as part of the contractual obligation. This too has many unsatisfactory elements. There are many uncertainties in operating an enterprise. Profitability is affected by prices, markets, and a host of other things. An enterprise's profit levels may be quite high now, but may fall once competition comes into the picture. As technology improves, and as products are changed and upgraded, competition also becomes more intense. All of these things mean that uncertainties abound in terms of future profit levels. Some things are not determined by the enterprise itself at all. No matter how profitability may have been in the past, profitability in the future may not be reliably predictable.

The next issue to deal with is paying back loans after figuring the tax that an enterprise must pay. Enterprises should return loans in after-tax income. However, loans that were used for investment and the upgrading of technology should be figured as before-tax repayments that incorporate a depreciation allowance. According to concepts used in a commodity economy, capital investment is a necessary cost in the production of products, but the use of that capital should be figured over a long period of time. It should be amortized according to a depreciation period and depreciation rate in the years after the capital is formed. If loans funds were used to purchase equipment, a portion of the investment should be repaid through depreciation and amortization. Naturally, the depreciation rate should be reasonable. It should reflect standard practices of installment payments for the use of capital. Moreover, the amortized funds should no longer be consolidated or "pooled" by the central government through such means as the "two funds."

Given the above, the whole issue of whether loans should be paid back in before-tax or after-tax income should be further clarified and defined. Saying in broad terms that loans should be paid back in after-tax revenues can lead to different understandings.

PROBLEMATIC WAYS OF THINKING ABOUT A SEPARATION OF TAXES AND PROFITS

1   The idea of separating out taxes and profits inherits the basic thinking behind the *cheng-bao* or contract system. Tax authorities are not charged with actively promoting fair competition. Instead, they actually try to have a low level of standardization of tax revenues. They do not worry about whether or not after-tax amounts serve to standardize profit rates of different enterprises. It is not realistic to think we can standardize taxes, even at low tax rates, while we are still operating under highly distorted situations of all kinds. Trying to do so is not only logically inconsistent but has a bit of a self-deceptive flavor to it.

2   The proposal to separate out taxes and profits does not take into account any corrections for existing distortions. It pays undue attention to the distribution of enterprise profits. It focuses too much on the income tax and the after-tax profit and therefore overlooks reforms that address distortions of the tax base and reform of the indirect tax. In fact, there is still enormous potential in reform of the indirect tax and other forms of taxes, and we should be able to exploit these in terms of gaining more financial revenue.

3   The thinking about separation of taxes and profit is highly colored by the department that is involved. Tax revenue departments would like to standardize tax revenues. They would also like to ensure stable national fiscal revenues. Nevertheless, they fail to realize that tax revenues are a powerful form of economic leverage in promoting economic growth and creating competitive mechanisms. These departments also have a responsibility to push forward reform. To a large extent, the thinking that is behind a separation of taxes and

profit accepts the current degree of inequality. It accepts the phenomenon of bargaining. It also, however, wishes to push off this bargaining process and any unfair results onto the shoulders of the State Asset Commission or other departments in charge.

The idea behind such thinking is that problems can be pushed onto other government departments that are then forced to bargain with enterprises on a one-to-one basis and negotiate contracts. Such things as appropriation of fixed assets, land rent differentials, unreasonable prices, and welfare and retirement pensions become "not my fault." The fact is that all these issues are a problem and an opportunity not only for the State Asset Commission but for local governments as well, including local industrial management bureaus. If we simply hand off any intractable problems to other departments, not only will we be operating under highly arbitrary conditions, but we may create a hotbed of "using power to seek personal advantage."

4   The thinking behind separating out profits and taxes fails to take into consideration the integrated nature of reforms. It views tax revenues and prices as independent things that do not need to be coordinated. It has not figured out how to coordinate the gradual elimination of price distortions. The problem is one of perception. In reforms that are oriented in the direction of a commodity economy, adopting different taxes means using market-economy tax models and design to a large degree. Before market competition has formed in any real sense, however, and when price reform is not proceeding in parallel, can tax reform achieve its objectives all on its own? We have three options. One is to wait for all conditions to be thoroughly ripe before proceeding. The second is to have each sub-system try to handle things on its own. The third is to recognize the need for coordination and have various reforms reinforce one another.

5   The thinking behind separating out profits and taxes also fails to take into full consideration how we straighten out the relationships among our public finance, banking system, and enterprises. Right now, there are rather a lot of problems in how our public finance system, our banks, and our enterprises relate to one another.

In terms of the relationship between public finance and banks, our finance departments that are in the red make overdrafts from banks as a way to continue to disburse funds. Meanwhile, they do not adopt any standardized practices with respect to taxing specialized banks. Planning departments give lower levels of authority the task of making "planning-type loans," which puts a mandatory spin on making loans that will mostly not be repaid. This forces banks to take on the burden that by all rights should have been borne by public finance. Problems like these lead to highly unclear relationships between public finance departments and banks.

In terms of the relationship between banks and enterprises, given our fixed interest-rate system, when banks make loans to enterprises they make no allowance for different levels of risk. There are no normal mechanisms for getting different returns for different risks. Meanwhile, we do not have any reasonable ratio between the capital reserves of a bank and its loan portfolio, that is, the capital-to-debt ratio. When enterprises start losing money, therefore, loans generally turn into "bad accounts" or nonperforming loans. But since the loans were made with the intent of fulfilling some administrative policy or other, the non-performing loans are not considered to be the fault of bank operations. When, on the contrary, an enterprise is successful, it is able to make much higher returns off borrowed money than would normally be acceptable given that its cost of capital is so low. In other words, it makes excessive profits.

All of these abnormally chaotic relationships among our financial departments, banks, and enterprises must be rectified via the actions of fiscal and tax reform.

Unfortunately, the ideas that are behind a division of tax and profits strategy do not actually resolve this whole set of problems. Indeed, they preserve the ability of administrative departments to interfere in enterprise operations. Administrative departments are the ones determining how much an enterprise should contract to pay the department that has control over it, once the enterprise has paid its taxes. They are the ones determining what kinds of preferential treatment to extend to enterprises, including preferential treatment in getting loans. This infringes upon the autonomy of a bank's operations. It is not helpful in straightening out the whole situation.

The solution, the "way out," is to figure out where the distortions are and to deal with them. Fiscal and tax reform must revamp the system with the understanding that the aim is to eliminate distortions. We cannot let the existing distortions blur our line of vision. Instead, fiscal and tax reform must reexamine the tax base on which taxes are levied, it must adjust the structure of tax revenues, and must design a new model by which our public spending is paid out. The ultimate goal of economic-system reform is to move from an excessively centralized "centrally-planned economy" toward a "commodity economy with a plan" that encompasses fair competition. The design of the entire reform process must emphasize pressures of all kinds that force competitive mechanisms to achieve greater economic efficiency.

Design of the framework for fiscal and tax reform

All of our ways of thinking about fiscal and tax reform are constantly moving forward with the actual experience of reform, and with our ongoing theoretical explorations. Our current thinking is not something completely new but is a continuation of the thinking and framework that came before. It inherits the "two-step process of changing profits into taxes" and the guidance principles behind the 1986 plan for overall reform. Not only is it constantly being improved upon but it incorporates new situations and new experience. What I describe below has some differences with the fiscal and tax reform proposal that is being broadly publicized right now and that calls for separating out taxes and profits, contracts after tax, and repaying loans after tax. It attempts to be more courageous in its analysis and policy explorations.

The objectives and specific characteristics of fiscal and tax reform

Our efforts with respect to fiscal and tax reform should be oriented in the following four directions. The first is to eliminate distortions, promote competition, and speed up the pace of reforms that lead to a commodity economy. The second is to increase fiscal revenues and make sure that they are stable. It is to increase revenues in line with economic growth. The third is to change the distribution of revenue income in a fundamental way, as it relates both to the State versus enterprises and the central government versus local governments. The fourth is to increase coordination between reforms of the fiscal and tax and other reforms, so as to be able to deal with all kinds of changes in economic behavior that occur after reform.

This article focuses specifically on eliminating distortions and promoting competition, which are the priorities for this immediate period of reform.

Our conceptions about how to reform China's socialist economic system have formed gradually, and have been based on ever-greater self-understanding. The whole series of economic reforms over this past dozen years have not only made progress over our traditional centrally-planned economic system but they have also attempted to break down and eradicate old systems and erect new ones with the aim of preserving and improving our essential socialist nature. Our reforms have improved economic efficiency and growth capacity to a large extent. They have set up mechanisms for more efficient allocation of resources. They have created mechanisms for incentives that rely to a greater degree on the market.

Fiscal and tax reform is only one part of the comprehensive proposal for reform. Fiscal policies are not almighty and they cannot resolve all problems in our economy. However, our immediate fiscal and tax policies can go a long way in eliminating distortions, promoting competition, and accelerating reform. By ensuring revenues and maintaining our fiscal balance, moreover, they can play a major role in the overall process of reform.

Right now, we are seeing a fairly fast drop in the percentage of revenues that comes from fiscal sources, so fiscal and tax reform are particularly important to ensure that our revenues are adequate for us to perform existing government functions, as well as those we envisage in our proposed reforms.

We can no longer rely solely on increasing central control as a way to increase fiscal revenues. Rather, an increase in revenues needs to be achieved through eliminating distortions, increasing competition, and expanding the tax base. We need to promote more rational structures and greater efficiency that can then serve as the basis for greater tax income. At the same time, we need to reform the administrative system that deals with tax collection and tax revenues. We must emphasize the "tax sharing system" (between central and local governments), and the separation of the "three authorities" at all levels of government, that is, separation of the three governmental functions of making rules, enforcing rules, and regulatory oversight.

Our current reform proposal is both an extension of what came earlier and a further development of its way of thinking. We first had a two-step process of changing profits into taxes, and then the fiscal and tax system reform of 1986.

One unique feature of the 1986 reform was that it emphasized the indivisible nature of reforms to do with prices, taxes, public finance, banking, domestic and foreign trade, and enterprises. For that reason, it was called "accompanying" or "integrated" reforms. A second feature was that it encouraged price reform as soon as possible in order to create conditions for equal competition among enterprises and accelerate their participation in a competitive marketplace. A third feature was the very explicit "tax sharing system" between the central and local governments.

The main principle in this was that any forms of tax that might negatively affect the economic efficiency of the entire system should be designated as national taxes. Any forms of tax that would not severely affect the behavior of local governments and that would instead benefit local government income should be designated as local taxes and should go to local governments. Local governments were to pull out of any operations and interference in the business of profit-making production. They were to grant further autonomy in decision-making to enterprises. Meanwhile, local governments were to be granted more decision-making autonomy over projects that required a reasonable outlay of public spending. The design of our current proposed fiscal and tax system continues towards orientation of the points described above, and adheres to the same principles. It goes further in stressing that we must reduce the three main "distortions," and it emphasizes the necessity of speeding up competitive conditions.

Economic progress has now created new demands. In 1988, given clear inflation, we adopted stabilizing measures and gradually benefited from those. We used fairly restrictive fiscal and monetary policies to control aggregate demand. Certain problems in the economy were moderated as a result, allowing some price reforms to be implemented and allowing us to reduce price distortions somewhat. In the second half of 1989 and in 1990 we implemented various further price controls and reduced our subsidies on a number of import categories. Prices that we had frozen again in 1988 were gradually released. We reduced the distance between our actual economic situation and a "competitive marketplace."

Since 1987, we have promoted a strategy for outward-oriented development. We have emphasized bringing in competition from outside, and participation in the division of labor in international markets. Having controlled aggregate demand, our growth in foreign trade has been quite good. Introducing external competition has corrected some systemic problems that were not ideal. Some prices are moving more in the direction of prices on international markets. Given this new environment, enterprises are gradually moving toward greater reality in the pricing of their costs. This applies particularly to foreign-invested enterprises as well as private and State funding, and to privately-owned enterprises and town-and-village enterprises. Cost management is now coming more in line with the standards of competitive markets and international practices.

The average profit rate on sales fell from 27 percent in 1978 to 18 percent in 1987 and in 1990 was roughly 13 percent. This is a necessary trend as competition picks up. If we were truly to have equal competition, the average profit rate on sales would be roughly 5 percent. In this process, the irrational constraints of the old system are now mainly concentrated in large- and medium-sized State-Owned Enterprises. This makes them less dynamic and increases the need to accelerate further reforms in this area.

At the same time, we have seen a relatively fast drop in fiscal revenues and we are experiencing serious budget deficits. We also see large quantities of "command-type" loans being made, which means that problems that should have been addressed by public funds are now being shifted onto banks. The result has been that enterprises are faced with large amounts of triangular debt, in which three parties owe one another money. This is an indication of a severe worsening of discipline in fiscal affairs. The problems relating to large- and medium-sized State-Owned Enterprises are most pronounced. New circumstances are exacerbating the conflicts and problems are becoming quite complex. It is hard to achieve any results by having just one department carry out reforms so we are placing much greater demands on coordinated sets of reforms.

The ongoing increase in bargaining behavior and a system characterized by administrative-type division of power are making the phenomenon of blockaded markets ever more apparent. This is increasing the potential for inflation. All of this requires that we reexamine the pace of reform and consider reform proposals that are more courageous and comprehensive.

Fiscal and tax reforms can play the following roles:

1   Fiscal and tax reform can play a direct role in increasing the overall level of fiscal revenues. This can be accomplished particularly through expanding the tax base and increasing the general level of tax revenues.
2   Fiscal and tax reform plays an absolutely vital role in resolving the relationship between the central and local governments, as well as in transforming the functions of both central and local governments.
3   Fiscal and tax reform plays an active role in furthering competition. It can create the conditions for fair competition among enterprises, and it can also reduce behavior that seeks to segregate markets. It helps in setting up a unified market.
4   Fiscal and tax reform plays an enormous role in terms of income distribution. Not only does it play a direct role in allocating individual income taxes, inheritance taxes, and gift taxes, but more importantly it helps with the process of separating out government authority from enterprise administration. It can reduce "rent-seeking behavior," artificial monopolies, and segregated markets. As a result, it can greatly reduce unfair income distribution that is caused by government officials and enterprises being in business together.

We cannot, however, use fiscal and tax reform to resolve the following problems:

1   Fiscal and tax reform cannot resolve the problem of unclear definition of property rights. It cannot resolve problems that result from distribution of benefits derived from property rights.

2   Tax revenues can only play a limited role in price systems. Tax-revenue policies can help rationalize prices and can supplement price distortions for a limited time, but they cannot substitute for prices themselves or play a decisive role in determining prices.

3   Fiscal and tax reform cannot resolve income distributions that are caused by the two-track pricing system. Instituting two different tax rates on income that is derived from "within the plan" and "outside the plan" does not work.

4   Fiscal and tax reform cannot provide an accurate measure of rents derived from resources and land use, nor can it regulate income from these things. In the absence of market prices for these things, fiscal and taxation measures can moderate the excessive inequality that results from occupying land or resources, but any such measures are transitional and temporary. They cannot become standardized approaches to resolving these issues.

A fiscal and tax reform proposal that aims for market competition

REVISE COST ACCOUNTING METHODS

1   As based on the principle of "more work more pay," enterprises should compensate people for their different contributions of differing amounts and kinds of manpower, and all such work should be entered into costs. All such welfare benefits as housing and pensions as they relate to labor should be incorporated in costs. Rents for housing and a portion of social security fees should be one of the components of costs.

2   We should increase depreciation allowances. As nearly as possible, depreciation timetables and methods should approximate the realities of time payments on use of capital (M). We should correct the former point of view that regarded depreciation as a kind of payment for the wear-and-tear on existing fixed assets. We should understand it conceptually as a percentage of capital costs that are allocated to production expenses over time.

REFORM THE INDIRECT TAX SYSTEM

1   As costs are made more "real," that is, are accounted for properly, we should considerably increase the tax base for indirect taxes and reduce the tax base for income taxes.

2   We should increase the scope within which a value-added tax is applied. A value-added tax should be imposed on both the wholesale arena and the large-scale retail arena. A value-added tax makes it easier to adopt unified tax rates with smaller step-level increases. Value-added taxes have several options for the tax base. These are generally the GNP type, the income type, and the consumption type of tax base. For now, there are certain benefits to China temporarily adopting the GNP-type of value-added tax base. On the one hand, the tax base is fairly large and on the other hand this enables us to

change the ways in which we control investment. It makes investment more cautious. Methods of collecting the value-added tax should be changed to a tax on top of prices (outside the price) and to tax withholding.

3   We should allow the ongoing existence of operating taxes and certain specific product taxes (these are a modified form of consumption taxes). However, we should control the scope within which these are applied to different product categories. Operating taxes should mainly be applied to retail and service industries that the value-added tax cannot deal with. The tax burden can be higher than the corresponding level of a value-added tax that would otherwise be paid. The aim is to have as much economic activity as possible shifted into categories in which we collect a value-added tax. In terms of imports and exports, we should completely end indirect taxes on all exported products. At the same time, we should apply an indirect tax to imported products. Customs duties on imported products are a supplementary form of additional income. We should reduce the price distortions that are caused by the structure of customs duties.

Adjustment of tax income on property or "ownership of factors"

1   *The current situation with respect to State-owned assets is highly complex.* Compensation for the use of such assets should be based on principles that are future-oriented and that do not rely on how things worked in the past. The price at which State-owned assets are valued should be a market price. Right now, a large percentage of our State-Owned Enterprises have insufficient registered capital and we need to supplement it with share capital. As a compromise method, on a temporary basis we can allow local governments to collect a tax on assets that is set at a fairly low tax rate. To a degree, this will reduce inequalities in enterprises. It will enable local governments to decide upon reduction and exemption of taxes as based on historical reasons as well as actual circumstances.

2   *We should adopt a different approach to land that is located in municipal centers and land in general.* This is in order to encourage a more optimal land-use pattern in large- and medium-sized cities in particular. It is to provide a motivation for certain industries to shift their operations to areas outside cities, while allowing high value-added industries to be in areas where there are better facilities. Land-use taxes and fees for land that is in municipal centers should be decided upon by local governments.

3   *Tax rates on resources should take the scarcity or abundance of the resource into account.* Such tax rates should look at the grade of the material and the distance required for transport. Tax brackets and development fees should be set at different levels and should be reasonable, so as to encourage equal competition. At the same time, taxes on resources can help address the problem of their waste and excessive use. They can encourage more effective use and more reasonable exploitation of resources.

4   *Reform of the income tax on enterprises.* As the tax base for enterprise income taxes gets smaller, the portion of enterprise income tax that goes toward

public revenues is being reduced. However, China has already set tax rates at a fairly low level on foreign-invested enterprises and enterprises owned by other forms of ownership. Because of this, we have a problem with policy continuity if we raise some tax rates. Since we emphasize the principle of equality in tax treatment, we can consider setting an income tax rate on all companies (enterprises) at a level of around 30 to 33 percent. Other than certain specific cases, we would then no longer extend preferential policies that reduce or exempt taxes on start-up enterprises over an initial period. By doing that, we would expand the tax base. We would apply a uniform tax treatment on collective enterprises, town-and-village enterprises, and privately-owned enterprises. We would not have different tax-revenue treatment depending on the "ownership form" of the entity. We could apply a low rate on particularly small enterprises, those with income that is only enough to support the wages of an average of three to five employees, in order to support job creation. This would incorporate a graduated tax. (From a theoretical perspective, however, we should not adopt a graduated tax with respect to enterprises.)

5 *The initial stage of developing a personal income tax and a salary tax.* In terms of our long-term goals, public revenues from individual income taxes should constitute a fairly high percentage of our total tax revenue. This will increase our ability to redistribute tax income. The international practice is to have a salary tax deducted in advance from a person's salary. This allows a government to implement its social security plans in a more solid way. This reform would also be done to enable enterprise reform, to enable enterprises to fire workers, and to set up a labor market. Certain basic conditions must apply before we can collect a personal income tax. We need a fairly sound and complete fiscal system and a fairly well advanced financial system that does not make as much use of cash transactions. Meanwhile, we will need a certain period of time for people to adjust psychologically to the idea of paying taxes. Because of this, our best option is to adopt a tax that deducts a certain amount in advance from salaries. For the relatively few people who have a fairly high income, we would have a voluntary system of reporting income and placing a tax on what people report. For now, we do not have enormous disparities in income. Moreover, the differences in income come primarily from distortions, insufficient competition, and administrative interference. At this current stage, we do not need to be overly careful about instituting a progressive income tax. We can use a few years to do the preparatory work for this. Instead, for now we should focus our direct-tax efforts on setting up a system that deducts taxes from wages and salaries. The ultimate goal of tax reform with respect to individual income taxes is to have a comprehensive integrated personal income tax system. If we put too much emphasis right now on the sources of income, all that does is create opportunities for people to evade taxes. It also makes the task of managing taxes more complex. For the time being, personal income taxes therefore cannot become a major source of income in government revenues. Over the long term, however, it will be extremely important as a means to redistribute income.

6 *Designing the tax-sharing system (between central and local governments).*
   a The design of the tax-sharing system should pay particular attention to the
      influence of the system on the behavior of governments at all levels. The
      tax categories, and especially the definition of large categories, should take
      into consideration which level of government would benefit most from the
      tax. At the same time, the tax should become an incentive mechanism that
      forces each level of government to behave in ways that are beneficial to
      the entire economy. In terms of the cost of collecting taxes, tax categories
      that local governments can handle in the easiest way, in terms of access
      to information, should accrue to local governments. This applies even
      if some categories of tax lead to economic behavior that involves some
      distortions. Tax categories that are closely related to local infrastructure
      development should belong to local governments. This will facilitate their
      task of creating jobs, increasing public facilities and basic infrastructure,
      and transforming their local government functions. Because of this, we
      need to achieve a complete and absolute separation of the tax bureaus of
      the central government and the tax bureaus of local governments.
   b We should not demand that the tax revenues of local governments be tied com-
      pletely to their public spending. After carrying out the reforms as described
      above, central fiscal revenues will increase while the percentage of fiscal
      expenditures that local governments have to carry will increase. To help bal-
      ance local budgets, therefore, the central government should provide local
      governments with fairly large amounts of transfer payments. If central allo-
      cations are not specified in terms of their ultimate use, they should be spent
      depending on specific conditions in the area—their populations, resources,
      natural conditions, economic development and income conditions, and so
      on. This should be carried out according to standardized formulas.
   c Local governments have independent authority to pass legislation on their
      own taxes. They should also have considerable autonomy in decision-
      making with respect to all tax categories that belong to local governments,
      including calculations of the tax base, formulation of tax rates, and meth-
      ods of collecting taxes. However, in principle, local governments cannot
      encroach upon the tax base and taxation methods that are national in
      character. As they move toward systems that are competitive, local gov-
      ernments should implement tax collection methods and should design tax
      systems that are reasonable, so as to be able to draw in more investment
      and manpower and grow their local economies.
   d In designing the "common-use tax," we should change our former way of
      thinking. This kind of tax takes advantage of the way local information is
      more accessible by local governments, who then help the central govern-
      ment collect taxes on behalf of the central government. This money is
      not to be collected by local governments in order to help them balance
      their budgets.
7 *Integrated policies that are put in place when prices are still severely distorted.* In industries where prices are still distorted, for example, grain

processing and oil refining, at present we still cannot use competitive mechanisms to put pressure on aggregate sums, nor can we rely totally on market sales to compensate according to our principle of "to each according to his labor." We should therefore carry out price reform as soon as possible. However, given that decision-making levels have not yet firmly resolved to implement price rationalization, we will need to use transitional methods. We can use calculating methods that use production variables to simulate the distribution results of market competition, then quantitative econometric methods to arrive at the actual production variables of the given industry. In this way, we would calculate an overall "large-bore" labor compensation that incorporates wages, bonuses, most welfare benefits, housing, health care, and retirement funds.

8 *Estimation of consolidated accounts.* In implementing the above reforms, a number of changes will occur in the consolidated list of categories of national tax revenues. If we assume that these changes occur in 1990, we can compare the projected change in tax revenues to what actually occurred in 1990. This will allow us to evaluate the design of our reform proposal. In 1990, China's GNP was RMB 1.76 trillion. The overall amounts and structure of fiscal revenues were as follows (see Table 4.1).

"Debt revenue" includes both overseas borrowing and income from domestic debt instruments. Subsidies to loss-making enterprises has already deducted out income from those enterprises. The taxes from industry and commerce include the salt tax, a special tax on fuel oil, and a tax on construction. They do not include income taxes on State-Owned Enterprises or "adjustment taxes" on State-Owned Enterprises The agricultural and animal husbandry tax includes a deed tax and a land-use tax on farmland.

Table 4.1 1990 fiscal revenue structure (units: RMB 100 million)

Total fiscal revenues		*3,312.60*
All different categories		2,821.86
of which:	Industrial and commercial tax revenues	1,970.87
	Customs duties	159.01
	Agricultural and animal husbandry taxes	87.86
Enterprise income		78.30
Debt revenue		375.45
Development funds from energy, transport, and major construction projects		185.08
Other		430.74
Subsidies to loss-making enterprises		−578.88

Source: *China Statistical Yearbook 1991,* National Bureau of Statistics, China Statistics Press (Beijing), 1991

If we assume that the reform proposal as above is implemented, then changes in the income tax accounts of 1990 will be as follows:

1 The tax base of indirect taxes will increase. Since bonuses will be incorporated in wages, the payroll tax (in the form of a withholding tax) will also be included in the tax base of indirect taxes. Moreover, since costs will have increased once they are accounted for on an actual basis, the indirect tax base will increase by around one-third.

   The primary tax among indirect taxes is the value-added tax. This will adopt two different rates. At present, the 14 percent rate that China uses covers more items. Nevertheless, the tax ultimately paid by purchasers comes to around 17 percent due to a variety of other factors that include the business tax that is generally levied on materials and business transactions as well as foreign trade.

   We therefore use 17 percent as the standard value-added tax rate, and we use 5 to 8 percent as the rate on a small number of daily consumer items. For the purposes of this exercise, we adopt the GNP model of value-added tax. We estimate that the value-added tax can be levied on 85 percent of GNP, but that 10 percent of this amount should have the lower rate of 8 percent applied to it. Our tax revenues from value-added taxes therefore come to the following:

   GNP in 1990 × 10 percent × 8 percent + GNP in 1990 × 75 percent × 17 percent = 140.8 + 2244 = RMB 238.48 billion.

2 The tax on tobacco and alcohol and other such special consumer items comes to RMB 40 billion.

3 The payroll tax is calculated on the basis of that portion of the monetized income of urban residents that can be monitored and measured. This income comes to RMB 500 billion, which, at a 15 percent rate, results in tax revenue of RMB 75 billion. This means that local governments have RMB 50 billion to use as funds for social security.

4 Revenue from customs duties must place severe limits on any special "reductions and exemptions." Customs duties result in revenues of RMB 30 billion.

5 Enterprise profits that can be monitored and measured are estimated at 4 percent of GNP. (The actual figure is 6 percent but only some two-thirds of that is retrievable.) The tax-revenue income is therefore RMB 23.2 billion.

6 We reduce the scope of the business tax down to roughly 40 percent of the original level. Tax revenue from the business tax therefore is reduced from a previous RMB 50 billion down to RMB 20 billion.

7 We do not anticipate changing the agricultural tax or the tax on land use for now. We have not done enough grassroots-level work on this, so we are keeping the amount at RMB 7 billion.

8 We are keeping the amount of "other revenues" at RMB 30 billion, the resource tax at RMB 2 billion, the asset tax at RMB 3 billion, and the land-use tax at RMB 2 billion.

The result comes to total tax revenues of RMB 470.7 billion, which is 26.7 percent of GNP. Given losses when we begin to implement this system, the total may actually come down to 25 percent of GNP. Of this amount, revenues from the value-added tax would constitute 50 percent, or 13.56 percent of GNP.

The influence of the above reforms once they start to be implemented

The evolving structure of China's national income

The average financial status of enterprises: Once reforms are enacted as described above, we should expect certain changes in the structure of enterprise finances. Material inputs into production may change but their significance to society will be modest, so we overlook that consideration. Depreciation will increase by several times. This will be necessary to upgrade equipment and expand production in line with autonomous decision-making. At the same time, a portion of that depreciation will be retrieved to pay back loans for renovations. It will therefore more truly reflect the amortization of capital that is invested in production. Interest rates that enterprises have to pay will rise slightly, to meet a market equilibrium point. The cost of labor will increase very substantially since it will now incorporate the bonuses, housing, pensions and so on that were formerly taken out of profits. Plus we should calculate a payroll tax into the cost of labor. Given the above increases in costs, the indirect tax will have to increase by a substantial amount.

At the same time, enterprise profits will go down considerably. We should take note of the fact that profits previously had to cover the enterprise income tax, and energy and transportation funds, as well as bonuses, welfare benefits, and other payments. After reform, enterprises will pay relatively small amounts of income tax. Previously, only a portion of profits could go into investment in production. After reform, profits will go 100 percent into investment in production (that is, after the enterprise tax and if no dividends are paid out). Due to reduced profits, if retained income is insufficient, then enterprises will have to rely on direct or indirect financing to raise funds for new investment. Under these conditions, the *ex factory* price of goods should be expected to rise by about 10 percent. Circulation taxes refer to the value-added tax or the business tax on circulation; profits in this sphere will drop substantially to around one-third of what they were before.

Changes in the structure of GNP

If reform is carried out as designed, the value of industrial output will increase once the sources of GNP are adjusted. The reason is that industrial output was somewhat under-valued before. Artificial means depressed *ex factory* prices, meaning that a portion of production value was transmitted on to the circulation sphere. Agriculture will not change much with this reform. The drop in the commercial portion will indicate in very clear terms that China's tertiary industries are extremely vulnerable. Their standing in China's GNP is overly low. One of the reasons for this drop in standing is that *ex factory* prices will no longer be controlled and their entry into circulation will not be restricted. Competition will therefore lower selling prices. As time passes, however, the circulation sector will grow substantially once freer entry into this sector of the economy is allowed. An increase in the communications and transport sector will be a dynamic process. Competition will increase once market entry into this sector is allowed. This will ensure that the sector maintains a certain percentage of GNP. The reason for a decline in the percentage of the construction industry in the GNP structure is because reproduction that is of an "extensive" nature will decrease after reform adjustments are made. More efforts will begin to go into technological renovation and "intensive" type economic growth. After housing reform is implemented, however, this will change and this sector will again see a rise.

The distribution of the employed population in various types of industries will change after adjustments. The number employed in industrial departments will drop somewhat. The reason is that allowing competition into industrial enterprises will cause them to cut personnel. Those who are fired will shift to tertiary industries. This will be beneficial in reducing the costs of labor. In agriculture (by which I mean farming and not town-and-village enterprises), the rapid increase in town-and-village enterprises will slow down for a while and some people may return to working in agriculture. Employment in commerce and in communications and transport will increase very substantially. All kinds of restrictions that formerly applied to the circulation sphere will be eliminated, allowing entry into this market. This will provide new job opportunities, to the extent that this area may incorporate 20 percent of the current employed population in cities. The number of people employed in the construction industry may decline somewhat, but after housing reform is implemented the outlook for this sector will change. The total number of employed people will rise by roughly 5 to 10 percent. This will be highly significant in resolving our problems of finding jobs for people, especially once reform allows for bankruptcy of enterprises and those former employees become unemployed.

Within restructured GNP spending, the first step will see total national fiscal revenues increase by 5 to 7 percent. Not only will central government public spending not increase, however, it will show some decline. (This does not include transfer payments to local governments.) Public spending by local governments will rise to a fairly large extent given large central government allocations. Since depreciation allowances for enterprises will rise and profits will decline, from the perspective of the current (unreasonable) indicators, in overall terms the funds "outside the budget" will decline and spending outside the budget will also decline somewhat. Spending by urban households will be slightly less than it was before (this does not include spending on new housing, or paying into social security funds). The reason is that after the inflation of 1988, people's actual income levels were already eaten up by inflation. In addition, forceful measures were taken to control aggregate demand. This, plus the new financial systems of enterprises meant that consumption funds did not increase to any large degree. This diminished part of the GNP structure will be more apparent. What this means is that there has actually been a solution to the difficult task of controlling a ballooning of consumption funds. Nevertheless, what this means also is that disguised wages have been reduced and also disguised consumption subsidies. This has caused a portion of consumption derived at public expense to be shifted onto the consumption bill of citizens themselves. A slight increase in the spending of rural households is due to ongoing reductions in controls on agricultural prices. This has led to a slight increase in those prices.

Changes in how enterprises feel about all this

1   Competitive pressures have clearly intensified. Since profits have gone down, it is now less possible for enterprises to show high sales figures simply by lowering their profits. They now have to rely on real reductions in costs, improvements in quality, control over wages, and reductions in loans to be competitive in the market.

2   Since the profit component of an enterprise's business will be lower, enterprises will no longer need to put such time and effort into deciding upon the uses to which to put profits. They can put all retained earnings into business-type investments (including investments in human resources). Bonuses, welfare benefits and so on will already have been incorporated into wages. They will pay a 15 percent payroll tax with far greater transparency of everything. Managers and employees will not try to match the wages and bonuses of other peer enterprises, which will also be conducive to managing total demand. Reduced profits will also make it easier to calculate tax revenues and we should see less tax evasion.

3   Autonomy in the business decisions of enterprises will be improved enormously. This will apply particularly to depreciation allowances and how to employ people. Local governments will have greater responsibility for social security functions and will allow enterprises greater latitude in firing workers. Other aspects will allow for new job opportunities (policies that allow for freer market entry in various industries, enhanced employment training provided by local governments, and so on).

4   The relationships between enterprises and financial institutions will be clarified to a greater degree. Once enterprises have lower profits, they will rely more on "public capital" for investments to expand reproduction. Whether this involves direct or indirect financing, it will need the banking industry as intermediaries. Enterprises will be adopting open financial systems. They will have to maintain a healthy relationship between equity capital and debt. Otherwise, they will not be able to get loans at normal rates.

5   The overly close relationship between enterprises and local governments will be weakened. Enterprises already have what is required to make autonomous decisions in the various areas of production, supply, marketing, price

determination, taking out loans, and so on. Tax revenues will be standardized making enterprises into true independent economic entities as opposed to being under the supervision of "grandma" (the local government).

On strengthening the value-added tax

After reform, the tax base of the indirect tax will expand and indirect taxes may constitute 69 percent of total tax revenues. This figure incorporates the broad definition of indirect taxes, which includes product taxes, special consumption taxes, the business tax, customs duties, and so on. This percentage is on the high side when compared to other countries. However, when one thinks of the unique two-track situation in China's economy, it is appropriate that the level be this high at this particular stage. As preparatory work on the direct tax is carried out and we garner results, the percentage of the direct tax will gradually rise. Moreover, if China can manage to keep a fair level of income distribution, then the value-added tax will be effective and reasonable. We will not need to rely on direct taxes with their progressive effect to provide a regulating role in equalizing incomes (see Table 4.2).

Changes in the functions of local governments

1 The functions of the local people's congresses and the government will include the following: (a) enacting local legislation as under the framework of national legislation; (b) formulating regional development plans and strategies that guide development; (c) confirming investments to be made in such things as basic infrastructure and environmental rehabilitation through arrangements made in the local government budget, participating in investments in specific

Table 4.2 Dependence of countries categorized by per capita GNP in 1968 on indirect tax and custom duties

Per capita GNP (USD)	Number of countries	Share of indirect tax in total tax revenue (percent)	Share of custom duties in total tax revenue (percent)
Developing countries 100 and below	20	68	35
101–200	11	64	32
201–500	19	64	33
501–850	9	50	18
Highly developed countries above 850	15	32	4

Source: R. I. McKinnon: *Money and Capital in Economic Development.* SDX Joint Publishing Company, 1988

industries and electing to invest in appropriate orientations, as allowed for by a reasonable application of the tax sharing system; (d) promoting the development of regional resources and the protection of the natural environment, improving the investment environment, and into science, education, culture, and healthcare, improving all kinds of service industries and developing commerce; (e) running occupational education facilities, promoting job creation, attracting talent; (f) actively promoting and guiding the enterprise reform of the region, and participating in rectifying and rescuing backward enterprises during the transition period; (g) reducing and exempting regional taxes as necessary and extending policy subsidies in order to implement the region's income distribution policies (such as rent subsidies for housing, allowances for purchase of vegetables, poverty alleviation, rescuing backward enterprises, and so on); (h) carrying out design and exploration of the region's own reforms, including those related to land, housing, social security, and some employment policies; (i) handling local taxes which, under the "tax sharing system," mainly mean town-and-village enterprise income taxes, individual income taxes, municipal building taxes, payroll taxes, local resources taxes, and business taxes.

Local governments will no longer be responsible for macroeconomic issues, such as the quantity of money supply and price indexes for regional prices. They will no longer interfere in the business of local banks. Instead, local governments will focus more on improving the investment climate for investments in their area, on improving their natural and biological environments, and on job creation and education. They will focus more on being responsible to the people in their own area. At a more significant level, this transformation of local government functions will help local people conduct regulatory oversight over the performance of local governments. This will prepare the groundwork for moving to direct elections as the method of choosing the local government.

2   The relationship between local governments and enterprises. Local governments will no longer be in charge of managing and intervening in profit-making enterprises. Nevertheless, for a certain transition period, one of the transitional economic functions of local governments will be to help loss-making enterprises that are publicly owned. They are to facilitate a smooth transition by drawing up progressively decreasing subsidies for loss-making enterprises.

After fiscal and tax reform is carried out, one-third of enterprises may face losses as they are forced to compete. Some of these may be able to survive by improving their management, developing new products, adjusting their factor allocations and so on, but others will only survive a few years due to historical and other factors, and only then if various adjustments are made. For this, it will be necessary for the local government to determine a limited length of time in which such adjustments will be allowed. Local governments should increase their financial auditing of such enterprises as they provide progressively lower subsidies. They should choose "leadership teams" for these enterprises with care. They should strengthen "guidance measures" that are scientifically determined, in order to help them turn around their losses and become profitable. If this is not possible, then they should allow them to go bankrupt or be merged with other enterprises. These functions are closely related to the interests of local governments themselves, since the performance of local enterprises affects local employment. Excessive subsidies, meanwhile, will reduce the amount of funds that can be put to other uses, affecting the region's overall business climate.

Local governments may also carry out economic functions in other spheres, such as promoting the growth of all kinds of markets, helping to upgrade enterprise management structures including facilitating generational change in management, developing tertiary industries, helping local enterprises make use of their own comparative advantage through greater access to information, and helping factors become more mobile. Local governments should work hard to eradicate all barriers to unified markets and all forms of behavior that could be described as extortion, blackmail, and racketeering. They should create a more ideal economic and social environment for enterprises.

3   Fiscal balance of local governments. While local governments will have greater autonomy in decision-making with respect to tax revenues and public spending, they will also be responsible for maintaining a self-determined balance in accounts as they receive transfer payments from the central government. Double-entry bookkeeping is the internationally followed practice. Even though the United States does not implement this at the national level, many local governments adopt the method. Local governments in China should take advantage of its strengths while avoiding its shortcomings. Current-account revenues and expenditures should be in balance in the books of local governments. There absolutely must not be allowance for any deficit. Capital accounts must also balance out, and local governments must receive permission from the central government for the issuing of any debt instruments (bonds).

With respect to the efficiency with which public funds are spent and the cost of taking in fiscal revenues, local governments should bear a greater responsibility given that the country is so large. They should be responsible for handling more local spending and also for taking in taxes since they have the advantage of local information (and lower costs of tax collection). They are also more effective when it comes to not damaging the efficacy of local incentives (which helps prevent the distortion of local government behavior). They should handle those types of taxes that are directly related to the functions of local governments, and taxes on things that involve small sums and messy accounts but that still are necessary. When local governments have gaps in their fiscal accounts, this will be remedied with transfer payments from the central government. There are two types of central government transfer payments: one does not specify the use to which they should be put—the local government may decide on its own how to spend them. The other is allocated by the central government for specific projects.

Local governments have autonomy in issuing local government bonds, but this must be done with great caution and it also must first receive approval from the central government. The central government must confirm that the local government can pay back the debt, and it must confirm the social and economic benefits of issuing the debt.

4 The performance standards that apply to the economic work of local governments will include the following: (a) Improving the environment, which includes basic infrastructure and the ecological environment as well as the living environment, meaning public transport, housing, public service facilities, and public service endeavors. (b) Increasing employment opportunities, meeting the needs of ongoing growth of the local region. (c) Investing in human resource development. Developing universal education is one of the main responsibilities of local governments. At the same time, local governments should put effort into developing higher education as well as vocational-technical training, as a way to promote employment. (d) Social security as it relates to the economy. Payroll taxes are now becoming local taxes. The local government must handle pension funds properly, as well as unemployment relief and re-employment training. It must manage all matters to do with medical care and welfare for disabled people. (e) Improving the housing system, providing good housing conditions and facilitating more flexible relocation of people. (f) Promoting market development so that enterprises and local citizens benefit from markets. (g) Providing business information that comes from both international and domestic sources, so that business entities can provide quality service. (h) With respect to justice systems and regulatory supervision, establishing, improving upon, and maintaining the economic systems that allow them to function. This includes opposing monopolies, encouraging start-ups, promoting competition, and maintaining economic order.

5 The establishment of local tax systems. In implementing the tax-sharing system as described above, it will be necessary to reorganize tax bureaus in each local government. The two distinct functions of tax collection and tax management should be separated out, for both national taxes and local taxes. The current system has one tax bureau in each local government, and these should now be separated out into two bureaus. There will be a tax bureau that is administered by central-government authorities, and a bureau that is local. The attempt to set up a multi-tiered tax management system is being done to ensure that taxing authority is truly delegated to the level of the local government.

First, there must be national-level legislation on tax collection. Within the scope of that legislation, local governments will be allowed to enact their own tax legislation. Local laws cannot, however, encroach upon the national tax base. This is in order to ensure that national tax collection has priority, is unified, and is mandatory.

Similar principles must also be followed at the lower level of tax collection. There should be explicit rules that govern any extra taxes or supplementary taxes in local areas. Local governments can pass their own legislation on taxes, but the central government has the authority to review and cancel these as necessary. This should allow for a division of labor at the different levels of taxation.

Transforming the functions of central government organizations, and central-government public finance

After reform, the microeconomic functions of the central government will be reduced somewhat. Government organizations (administrative institutions) should shrink somewhat in total numbers given the change in functions and their budgets should be reduced by cutting a portion of public spending to them. The reorganization of central government organizations may be able to turn some government departments into "semi-private (non-government)" kinds of organizations. These will focus on "promotion" and "services," as opposed to "control." They will serve to coordinate relationships among enterprises.

Central-government public spending

Within State spending, quite an impressive percentage relates to fees for "economic construction." This is after deducting out national defense, administration costs, culture and education, and national debt payments. Statistics from relevant sources indicate that this has been the case ever since the country was founded. As a percentage of total spending allocated for "basic infrastructure," the percentage spent on "economic construction fees" has consistently been high. Within this percentage, quite a large amount is invested in profit-making projects.

As we go further in price reform, a fairly substantial portion of investment currently being made in energy and raw materials industries can be "drawn back" or recovered. These expenditures on the part of the State should be reduced. The purpose is to utilize limited funds in a more reasonable way. Within allocations for basic infrastructure, our current spending on culture and education is around 8 percent. This portion of spending should be the responsibility of local governments. Having the central government pay for these is going beyond the functions of "central government" and meddling in local affairs. Moreover, many smaller items are still inappropriately controlled by central finance and departments directly managed by central government. If we can stop this kind of thing, we will be able to reduce the pressures on our fiscal expenditures even more.

Spending by central finance should mainly be concentrated on such things as central government expenditures, national defense, some higher education costs, large-scale environmental remediation, science and technology development, and basic infrastructure facilities that are national in scope. Some basic infrastructure should use fees as much as possible and some should be paid for by local-government bonds and raising funds from the public. Central-government spending should have nothing at all to do with such things as profit-making enterprises or production-type enterprises.

Central government revenues mainly rely on collections by the State Tax Administration under the leadership of the central government. The State Tax Administration should have a reasonable salary structure and sufficient incentives to ensure good work. It should adhere to a system that rotates people out of office on a regular basis and that has a separation of the three powers. All of these things are internationally recognized as effective practices. If there are any overlapping taxes that are levied by both central and local governments, collection should be undertaken by local governments given the consideration of the costs of collection.

After implementing the above reforms, given that central finance revenues will grow substantially, while central government expenditures will decline in accord with lowered responsibilities (after allowing for transfer payments to local governments), it should be easier for the central government to achieve a balance in its accounts. Central finance will then make transfer payments to lower levels of government.

Transfer payments of the central government

While it is true that China's various regions differ greatly, this does not mean that we cannot apply some uniform laws to how we handle the issue of central versus local taxation. Population density differs greatly, degree of cultural and economic development differs greatly, and budget allocations that the central government makes must take these things into account. This does not mean that all budgeting considerations have to be decided upon by a one-on-one negotiation process.

Looking at how we currently handle the budgeting process of the central and local governments, we can see some regular patterns emerging on a nationwide basis despite the historical factors and negotiations that go into the decision-making process. Let us assume for the time being that our current local-government expenditures are reasonable. Then let us take the allocations made by the central government to local governments and conduct a statistical regression on a series of variables. From this, we can see whether or not there is any pattern to our existing allocations. These patterns would then be the "budgeting allocation formulas" for central government allocations to local governments. The distribution results of this regression do in fact approach our current reality to a considerable degree.

Among the results, there are five provinces where the error is less than RMB 100 million. In 11 provinces, it is less than RMB 200 million, and in 21 provinces it is less than RMB 300 million. From the results of this statistical analysis, all of the main indicators show that the resulting estimates are acceptable. What this means is that the predictable nature of certain patterns is quite clear-cut.

However, we do not accept the assumption that our current local-government expenditures are reasonable. If they were, we would have no need for reform. The error distribution in the equations also happens to show quite clearly that there is an arbitrarily subjective nature to the amounts of public finance that the central government allocates to local governments. We can analyze what the unreasonable elements are by looking at the regression coefficients of the variables in the equation. These give a different weighting to various decision-making factors in the current decision-making process.

With respect to formulating future budget allocations, we should not attempt to be as close as possible to the current situation. Instead, we should correct the unreasonable phenomena that can be seen in our current formulations. We should make the budgeting process more reasonable and more standardized and this is something that should be recognized quite explicitly.

Setting up social security, and its demands on fiscal and tax reform

The current status of China's social security system, and the four different independent systems

1   The social security system that applies to employees of State government organizations and institutions was set up in the early 1950s. Its expenses are paid for by State finances, out of the "wage funds" of State administrative expenditures. Employees are entitled to retirement benefits, publicly funded healthcare, disability insurance, relief payments when a person dies, various subsidies (such as for urban transport, water and electricity and rent subsidies, heating, and so on), as well as a host of other benefits such as canteens, kindergartens, bathing facilities, and recreational facilities.

2   The social security benefits of employees of State-Owned Enterprises are similar in most respects to those for State organizations and institutions. The expenses are paid mainly out of the enterprise's own "wage fund" and non-operating expenses, however. The State has ruled that State-Owned Enterprises may draw 3 percent out of their wage funds to pay for pensions. They may draw out 5 percent to pay for publicly-funded healthcare. Any gap in funding must be paid for out of non-operating expenses.

3   Social security benefits for employees of collective enterprises in towns and villages are very considerably different from one another. Expenses are paid for out of the profits of the enterprise. Each unit must decide on its own "standards" depending on economic circumstances. When possible, enterprises under a collective system of ownership provide benefits that are similar to those of State-Owned Enterprises.

4   Cooperative medical services were set up in the course of collectivizing agriculture in the 1950s. These generally only provide medical fees (not social security in general), with funds that are drawn from the limited "rural welfare funds" paid into by farmers themselves. Rural people who work in entities under a collective system of ownership may enjoy retirement benefits. A policy mandates that older rural people who have no children should enjoy what are known as the Five Guarantees, namely food, clothing, housing, medical care, and a burial. Once reform started, however, this system encountered

problems. The number of people enjoying the Five Guarantees has been declining every year since 1984. By 1988, it had gone down by 460,000 as compared to 1984, a drop of 16 percent. In the past couple of years, more attention has been focused on this problem, however, and in 1990 some 91 percent of those rural people entitled to the Five Guarantees were able to receive benefits.

The current social security system in China is unsuited to economic and social progress

1   China currently faces the problem of having a population that is aging very rapidly. Within 30 years, the senior population in the country will double. In 1980, the elderly constituted 8 percent of the total population. By 2010, this figure will be 15 percent, and by 2040, it will be 28 percent. That is, in 2010 there will be 191 million elderly in the country, and by 2040 that figure will go to 398 million.

China's current method of paying into and drawing out welfare funds means that the percentage of retirement funds drawn out of national income will gradually increase. The pay-as-you-go system will face problems given the need to cover the pensions of a rapidly aging population. In 1978, on average, 30.3 employees bore the cost of paying for one retired person. By 1990, 6.1 employees had to bear that cost. By the year 2000, it is predicted that payments made into a pension fund will require more than half of a person's total wages.

2   The social security system that is based on enterprises leads not only to unequal burdens on different enterprises but also to problems with it comes to reorganizing the enterprise. It keeps outmoded enterprises from being able to shut down, and it affects the speed of economic progress for those that should not be shut down.

3   The four different systems governing social welfare in China are each managed independently. This influences labor mobility among enterprises as well as departments. In addition, the current requirements for paying pensions at a certain age of retirement no longer conform to the health standards of the population at large or to longer life spans. One aspect of this is that enterprises and State institutions lose out on a large group of still-capable employees, as well as scientists, professors, and medical personnel who are highly experienced.

4   A system that provides social security only to those who earn a wage creates rather major disparities in welfare benefits nationwide. These are particularly apparent in the divide between urban and rural areas.

5   State organizations and institutions, as well as State-Owned Enterprises, bear the costs of all healthcare expenses. This allows for abuse, since many of the fees are "wasted." This waste may indeed become an ever more apparent reason for imbalances in fiscal budgets in the future.

Reform of social security systems and coordination of the relevant
fiscal and tax policies

1 Social security funds should come out of fiscal revenues, payroll taxes, enterprise profits, and workers' wages. The method of providing the actual money
   is best done by using "funds." We must improve the investment systems by
   which we manage social security funds so as to facilitate the accumulation of
   funds. Not only will this provide a reliable source of money for social security systems in the future, but it will become an important component of our
   capital markets and will help stimulate economic growth.
2 Right now, the diversity of social security systems is rather complex while
   funding of those systems is inadequate. For the time being, given that we
   must recognize this situation, all we can do is institute different policies for
   each category of social security. We should carry through with reform of our
   existing social security systems but on the principle that we do our utmost not
   to impinge upon the vested interests of employees who are entitled to social
   security. We have to move gradually as we transition to a better system.

We will need to reduce insurance benefits to new recruits into State organizations and institutions and State-Owned Enterprises. We should gradually
introduce a system of having a portion of benefits paid for by the individual
himself. We should increase the percentage of fees that the individual pays for
healthcare in particular, or raise the threshold of what insurance will pay for. At
the same time, we should implement a universal system of withholding taxes
from payrolls.

For employees in collectively-owned enterprises, enterprises invested in by
foreign entities, privately-owned enterprises, *ge-ti* (independent) enterprises, and
town-and-village enterprises, we should adopt a self-paying system with amounts
being deducted from salaries and paid into an account. This will be similar to mandatory savings in principle. Small amounts of overlapping withdrawals should be
allowed as a way to enable fairly low levels of insurance. We should adopt a voluntary system in rural areas, in which people pay in and take out pension amounts
that they themselves decide upon. At the same time, we should have a medical-
fund system that is planned and coordinated on a national basis and that is of a
mutual-assistance nature. We should encourage rural residents to participate in
the system.

Reform of our fiscal and tax system is a key part of overall economic reform.
Fiscal and tax policies are not all-powerful, but they can make a major contribution to eliminating our current distortions. They can stimulate greater competition
and accelerate the pace of other reforms. By now, our current situation is such
that implementing reforms should not be as hard as it was earlier. Not only are
underlying conditions more suitable now, but we are facing ever greater fiscal
problems. Not only is reform now possible, therefore, but it is imperative. In order
to ensure the probability of success, we should also institute new ways of thinking
that conform to the requirements of a commodity economy. We should design our

reform proposals with the use of analytical tools and economic and theoretical concepts that are in line with the laws of the market.

Notes

1 This was originally published in *Reform*, 1992, Vol. 6.
2 Source: *China Statistical Yearbook 1991*, National Bureau of Statistics, China Statistics Press (Beijing), 1991.
3 Su Xiaodong and others: "The *cheng-bao* system: realities and policy options," in *Economic Research*, 1990, Vol. 6; Yang Peixin: "Revitalize enterprises by adjusting taxes," in *World Economic Report*, July 20, 1987; "On adhering to and improving the *cheng-bao* system," in *Economic Research*, 1990, Vol. 3.

5 Different paths toward achieving economic structural reform[1]

(1993)

This paper looks at two approaches to reforming socialist economies, the "troika approach" and the "shock therapy approach," and discusses considerations surrounding each approach.

Different ways of thinking about reform, and related controversies

In recent years, one particular way of thinking has been popular among the conceptual approaches to taking centrally-planned economies in the direction of market-economies. That could be summed up as a kind of "reform troika." The troika is composed of marketization, privatization, and democratization. Among these, democratization is regarded as providing the basis for determining that reform must be carried out. Meanwhile, marketization and privatization are meant to be carried out to the maximum extent possible within the overall package of reforms.

A few years ago, this troika approach was universally seen as necessary for carrying out reform of a socialist economy. Economists from both socialist economies and developing economies accepted this thinking and terminology.

In what follows, I use the term G1 to represent this kind of thinking, as a way to distinguish it from another way of thinking that I will present below. G1 stands for "Group 1."

Many eastern European countries have followed a path that closely approximates the recommendations of G1. Some of these reforms have been what could be called "radical," in that they implemented or approximated a Big Bang kind of so-called shock therapy. The idea behind the troika is that if all three kinds of reform are not undertaken at the same time, then the ultimate result will fail. Within a socialist economy, therefore, market-oriented reform must be complemented by privatization and democratization. In a country such as China, this view holds that trying to "marketize" the economy while the country still adheres to public ownership will simply be wasted effort.

Meanwhile, the subject of a "sequence of reforms" has been a hot topic at various times among economists and policy makers of both socialist economies and developing economies. Most recently, the opinion of the broadly held G1 idea feels that this sequenced approach should simply be abandoned. It is too problematic. Two reasons are given for this. One is that there is a logical connection between the troika and all of the various components of marketization (which include prices, taxes, public finance, banking, trade, social security). Because of that, these should be implemented concurrently. The second is that we lack sufficient capacity, knowledge, and expertise, and we also face political issues, in trying to reform any other way. A government that is in the midst of "switching tracks," transitioning from one system to another, may launch reform but then will never have the capacity to manage the process. It can initiate reform but the reform must then follow its own course without interference.

In this view, the best option, therefore, is to open out all spheres of the economy to all kinds of reform and not be concerned about sequencing actions. We should not attempt to promote only those things that we know we currently are able to promote.

Shock therapy, and particularly the process of privatizing on a large scale, requires a redistribution of the wealth of society. It requires the broad-based readjustment of interests among groups. In this process, we unavoidably will see the appearance of unfair or arbitrary wealth distribution. This is a highly sensitive topic to both the public at large and all interest groups. Because of that, it is very easy to come up against problems, and it is highly controversial. What G1 says in response to this is that the current system is already highly arbitrary in how it distributes wealth. Using another arbitrary system to replace this one does not generate any new mistakes.

However, the experiences in eastern Europe and the entities formerly in the Soviet Union are not highly encouraging in this regard. Indeed, many people criticize those countries for not, in fact, having followed any sequenced process. Moreover, substituting one arbitrary situation for another is not a policy decision that can easily be taken. Meanwhile, China has been taking a different route to reform that is perhaps not as bad as what has been predicted by G1.

Economists in socialist countries find themselves in different kinds of environments, yet all are faced with constraints that are non-negotiable. In China, for example, market-oriented reform, reform that attempts to relax the controls of central planning, faces the following kinds of constraints:

- Such reform allows for the development of a diversity of forms of ownership, but at the same time must adhere to public ownership.
- Such reform must do its utmost to prevent the eruption of large-scale chaos. It must preserve stability in the course of transition.
- Such reform must carry out redistribution of wealth within the limits of what the public can tolerate, which also means taking the short-term limits of tolerance into account.

Leadership levels of a government generally only initiate reforms when a crisis is upon them. For example, China's reform only started when the Cultural Revolution had occurred and indeed had progressed to its final stages. Unless a crisis reaches its ultimate intensity, leadership levels are inclined to opt for an incremental process of transition. This may not be the optimal choice but it is one that is determined by immediate balance-of-power considerations, and this is understandable.

Meanwhile, the public at large is also often unprepared for violent change. As a result, economists are invited to present reform proposals that contain the smallest amount of change and that lay out how to compromise, how to organize reform steps in ways that may resolve the problems. These economists too have essentially no room to move in, no way to attempt a fundamental revision given the constraints as described above.

The real question is whether or not there is any solution at all.

For ease of discussion, we have very approximately divided reform thinking into two groups, call them G1 and G2. G1 emphasizes the troika approach to reform, and the necessity of the Big Bang and shock therapy. It says that the basket of reform proposals must be as large as possible. G2, in contrast, feels it must live within the constraints as posed above. It believes there is indeed a solution to reform if the reform is arranged in the proper sequence. It highlights the marketization part of the troika. It chooses to have reform proposals in the overall package that are manageable at each stage of the transition process.

Faced with varying constraints and different environments, G1 and G2 and the economists in each also differ among themselves on solutions and ideas. At a minimum, the debate between G1 and G2 includes some of the following issues.

G2 may recognize that the political leadership (of China) has a commitment to reform and the possibility of implementing a transformation of its system. G1 may, on the other hand, believe that there is no way to create leadership within the existing system that is able to undertake real reform prior to large-scale democratization. G1 may feel that market-oriented "switching of the tracks" is above and beyond the ability of socialist leadership levels.

G2 takes political and social stability into account when looking at options and is more inclined to be cautious or "prudent" with respect to redistributing wealth. G2 feels that political and social stability can help preserve the commitment to ongoing reform and that such reform will swiftly bring about an improved economy. G1, on the other hand, is much less concerned about the sensitivities of redistribution and the dangers of political instability.

G2 recognizes that an enormous number of changes need to happen in the course of switching tracks from one system to another. It feels that the process of democratic decision-making is really too slow to deal with everything. Therefore, reform needs the strong hand of administrative control. Moreover, unduly hasty democratization may damage the government's standing in the process of switching tracks. Some leadership levels might deviate toward nationalistic tendencies for the sake of political maneuvering, and therefore reduce the efforts that government is able to put into real change. G1, on the other hand, tends to emphasize that democracy can provide the legal entities in a market economy with accurate policy options. These then replace the role of government as the transition process becomes more automatic.

In the eyes of G1, G2 is overly optimistic. G1 feels that G2 is too eager to sat-isfy short-term political needs and, as a result, violates the fundamental principles of economics. G2 disputes this, saying that every limited action taken to push forward reform results in the gradual accumulation of major change in the end. Therefore, the main requirement is to preserve the forward momentum of reform. G2 feels that excessive promises on the political front as a precondition for reform can lead to a great deal of bargaining that can only delay reform actions.

Some people use the terms "radical" (*ji-jin*, moving forward in aggressive steps) and "incremental" (*jian-jin*, moving forward in gradual steps) to describe two ways of thinking about reform. However, both of these terms are relative. They can be understood in different ways depending on the context. For example, in western discussions, the term radical refers to things like shock therapy. Those who espouse a more incremental approach emphasize the sequential nature of reforms and the operability of each step, but they do not regard each step as being in any way "small." In some socialist economies, "radicals" are closer to what those in the west would view as "incrementals." Incrementals, on the other hand, cover a broad range of things, from mild marketization to slow improvements in a planned economy.

Is privatization a rapid and also effective path for reform?

Let us assume that privatization of State-Owned Enterprises is a necessary part of economic reform, indeed of core importance, as argued by some western econo-mists. The question that this section seeks to explore is whether or not there is a fast-track and effective reform method that also conforms to the logic of the G1 point of view.

Auctioning State-Owned Enterprises

Auctioning State-Owned Enterprises to investors and the public at large, who put up capital to buy them, requires a long time. First, potential buyers for State-Owned Enterprises need time to conduct due diligence by gathering information that has already been made public. In the past, we lacked adequate market mecha-nisms plus accounting standards were bewildering at best. People now therefore need time to confirm financial data that has only recently been modified to con-form to new accounting rules. After that, they need to compare the data with other State-Owned Enterprises and companies, so as to make judgments about how competitive companies might be in certain lines of business, and to think about how profitable they might be. (Note: profit potential and share prices are deter-mined by the competitiveness of specific industries, but this is a relative yardstick. Prior to doing detailed research on other companies, it is impossible to know how just one State-Owned Enterprise weighs in the balance.) All of these things are necessary steps before a buyer can reach any determination about price.

The preparatory work that a seller has to undertake includes asset evaluation, financial reconfiguration, and so on, and this too takes time. Nevertheless, many enterprises can be undertaking this process at the same time (if there are a sufficient number of experts to do the work). In what follows, I therefore do not take into account the time required by the seller. For the buyer, though, an auction process must be carried out in the proper sequence.

Let us assume we want to auction one State-Owned Enterprise each week. In one year, we could sell 52 of them. China's economy is large, however, and contains roughly 4,000 large-scale State-Owned Enterprises. Some local State-Owned Enterprises could be sold *in situ*, so to a degree several auctions could be held concurrently. Buyers might not be willing to accept a wide range of auctions happening concurrently, however, since it makes effective comparison more difficult. They might not be able to bid as a result.

Who might buyers be? Generally speaking, they could be citizens, institutional investors, and foreign investors. In socialist economies, however, institutional investors are also State-owned, while those people who truly believe in private property do not like companies in which control shares are held by the State. Such people therefore exclude the institutional buyers as potential buyers.

Meanwhile, the total gross assets of China's industrial State-Owned Enterprises are estimated at around RMB 2 trillion. The entire amount of savings that Chinese people hold in banks comes to a total of just around RMB 1 trillion. (We must remember that banks are the only place people can put their savings, given that we have not developed capital markets.) How enthusiastic are people going to be about taking their savings out of banks and buying shares in State-Owned Enterprises? Right now, the answer to that question is unclear. In the case of eastern Europe, in the early period, before many distortions were corrected, it was not that easy for foreign capital to come in. Because of that, not only were there problems in terms of how quickly real auctions of any true value could be held, but there were problems in knowing who the buyers might be and where the capital was going to come from.

Employee participation in ownership and management buyouts (MBO)

One method of privatizing quickly involves having employees participate in ownership. Looking at the lessons learned from Yugoslavia, however, with its worker self-governance (autonomy), most economists feel that only a small portion of shares should be sold, or assigned for no cost, to employees. (If sold, then this means sold at a very low cost.) However, "a small portion" can quickly expand in meaning. In past discussions, we talked about around 10 percent but recently some people believe that 30 percent might be acceptable. The reason may be that we lack other ways to privatize quickly on any major scale.

Whether or not worker participation in ownership is fair and just is highly debatable. Different industries and enterprises are capital-intensive and labor-intensive to different degrees. If 30 percent of a capital-intensive factory is distributed out to a small number of workers, say people who are employed in a petrochemical factory, then each receives shares that are worth considerable value. If a labor-intensive factory is distributed among workers, each receives much less. This issue of fairness can easily lead to political or social instability.

The method known as MBO, for management buyouts, sells a portion of shares (say 5 percent) at a low price to the management of a given enterprise. For many reasons, this is an attractive proposition. However, this also involves going about things in the right sequence. If, for example, it is done under our current economic system, and we do not differentiate between capable managers and "government officials," then the management buyout can be somewhat arbitrary. It may well turn into a situation where the bureaucrats buy the entity and not the managers. Moreover, the public may have a strong negative reaction to the unfairness of such "redistribution." At a certain stage in our transition, once we are able to confirm who capable managers are, management buyouts may indeed be a good option. In the initial stage of reform, however, management buyouts may not be of great help. They cannot assist in any kind of "radical" privatization.

Using share vouchers for shares

In thinking about how to transform property rights and distribute assets, the idea of vouchers as a form of share ownership is quite attractive. These were proposed by some Chinese economists in 1986 and 1987. In reforming State-Owned Enterprises through vouchers, China could institute a virtual-capital form of share ownership that would enable enterprises to become "legal persons" and that would transform a State-owned system into an institutional shareholding system. At the same time, it would not be the same as privatization.

Compared to other methods, vouchers have the following virtues: (1) They represent a fair and equal method to the public at large, which is highly important to a socialist society with a long tradition of equality. (2) There is not enough capital within China to purchase all of the assets that are intended for privatization in the country. Issuing share vouchers can help resolve this problem. (3) The process eliminates any over-reliance on employees, and thereby avoids "worker self-rule". (4) The issuing of vouchers encourages more people to pay attention to the capital markets and the companies in which they are invested. (5) The process can generate public enthusiasm for privatization and the support of society at large since each person appears to be receiving "extra" assets.

G2 feels that vouchers are a good start, but just the beginning of the process of privatization. It will still take a long time for the new owners to play a positive and proper role in the market economy. Once vouchers are distributed out to the public, there will still be two different ways to change the ownership of State-Owned Enterprises. One is auctions; the other is by "random assignment."

I discuss auctions first. Other than a difference in the source of the capital, the process of auctioning is the same as described above. It includes changing accounting practices, making entities into legal persons, appraising their assets and making everything open and transparent. After all of that, potential buyers can review State-Owned Enterprises one by one, make comparisons, and decide on how much they are willing to bid. As noted above, this will take time. Since some people face cash flow issues, prior to this time they may well have sold their shares by transferring them to others at a low price. As a result, shares will tend to concentrate in the hands of those employees who "get rich first," or in the hands of institutional investors. For enterprises that are being privatized, this is a good thing since it is good to have professional investors on the board. However, since wealth was being generated by unequal cash flow situations and at unfair prices, it can also be a source of public resentment.

The second way to change ownership is by "random assignment." This means using a computerized "random-number generator" to distribute equity in all State-Owned Enterprises among voucher holders at a roughly estimated price. Once that is done, we then officially make enterprises into legal persons, appraise their value, and begin trading their shares. Each investor starts out with a diverse port-folio of shares but can restructure them as he wishes. This can very definitely speed up the process of the first step in transforming ownership. However, it will take a long time to get to the second step, namely making sure that owners have adequate information and knowledge to make an active, voluntary, and proper contribution on the board of directors.

In the whole process of privatization, the first step is actually fairly superficial. Once random assignment is done, but before the rest of the time-consuming work is completed, the owners and/or investors are actually in a passive position. They have no way to participate actively in any decisions, nor do they need to, since they can sit back and wait. When they get the price they want, they simply sell their shares. The whole purpose of privatization is not merely to privatize assets in name but to create mechanisms whereby private persons utilize property rights. Until new systems replace previous systems of State ownership, and new owners actively play a different kind of role, the process is not really meaningful. For that reason, simply speeding up the first step in the process is not the fundamental issue.

Let us assume that it takes time for the large body of voucher holders to learn how to handle their equity or their vouchers. It takes time for China to form pro-fessional institutions (such as accounting firms, law offices, brokers, consulting companies, stock markets and so on.) It takes time to train up people in these institutions. No matter what, it is going to be a while before new owners have the qualifications and interest to play an active role.

At this point, G1 might say that the great majority of shareholders actually do not need anything more than limited experience and knowledge since they will rely on professional institutions. As we know, however, professional institutions in capital markets are (currently) all operated by foreigners. It is quite easy to say these things, but it is absolutely not going to be easy to convince the public and China's politicians to let foreigners handle China's assets via foreign-controlled institutions and capital markets.

Handling the privatization of smaller enterprises is easier and can be done in many ways. Some are quite effective and China, among other economies, is doing fairly well in this regard. The redistribution of wealth may well not be all that fair. Since the quantity of assets being redistributed is not so great, however, and since redistribution is limited in coverage, the degree of unfairness is not such that it will threaten social stability. The difficulties arise more with large- and medium-sized State-Owned Enterprises. Among these, some are quite capital intensive. Since China's economy is large and the number of its large enterprises is substantial, privatization presents much greater problems.

There may be other methods on the list of how to privatize quickly, in addition to the views and ideas presented above. These still need to be evaluated. If we cannot find ways in which to privatize quickly, and on a large scale, the question is why do we need to put privatization in our immediate package of reforms? Especially since we are at the initial stage of switching tracks right now, why should we risk high-cost measures in terms of social and political turmoil? Can it be that the reason relates to some kind of economic "religion"? Or is it because some people prefer not to recognize that we might be able to change our previous highly centralized planning system in a smooth way? I do not see why we should not adopt a reasonable sequence of reform measures based on the proper timing and interrelated nature of what needs to be done.

Coordinating the initial stage of reform: analyzing China's experience

Based on what has been said above about the constraints on socialist economies, together with opinions on democratization and privatization, it is necessary to think also about the minimum basket of proposals that is feasible in this initial period of switching tracks. That is, what is the minimum a country must do to create conditions that still serve as an engine for ongoing reform?

In this article, I propose that the minimum package plan could be described as the following: "a relatively aggressive form of marketization plus initial political reform plus turning enterprises into legal persons (corporations)."

Certain things can be put to later stages in the whole process, that is, things that are admirable but not required at this initial stage. Once the basic framework of an economic system has shifted from "centrally-planned economy" toward "market economy," released productivity will also become a driving force for ongoing reform. This opinion about countries in general also comes closer to people's observations about and analysis of China (also Asian newly-industrializing economies in terms of economic liberalization). Experiences in this regard have both positive and negative aspects. China's reform has basically been successful but there are areas in which it could have done better. It could, for example, have been done more quickly, while there are still issues waiting to be addressed by policy determinations and real action.

While the former Soviet Union was firmly pushing forward an "open" kind of democratization, some observers seem to have overlooked the fact that China was carrying out initial stages of democratization as well. Observers described China's reforms as purely economic, not political. In fact, China was already taking steps in around 1978 that were admittedly preliminary but still extremely important in terms of political reform. These changed the political mode of thinking at the very highest levels of decision-making in the country. The main actions in this regard were:

- Criticizing the socio-economic system that prevailed during the Cultural Revolution as being a mistaken "leftist" deviation and a dogmatic approach.
- Putting forward economic development as the priority.
- Confirming the new principle that "experience is the sole criterion by which truth can be tested."
- Formulating the new constitution and, following on from that, gradually enacting a new set of laws and regulations.
- Overthrowing the "Gang of Four," and eliminating the remnants of its influence.
- Releasing (from incarceration and political limbo) cadres who adhered to a fairly new way of thinking and putting them in (government) positions once again.
- Reconfirming the role of market mechanisms and related concepts.
- Restoring and improving upon democratic systems under the leadership of the Communist Party, that is, the people's congresses and the political consultative committees.
- Reaffirming the role of intellectuals, and others.

One of the consequences of these political reforms was that they successfully changed the leadership tier in the country and put the new leadership on a standing that was relatively stable. This made it possible to pass a number of forceful reform measures. The main energies of the government could now be focused on designing and implementing reform.

At the same time, the broadening of democracy was helpful in preserving a strong leadership tier, because the great majority of people in the country supported reform. This kind of democracy did not lead to intense competition among politicians, and such competition might well have led to a tendency to promote nationalistic fervor on the part of politicians and might have diverted attention away from reform.

Another important consequence was greater freedom and autonomy in economic rights, as established by a revised constitution and new laws, regulations, and policies. This process occurred in the midst of and was formed as a result of tremendous debate among various schools of thought. This whole process served to lay the foundation for reform that was ultimately market-oriented.

We can recognize a similar course of events in observing the relationship between political and economic reform among newly-industrializing economies. This indicates that initial political reform is necessary—the question then becomes how far it should go, and how fast. This will be determined by a balance between two considerations: the firm resolve to continue with reform and "switching tracks," and the desire to maintain the stability of the government.

A reasonable order of things would be as follows: first, carry out the initial stages of political reform, follow that with relatively forceful and effective economic reform, then deepen the establishment of democratic systems on the basis of a higher level of economic wellbeing.

Based on China's experience in the initial stages of reform, the core aspect of economic reform has involved proposals relating to marketization. This has improved the efficiency of resource allocation and the efficiency of enterprise operations, as well as maintained the momentum for ongoing reforms. In the reform period between 1978 and 1992, the public gradually came to accept "marketization" concepts and the idea of a market economy. The great majority of reform actions were, in fact, being pursued along the path of marketization. This kind of "incremental" marketization had its advantages but also its drawbacks, as follows:

1   Progress in reform followed along with gradual changes in the mentality of the public as well as leadership levels. Reform demanded a material or "real" change in people's way of thinking and was the subject of interminable debate. Each major step taken in any policy change always required a following period in which results that had been "released" by the policy could be made manifest and so that the public could become aware of its advantages. This then allowed those who were carrying out reform to win the support of the masses in the course of debate. Meanwhile, ongoing production and trade were not impacted in a noticeable way.
2   Marketization was a relatively slow process. This allowed some reform opportunities to slip by that might have been more effective. Meanwhile, concurrently running a centrally-planned system as we instituted a market economy unavoidably meant we had inflation, rent-seeking, corruption, and unfair income distribution. This damaged or had the potential to damage political and economic stability as well as the resolve to continue with reforms.

In analyzing both sides of the experience, my own opinion is that China's marketization is not only necessary but could perhaps be done more quickly and more effectively. It could be incorporated in better ways into our package of reforms. This overall package would include the following necessary reforms.

Price reform

This includes releasing (liberalizing) prices and regulating prices in a transitional way, in order to reduce the gap between the market equilibrium point and our existing prices. In sectors where prices are extremely distorted, instant release of all prices would bring about insurmountable pressures and many producers could not survive. That means they could no longer continue to employ people. Dividing price liberalization into two or three linked steps would be more beneficial to producers in giving them time to reorganize during the transition. However, in overall terms, price reform should be fairly fast and fairly timely, so that there is sufficient pressure on producers although not too much. Producers should be forced to come to terms with reorganizing themselves and with the need to face international market competition.

Public finance reform

We must set up a new tax system in order to accommodate and support fair competition in markets, competition that operates under equal conditions. Under the old system, tax collection relied to a great extent on State-Owned Enterprises. The products of many State-Owned Enterprises also served to keep prices high. We must reform the role that accounting plays and make sure that it reflects real costs and profits.

In terms of budgeting, we must put a stop to State investment in profit-making industries. Public spending must be in line with the new functions of government within a market economy.

Banking reform and reform of the non-banking financial sector

We should set up and improve upon a two-tiered system of banking. In this system, a central bank should focus its attention on monetary objectives and supervisory regulation. We should change the Soviet type of "specialized banks" into commercial banks that the government cannot "command," and these commercial banks should be in competition with one another. We should separate out "policy-type loans" from "commercial-type loans." Government should not involve itself directly in any commercial type of credit. We should, meanwhile, develop money markets and related financial tools. We should gradually develop capital markets and the basic infrastructure and systems that go along with them. Since these take a long time to mature, we should start the process as soon as possible in the course of our reforms.

Foreign trade reform

We should set the exchange rate on the principle of equilibrium or we should let rates float as determined by the market. We should adopt policies that allow for free entry into foreign exchange dealing, and that allow for equal competition. We should eliminate import and export subsidies, and reduce quantitative restrictions.

Enterprise reform

We should separate out "operating rights" of large- and medium-sized enterprises from "ownership rights," whether these enterprises are State-owned or owned by collectives. The goal of managers should be to optimize profits or to optimize the share price of the enterprise.

We should turn companies into legal persons. Decision-making authority as under autonomous operating practices should be assigned to management personnel. We must change the accounting systems that currently apply to enterprises and make them suitable for a market economy. We should not only allow but should encourage the growth of diverse forms of ownership. These would include private ownership and public ownership that is not State-owned.

Reform of the social security system

We should set up new institutions that are responsible for pensions, healthcare insurance, and unemployment insurance. At the same time, we should no longer have the administrators of enterprises handle these things. We should get rid of the system whereby enterprises are responsible for providing low-cost housing to their employees. At the enterprise and municipal levels of administration, we should privatize and commercialize existing housing. We should reduce housing subsidies. We should encourage greater mobility of labor and allocate human resources in better ways. In releasing enterprises from social responsibilities, we should push them toward the new objective of maximizing profits.

As unemployment guarantees and the responsibility for housing are shifted away from enterprises, we should make sure that there are alternative "socialized" institutions to deal with problems in order to ensure social stability. We must make sure that people can be adequately linked in to such institutions.

Reform of the government's economic functions

Other than administrative tasks in the course of switching tracks, the basic functions of the government must shift away from the centrally-planned economy mode to a mode that is suited to a market economy. Government should now use indirect policy tools and not mandatory commands to achieve its macroeconomic objectives. It should focus its efforts on providing public services and publicly-used assets, as well as maintaining macroeconomic stability. It should not directly interfere in the operations of any enterprise.

In accomplishing the package of reforms as described above, policy formulation involves three main aspects.

First, we must maintain macroeconomic stability. That is, we must keep a low or at least tolerable level of inflation. Inflation can damage any desire for swift reform and can prolong the process or even reverse it. Price reform involves reconstructing our entire price system, which will inevitably lead to inflation. Misguided macroeconomic policies may create inflation that is beyond the acceptable, however, which not only will make for problems between the government and the people but will make it hard to carry on smoothly with reform.

Second, we must maintain and also increase the percentage of savings in gross domestic product (GDP). Economic growth will depend not only on reform but also on savings. People generally use the rate of economic growth as the yardstick by which to measure the results of reform. In socialist societies, savings are often mandatory given the existence of shortages and standing in line for products. Since reform may be able to change the phenomenon of shortages, savings may go down as a result. The key thing will be to implement appropriate policies for interest rates, consumer credit, and other relevant areas. Based on a voluntary approach, our aim is to restore a high rate of savings so that new investment can generate higher economic growth and demonstrate the results of reform.

Third, we should change our mode of foreign trade in a stable manner so that we provide time for our foreign trade companies. We should not exceed the ability of those companies to deal with sudden change (such as a sudden suspension of trade with the Council for Mutual Economic Assistance). As we switch tracks by carrying out foreign trade reforms, we should allow some parallel regulations to occur at the same time, such as free trade using hard currency, counter-trade, border exchange, and government-to-government trade agreements. The purpose of trade is not just to gain hard currency and carry on exchange with industrialized economies but also to realize mutual comparative advantage with Third World countries as one way to keep up our employment. Between 1988 and 1991, reformers in the former Soviet Union and eastern Europe insisted on settling trade with China in hard currency. Policy makers in China agreed with this on the one hand, while continuing to encourage counter-trade and border trade in bartered goods, even though paying in hard currency was not a problem for China.

The points noted above are intended to show that we need not sacrifice many objectives of a socialist economy as we implement new reform mechanisms. Transition that is done through meticulous and pragmatic ways, reform that is coordinated, properly sequenced, and manageable can improve reform results as well as economic welfare. All of this is fully in line with the objectives of reform. In contrast, the views of G1 seem to feel that our former socialist economy cannot be reformed. Therefore we should replace it at any cost, no matter how large that cost.

Performance of enterprises that are within the public sector during the course of transition

Reform of our public sector, and particularly the State-owned sector, is meant to find new operating methods for public ownership—it is not aimed at privatizing all publicly owned industrial assets. As reform moves further into later stages, we will include the restructuring of the State-owned system in our overall reform package. As noted above, this will take many years. Because of that, we do not necessarily need to include it in the initial stage of reform nor will it make major contributions to the economy in this stage. Nevertheless, it is precisely because it will take time to set up new forms of ownership and mature capital markets that we need to start the process as soon as possible. We need to make sure that reform achieves certain progress now in order to meet the demands of reform later on.

In current economic thinking around the world, the prevailing view is that there is absolutely no hope for public ownership at all. Performance of companies held in the public sector are uniformly terrible, including those of China, and such companies cannot be saved. There is no need even to discuss the issue unless privatization is part of the discussion. In order to test this opinion, and clarify whether or not the public sector can indeed be reformed, we should carry out thorough observation and empirical analysis. China can serve as one example in the process. Popular opinion holds that the greatest part of economic growth is being achieved in China's non-public sector. It is being driven by the privately-owned sector and Sino-foreign joint ventures. Meanwhile, the way our exports are prospering can be attributed to the special economic zones and the two "special provinces" in the south. At the same time, losses in the public sector are severe, requiring ever increasing amounts of government subsidies.

What I attempt to do in the following section is show that this portrayal of the situation is distorted. I try to use a minimum of statistics and supporting material to do this.

I divide the analysis into three periods in order to analyze more clearly how China's State-Owned Enterprises have performed and how that performance has changed. The years between 1978 and 1988 represent the initial period of reform. Between 1989 and 1991, we had a period of "rectification" and anti-inflationary policies. Since 1992, we have entered a new period.

Between 1978 and 1988, the gross industrial output of China's State-owned industrial sector grew at an average rate of 8.5 percent (according to the *China Statistical Yearbook 1992*[2]). This was in the top ranks of other economies around the world. "Collective ownership" is regarded as a different form of public ownership, and as such its industrial sector grew at an average annual rate of 19.5 percent. Meanwhile, the privately-owned sector as well as foreign-direct-investment sector grew at an even faster pace, but these grew from a base figure that was very small. By the end of 1988, these two sectors as well as others under the general heading of "*ge-ti*" or individual ownership held 7.06 percent of industrial output. In 1978 the figure was too small to be recorded. If these non-publicly owned sectors had not developed, China's industrial output would have been growing at a rate of 11.03 percent, slightly lower than the actual rate of growth of 11.84 percent. The improved performance of the publicly-owned sector is quite apparent. The contribution of public-sector growth to overall growth is not only substantial but it constitutes the dominant share of growth.

The speed at which foreign trade has grown in the special economic zones and southern provinces (which generally refers to Guangdong and Fujian) is quite high, but one cannot say these are the sole source of export performance. In 1991, the export volume of our four special economic zones came to around 7 percent of China's total exports. Guangdong province held around 17 percent of the total (excluding Shenzhen). Fujian came to 4.6 percent.[3] The remaining volume of exports is distributed broadly among a number of provinces. Export trade is growing quickly from China's interior provinces as well. Between 1985 and 1991, the average rate of growth of exports of all interior provinces came to 18.4 percent. This was higher than the average growth rate of exports nationwide (15.3 percent).[4] These statistics do not incorporate goods that were produced in the interior but then exported by foreign trade organizations along the coast.

In China, State-Owned Enterprises hold the largest share of the production of capital goods and the inputs for manufacturing. Their share of consumer goods production is relatively small. The reasons for both of these relate to market-entry policies and the way China adhered to the former Soviet model in its bias toward heavy industry. Between 1989 and 1991, during the anti-inflation period, the government relied too much on limiting investment in fixed assets in order to reduce aggregate demand. Investment in fixed assets fell sharply as a result. In 1989, investment was 77.65 percent what it had been in 1988. In 1990, investment was 70.88 percent what it had been in 1988.[5]

Since a reliable deflator is not available, this calculation uses the retail price index to make figures comparable. (The inflation rate in 1988 was 18.5 percent and in 1989 it was 17.8 percent, but the price index for capital goods is not available.[6])

Our reduction of aggregate demand mainly damaged State-Owned Enterprises, which enabled many observers to take note of the comparative problems between the State-owned sector and other sectors. It was said that one-third of State-Owned Enterprises were making a loss and "eating public subsides," one-third were breaking even (or being moderately subsidized), and only one-third were profitable. This was not so surprising during a period in which competition was taking down the average profitability in the context of a market economy, particularly during the period of contraction. What's more, we were in a period in which profit objectives were subject to negotiation, and in which the tax on profits was 55 percent. Given those considerations plus many other "apportionments" (fees and expenses allocated out to entities), China's State-Owned Enterprises had sufficient motivation to try to break even.

Meanwhile, total State subsidies to State-Owned Enterprises during this period came to only 2.5 percent of GDP (roughly RMB 51 billion in 1991). Around one-fourth of the subsidies went to energy sectors, so that they could provide energy at nationally-mandated low prices. Another one-fourth went to sectors producing other basic necessities, again in order to keep prices low. These subsidies should be eliminated, but they are not sufficient evidence to prove that State-Owned Enterprises are totally incapable of being reformed. In many market economies, social welfare objectives are achieved through the use of transfer payments or tax reductions for low-income households. The total volume of such transfer payments is substantial. In China, these payments are incorporated into losses of State-Owned Enterprises.

In the second half of 1991, capital investment began to increase again and the industrial output of State-Owned Enterprises showed a clear increase while losses began to decline. Statistics from 1992 indicate that they will maintain this outlook.

When comparing our methods of accounting with those of Western accounting methods, we can see that some figures are exaggerated while others are under-estimated. I list some of the rarely noticed ways in which we under-estimate figures here.

In order to evade heavy taxes and give themselves more flexibility, many State-Owned Enterprises set up the equivalent of "private plots," that is, areas of business activity that they retain for their own use. They set up new enterprises that may appear to be "collectively owned" on the surface, or may seem to come under different forms of ownership, but in fact that are wholly-owned subsidiaries of the State-Owned Enterprise. Through "internal" exchange with these entities,

State-Owned Enterprises shift a large amount of their value-added or their profits over to them.

When a State-Owned Enterprise finds a foreign investor or partner and turns itself into a joint venture or cooperative entity, it then falls into a different category of statistics that apply to different ownership sectors. All of its output value, assets, and growth are accounted for outside of State-Owned Enterprise statistics, so that the impact on those statistics is purely negative. Meanwhile, our "opening" policies provide incentives for State-Owned Enterprises to try to attract in foreign capital and technology. Some State-Owned Enterprises are therefore more than happy to set up spurious types of joint ventures with "fake foreign devils."

Some State-Owned Enterprises provide goods to entities they are in league with at the low prices mandated by the government, ostensibly in order to "meet basic public needs." It is clear that such transactions should be excluded from valid statistics when comparing them with transactions done by other forms of ownership.

All these factors and others serve to under-estimate the potential of State-Owned Enterprises. All of them need to be reformed. Moreover, they are in fact defects in our system that can be reformed. My reason for pointing out these problems is not to defend the existing defects of our system but rather to make it clear that restructuring (while not completely privatizing) State-Owned Enterprises is something on which our economic circles should focus more attention.

Through the observations made in this article, I try to point out that a large part of the problems of State-Owned Enterprises do not in fact relate to productivity. These entities can in fact increase production within the context of a market. They can renovate their factors of production, improve quality, and meet the competition. Their most outstanding problem is that nobody represents ownership rights. State assets are constantly being eroded (stripped) and lost as a result.

The managers of the enterprises themselves are among those doing the "eroding." Their methods include direct appropriation of assets, siphoning or "infringement upon" profits, and improper accounting for costs. If we do indeed see that the share of State-Owned Enterprises in the national economy is declining precipitously, I'm afraid it must be said that this to a large extent is related to the "flowing out" or asset stripping of State-owned assets. Because of this, the substance of our reforms must include not only orienting State-Owned Enterprises in the direction of the market and expanding their operating authority, but it must include restructuring the framework of property rights.

Straightening out the rights and accountabilities that apply to property rights in State-Owned Enterprises

In this article, I have emphasized that the primary focus of reform of State-Owned Enterprises in the initial period of reform is "marketization" and making enterprises into "legal persons." Restructuring the property rights of State-Owned Enterprises will take many years. Therefore it should start in the early period of reform.

One of G2's reform proposals involves finding a better replacement for responsibilities currently borne by public ownership. That could mean institutional shareholders and investors. This could also be a way to avoid the highly sensitive topic of redistributing public assets in this early period of restructuring.

Before describing this proposal in brief below, I would like to review some of our basic understandings about property rights.

- Market exchange should be done on the basis of property rights that are clearly defined. Agents who are authorized to represent the "owners" of the assets or property rights should do so in ways that are made explicit. In socialist economies, the "owners" of State-Owned Enterprises are at a far remove from the enterprises themselves. Because of this, to the greatest degree possible, agents must have valid authorization if they are to act on behalf of the owners.
- Within market economies, numerous shareholders can be the owners of large listed companies, and the Board of Directors then serves as the agent for these shareholders. The Board itself is composed of professional staff or others who are qualified to hold such responsibility. The shareholders themselves, however, maintain the ultimate power to choose the Board of Directors.
- There must be a competitive context for choosing a Board of Directors, so that people who are authorizing others to serve on their behalf can evaluate the performance of their agents.
- For large enterprises, the widely accepted practice is to have a shareholding-type company that separates out operating authority (management) from ownership. This practice requires a clear definition of how ownership can balance and constrain operating authority.
- Given the limits to how much information can be handled and limits to organizational capacities, a shareholding company or an investment company cannot supervise an unlimited number of subsidiaries. Such an organization can reasonably manage between ten and 30 subsidiary entities.
- There must be a clear definition of who the ultimate owners are when shareholding companies are held by institutional investors.

The above items should also represent a prescription for treating the problems we currently face with our ownership structures.

G2's design of the new structure of public ownership could be sketched out as in Figure 5.1.

C_i where ($i = 1$ to n) represent shareholders, including shareholding companies, and investing companies.

C_{ij} where ($j = 1$ to m) represent subsidiaries that are either shareholders of or investors in C.

"E_{ijk}" where ($ijk = 1$ to K) represent industrial-type State-Owned Enterprises that have been transformed and are now owned by C_{ij}.

n, m, and K represent dimensions and refer to the number of enterprises that can be operated and managed, which should range between ten and 30.

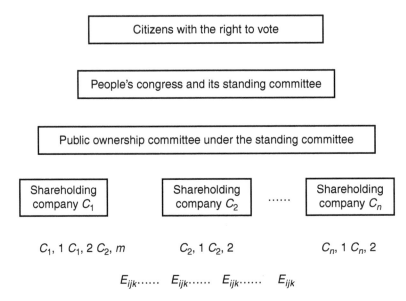

Figure 5.1 Structure of ownership rights

We allow for cross-holdings both on a horizontal and vertical basis and we allow for alliances of shareholding. C_i and C_{ij} are not particular to any specific industry.

China has between 1,000 and 27,000 State-Owned Enterprises that can be encompassed within this dynamic ownership framework. Within the framework, C_i, C_{ij}, and large-scale E should be allowed to list shares on the market. They may then be in competition with one another, and be evaluated by the market, which allows both the owners and the board of each to compare corporate results with others.

The ultimate Board of Directors is the "Committee of the publicly owned sector under the People's Congresses." This committee is selected by the standing committee of people's congresses. It represents the former system of State ownership. On the basis of the business results of C_i, it is responsible in a professional capacity for arranging for the members of the boards of directors of C_i (with $i = 1$ to n).

Policy decisions of the committee, votes, and all speeches must be made public. The electorate can therefore observe the behavior of every single member of the committee. Board members of all the boards of directors of C_i to C_{ij} must have gone through a selection process by the governmental tier above it. The higher authority may pay appropriate compensation to such agents in accordance with their capacities. In C_i, C_{ij}, and E_{ijk}, operating authority and ownership are separated out by setting up mechanisms that balance power.

China's original State-Owned Enterprises have all carried high levels of debt. Given high debt-to-equity ratios, their capital is insufficient. Therefore it is generally not necessary for E_{ijk} to distribute bonuses to C_{ij} and other share-holders until capital is replenished. Both C_{ij} and C_i aim to achieve share price maximization. C_i does not distribute bonuses (extra dividends) to the committee. Any expenses of the standing committee of people's congresses and government expenditures rely entirely on public-spending (government) budgets.

Some independent consulting enterprises, law firms, accounting firms, stock exchange markets, agents and board directors may also play a positive role in serving the framework. Each act of each director is subject to supervisory over-sight and balancing by others. In the past, the government played several roles combined into one, including policy maker, owner of State-Owned Enterprises and enterprise manager. The State should now focus solely on making the policies and rules that enable fair market competition.

If some State-Owned Enterprises can be re-defined as entities of local gov-ernment (including provincial) public ownership, the framework as described in Figure 5.1 may be applied as well. It can serve to transform local medium-sized State-Owned Enterprises. Transforming enterprises can then be done simultane-ously throughout the country, expediting the whole process.

Let us now look at the process of actually creating this new framework.

We could call the capital that the people's congresses grant to shareholding companies for purchasing State-Owned Enterprises "virtual capital." (Such capi-tal represents the funds that the committees selected by the standing committee of the people's congresses grant to C_i ($i = 1$, n).) It is similar to vouchers, however, so in future we will use the term vouchers afterwards.

The committee only allocated a certain number of vouchers, which is then equivalent to its investment in C_i ($i = 1$ to n).

C_i (shareholding companies or investment companies) may be selected from among existing large-sized banks and investment companies.

C_i ($i = 1$, n) is owned by or partially owned by the committee on behalf of the public.

C_i uses the vouchers it obtains to invest in and form C_{ij} ($j = 1$, m). (That is, to invest in subsidiaries that are either shareholders or investors in C.)

As incorporation of State-Owned Enterprises is carried, as entities become legal persons, we may want to select certain entities for being listed on the stock market in a proper sequential order. C_{ij} can then use its own vouchers to buy some shares, but this does not preclude regular people from using real money to buy shares as well.

The nationwide requirements of this process, including various procedures, should take a minimum of five years given the large scale of China's econ-omy. New owners can be active from the start, however, given the necessary information.

In this process, the State has not actually sold the State-owned assets of State-Owned Enterprises because the committee is now the owner of C_i ($i = 1$, n).

In the balance sheet of C_i, the equity of E_{ijk} ($j = 1$, m; $k = 1$, K) is gathered through the equity of C_{ij} ($j = 1$, m) and is now expressed as the property rights owned by C_i. Therefore, re-distribution of public wealth is not at issue here. The process of transformation is also a process by which the stock market, its affiliated institutions, and its agents can gradually develop and accumulate experience. Since large banks have participated in the establishment of C_i, as ownership conversion proceeds, any of E_{ijk} that suffer from severe capital shortages can conduct debt-equity swaps.

At the outset, the committee can allow all the C_i to use 1 percent of the prescribed number of vouchers for the purchase of or in exchange for office buildings and facilities. C_i can do the same with respect to C_{ij}. The new structure of public ownership and its transformation will mean that many existing industrial departments and their affiliates will now be eliminated. As a result, many government office buildings will become available for sale.

Staff that formerly worked in these departments can now become candidates to fulfill different positions within C_i and C_{ij}.

C_{ij} may draw a very small portion of funds from E_{ijk} ($k = 1$, K) to cover daily expenses, as per a fixed percentage of the equity value. This may be included in the cost accounting of E_{ijk} to cover such expenditures of C_{ij}. C_i may also do the same with C_{ij}.

Decisions about wages and bonuses are made by higher levels and are paid by higher levels in a top–down fashion. The committee pays all members of the boards of directors of C_i.

Each C_i board of directors in turn pays salaries to C_i managers from C_i operating accounts. C_i managers in turn use C_i operating accounts to pay the boards of directors of C_{ij} ($j = 1$, m).

Each C_{ij} board of directors decides upon the salaries of C_{ij} managers, and pays from C_{ij} operating accounts. C_{ij} managers pay directors of E_{ijk} ($k = 1$, K) from their own operation fees; each E_{ijk} board of directors decides salary payment to E_{ijk} managers based on E_{ijk} operation fees; and E_{ijk} managers use E_{ijk} operation fees to pay their employees. Since the objective of managers in most cases is to maximize share prices, stock options may also be used in the framework as a part of the incentive for managers.

One severe problem that China's State-Owned Enterprises face is their excessive burden of social security. They must pay for pension costs, health insurance and unemployment compensation, as well as offer low-rent housing, for all employees and retirees. Market-oriented reform must free enterprises from such responsibilities. The primary objective of enterprises must be to maximize profits and share price. In the structure designed here, C_i will establish pension funds and health insurance funds and set up real estate departments for fulfilling housing-related functions.

During the process of transformation, when C_{ij} makes an offer to buy E_{ijk} it needs to evaluate the latter's burden of pension, healthcare and support for surplus employees as well as the resources to implement these functions, such as the housing and other social security facilities owned by each specific E_{ijk}. Knowing these, C_{ij} can include all the re-arrangements in its offer and such evaluation should not only be static but also dynamic. When ownership of E_{ijk} is transferred to C_{ij} the accumulated social security benefits of E_{ijk} will be transferred to those institutions carrying out implementation of C_i via C_{ij}.

Later, E_{ijk} employees will be paid with real wages, with which they can themselves pay for rent or buy apartments via mortgage loans, with which they can pay pension and health insurance on a monthly basis, and with which they can pay payroll tax for their basic social security (if this is indeed established).

In the future, E_{ijk} employees will not be limited to using their own C_i functional institutions, but may prudently choose social security institutions that they believe suit their needs, depending on services and value-added performance. In this regard, C_i can also sell or buy its resources and obligations and professionalize these functions. Another advantage of this whole process is that people will pay much closer attention to the performance of C_i since that performance relates to their own pensions. This will be of considerable help to the work of the committee.

A parallel process could apply to share participation by employees. Within a certain limited quota of total E_{ijk} equity, some E_{ijk} can motivate their managers by providing them with stock options as compensation.

When transformation is a little further along, C_i and C_{ij} can use other financial vehicles, such as mutual funds and corporate bonds, to raise funds. The boards of directors of E_{ijk} can also decide to distribute dividends to C_{ij}, so that they may invest in other profitable industries.

Joint shareholding means that several C_{ij} with different "i" jointly hold the equity of E_{ijk}. Though this is not expressed in the illustration here, it should be allowed to exist. It will not undermine the above framework. For the sake of clear and convenient illustration of the concept, however, this paper only introduces the top level of the framework.

Conclusion

This article points out that in the initial stage of reforming any socialist economy the minimum package of reforms incorporates less than what is envisaged by the "troika" approach. This smaller reform package generally includes initial political reform, fairly fast marketization, and fairly early restructuring of State-Owned Enterprises. China's reform basically belongs to this type.

Nevertheless, since China was in fact incapable of marketizing at a sufficiently fast pace, it lost out on certain opportunities. This created some problems, as described below.

- The economy ran into a fiscal deficit and also had a negative balance in its international payments. This led to economic instability and the wavering of reform (or the need to repeat reforms). This was highly correlated with the simultaneous coexistence in China of rules governing a centrally-planned economy and those governing a market economy. Such concurrent rules applied to both micro and macroeconomic aspects of the economy.

- Corruption increased dramatically among those administering the economy. The process of shifting tracks from one system to another presented opportunities for rent-seeking and rent-setting activities.
- The process generated unequal distribution of incomes. The reasons for this included mainly unfair competition and rent-seeking activities, as well as the stripping of State-Owned Enterprise assets.
- Resource allocation has not in fact improved to an acceptable level.

Another problem with China's reform is that we have not yet achieved consensus on how to restructure the property rights of State-Owned Enterprises. This is true despite the fact that there is broad recognition within the country of the need to do this. This article therefore reiterates my own opinion on the subject.

Reform that is guided by government and managed in a sequenced process (if that is possible) is to be recommended over reform that is carried out along a maximum frontier. Considerations that relate to such sequencing are the following: first, all aspects of reform must have a logical sequence and coordinated connections; second, they must provide for ongoing momentum of reform (they should balance marginal economic effects and marginal political effects under different conditions); third, our administrative capacities must be sufficient to carry out the process.

This sequence involves first carrying out initial political reform, then marketization that is relatively more effective than it has been in the recent past, and finally straightening out property rights relationships in State-Owned Enterprises on a comprehensive basis.

Democracy and human rights will definitely follow in this process, based on a shift toward public elections. In terms of marketization, we should rapidly undertake reform actions that bring a swift improvement in efficiency (such as incentive mechanisms, releasing controls on the prices of consumer goods, and so on). We should start these actions as soon as possible. As for actions that reduce social welfare and security, we should arrange for those to be implemented in concert with (or bundled with) other actions that improve results.

Deciding on radical or incremental reform depends on economic conditions and particularly on crisis conditions. Our government administration generally prefers incremental reform, but that means that we must begin reforms before a crisis takes hold. Otherwise we will no longer have the ability to choose between an incremental path and one that is more radical.

Economists should not hold to one specific value or one specific belief. They must seek truth within an evolving world. This article believes that privatization may not be the sole way to reform a socialist economy. There may be other ways to restructure and resolve property rights within State-Owned Enterprises. A diversified path toward economic growth and economic reform definitely helps economists gain more empirical knowledge and it should therefore be welcomed.

Economists should also provide concrete techniques that help resolve problems in the real economy. These include techniques that provide certain constraints in the process of transition. The task of economists is to be conscientious in trying to find solutions. It is not our task to declare prematurely that there is simply nothing to be done.

Notes

1 This was originally a speech given by the author, which was then published in the magazine *Reform* in the second volume of 1993. The co-author of this article was Yin Wenquan. The speech was given at MIT, with World Bank vice president Stanley Fisher serving as commentator. The occasion was a meeting of the American Social Science Association (ASSA) on "Different transition strategies for moving toward market economies."
2 *China Statistical Yearbook 1992*, National Bureau of Statistics, China Statistics Press (Beijing), 1992.
3 These statistics come from pages 54 and 55 of the *China Foreign Economic and Trade Yearbook 1992*, National Bureau of Statistics, China Statistics Press (Beijing), 1992.
4 The source of the 1985 data came from page 329 of the *China Foreign Economic and Trade Yearbook 1987*, National Bureau of Statistics, China Statistics Press (Beijing), 1987.
5 As mentioned on page 145 of the *China Statistical Yearbook 1992*, National Bureau of Statistics, China Statistics Press (Beijing), 1992.
6 Page 237 of the *China Statistical Yearbook 1992*, National Bureau of Statistics, China Statistics Press (Beijing), 1992.

6 The role of liberalized foreign trade in creating a more reasonable pricing system[1]

(November 1993)

Reform of the economic structure is sometimes derived from proactive efforts and sometimes from a passive response to one kind of pressure or another. To an extent, China's price distortions have been corrected by proactive economic reforms, while other changes have been the result of the "passive" kind of response. We could call this second category a "passive type of price evolution."

Proactive price reform means taking intentional steps to reduce price distortions or to correct them. Such things include releasing prices from price controls so as to enable them to approach market-determined rates. Where the market is not effective, they include taking administrative action to set prices in ways that will realize a balance in supply and demand as much as possible. Voluntary actions involve recognizing the negative effect that price distortions have on resource allocation, as well as the negative side effects they have on income distribution. They involve taking action to reduce those distortions. The passive form of price evolution points to ways in which reform measures already being taken in other areas unavoidably have a "transmission effect" that influences prices as well. The transmission effect was not intentional. Rather, it is uncontrollable. This transmitted response gradually must be accepted in the form of price changes.

In terms of opening up foreign trade and allowing greater market entry into foreign trade business, most among us would like to participate in the international division of labor and enjoy the benefits of international exchange. Many are not, however, prepared to accept that this will also change our domestic price structures, that international markets will affect domestic markets. From this perspective, the impact of international-market prices is one kind of the passive-type of price evolution. Since the start of reform and opening up, this particular process has in fact had a massive effect on the relative structures of our domestic pricing. That is, it has greatly influenced the prices of some goods relative to others.

Indeed, among all passive types of price changes within China, the enormous influence of international price structures is the most pronounced. At present, our domestic prices are gradually drawing closer to international market prices. Our domestic pricing departments have never wanted to use international prices as reference standards for domestic market prices since they believe that such prices are inconsistent with our domestic situation. Foreign prices are controlled by the "old international order," the order by which capitalist nations manipulated prices. Nevertheless, opening up to the outside has not only opened channels for cultural and scientific exchange, but even more importantly it has broadened our degree of openness in economic terms. It has expanded imports and exports, and attracted in foreign investment ("foreign-funded enterprises of the three kinds). All of these things have generated an incremental and cumulative effective on prices that is extremely important.

As shown in Table 6.1, the total volume of China's imports and exports already represents a fairly substantial share of the country's GNP. In terms of imports, the variety of product categories has increased greatly, competition has gradually grown, and trade companies are more autonomous and now implementing the policy of being responsible for both profits and losses. The domestic pricing of a number of products that have been imported now relies on the internationally set price as the basis of comparison.

Competition from imported goods is also having a profound influence on domestic pricing of goods. When imports are not only low-priced but more reliable in terms of quality, then it becomes harder to sell our domestic production of the same item. Most of our manufactured goods are still inferior to imported goods when it comes to quality. Customs duties are also fairly high, which allows for a certain degree of protectionism. For the majority of products, however, the role being played by import competition is quite apparent.

For example, China has set customs duties on the import of raw materials at a fairly low level in order to promote and encourage raw materials imports. This has gradually affected the input prices of many products being produced in China, including steel, materials for the chemical industry, chemical fibers, and so on. Many enterprises make use of imported materials in their production right now, so it is unavoidable that the pricing of their products will draw closer to those of international markets. Meanwhile, we adopt a variety of protectionist and import-substitution measures to limit the import of manufactured (finished) goods. Nevertheless, even here the international markets will ultimately have a major effect on China's domestic markets.

China's importing system itself has been undergoing major change, which has unavoidably impacted our domestic pricing. Since reform of the foreign trade system began, the following changes have occurred to strengthen competition.

First, the number of companies that are allowed to carry out importing has increased enormously. In the course of their operations, these companies conduct

Table 6.1 The degree to which China's economy is open

Year	Import and export volume as a percentage of GNP	Import volume as a percentage of GNP	Export volume as a percentage of GNP
1978	9.9	5.22	4.67
1985	24.2	14.7	9.45
1990	31.9	14.8	17.1

Source: *China Statistical Yearbook 1991*, China Statistical Publishing House, 1991

business according to the needs of the department (with which they are affiliated) or their local area. The old centrally-controlled system cannot impose strict controls on this whole process, including the way in which domestic prices are set on imported products. Since many imported products are in categories that have now been "released" or "liberalized," the companies have autonomous decision-making authority over operations. This stimulates the growth of a competitive pattern.

Second, we now allow the importation of some raw materials to be done on a "decentralized" as opposed to centrally-controlled basis. This allows entities to carry out direct wholesale purchases of raw materials, as well as imported items to be used as inputs in industrial production. We allow "piecemeal" imports of smaller quantities to be used in steel production, chemical fertilizers, and so on. This policy implementation has had a massive effect on the domestic pricing of some primary products and intermediate input products in China. It has brought competition in its wake.

Third, we have granted authority to lower levels of government administration to do the review and approval process for granting import licenses. The pressures of reform gradually forced this change in authority. From being concentrated at the central level of government, it was gradually opened up until a large portion of imported goods no longer need licenses at all. Although some imported items still have quantitative restrictions, the permission process for granting licenses to import these things has been passed down to local governments. This too has increased competition.

Fourth, the practice of illegal smuggling has impacted domestic prices. The imported supply of some goods is restricted by prohibitively high customs duties. China has a very long coastline. When duties are too high, this only contributes to the practice of smuggling—the higher the duties, the more the smuggling. Large amounts of smuggled goods have a clear impact on the pricing of domestic goods that were originally supposed to be protected by high customs duties. The result is a fall in domestic prices of these goods.

Fifth, foreign-invested enterprises are now participating in domestic competition, particularly those making high-tech and import-substitution products. Policies allow these to enter into domestic markets, and they then create price competition. Such enterprises have the option to choose between imported or domestically-produced raw materials. They may also set the prices of goods they make themselves. By now, this kind of competition has already become extremely important.

The above five changes in China's situation are already generating competition within the import arena which is having a tremendous impact on the structure of our domestic pricing.

As for exports, the competition in this sphere is having an even greater impact on price structures in China than the import arena. Products that are cheap in China tend to be either raw materials or products with only a small amount of value-added or processing. Competition to buy these goods for export will continue until their prices approach international market levels. By now, under the influence of this kind of competition to export, prices of China's foodstuffs and minerals are already approaching international levels. In the past, our domestic prices for finished goods were relatively high so that exporting was generally not profitable. To compete, our exporters must now try to sell products that are more advanced in terms of function, quality, and standards. At the same time, they must have the freedom to choose what raw materials and components go into their products, if they intend to be able to compete. This clearly has improved the structure of inputs going into production. Both of these two factors are gradually leading to a lowering of the overly high prices of our finished goods.

The main challenges confronting China's exports are as follows. First, there is a "buyers' battle" going on among the government(s), State-owned foreign trade companies, and the various producers of products in the country for export goods. They are contending with one another for product to export and the resulting conflict has been intense although by now it is diminishing somewhat because fewer and fewer products still earn exceptionally high profits. The State has tried to increase controls but the fact is that the State has made clear concessions to those handling foreign trade as well as producers. Once the concessions are made, domestic price distortions are reduced.

Products that can be exported do not account for all products in China's product market, but they will account for an increasingly large share as the Chinese government further "opens up" the country. In the past, China's price distortions were characterized by unreasonable comparative pricing between primary products and finished goods. Those are now being corrected within the categories of goods that are released for foreign trade.

Second, as inflation occurs in China, finished goods that are exported must bear the cost of higher inputs because of a depreciating currency. Overall, however, the higher cost due to currency exchange is lower than the rise in the overall price level in the country. At the same time, prices of our exported products are not increasing too much given ongoing development of manufactured goods, improvements in types of product being produced, and increased competition. Right now, many electronic products are being exported on a profitable basis while they were formerly exported at a loss. The domestic price levels for quite a few primary products such as grain oils, specialty food products, Chinese medicine, and so on are already more on a par with international markets than they were. They are catching up with finished goods when both categories are compared with prices on the international market. Among the category of "finished goods," internal consistency in pricing has also been achieved to a degree.

All of these things are evidence of the fact that participating in international market competition is a necessary trend. The trend will enable exports to have an increasing influence on rationalizing our domestic price structure.

Third, now that foreign-invested enterprises (of three types) are allowed to export as well, this is having a massive "transmittal effect" within China. If production of something is quite competitive within China, then foreign investment is eager to participate in it, which creates competition. The foreign-invested entity uses management practices that are not constrained by government controls—they are "free enterprise" methods. Such practices include the freedom to choose inputs that are either produced inside China or imported from outside China. What's more, these enterprises have the freedom to choose their technologies and their personnel. This puts very considerable pressure on industries in the same field within China.

Take bicycles as one example. In the past, China exported outdated styles yet found it hard to change this practice. Now, not only are foreign-invested entities seizing the opportunity to make higher profits from new models, but they are threatening China's own production in the domestic markets that China once controlled. In terms of management systems, our domestic producers must begin to emulate those of foreign-invested entities or they will find it hard to be competitive when it comes to exporting. All of these things are leading to changes in the structure of China's prices.

Fourth, people are gradually realizing that it is absolutely necessary for us to allow freer market entry into export areas. We must allow for competition in this arena. In the past, China monopolized the markets in Hong Kong and Macao for such things as fruit and vegetables, because of proximity and the ease of transportation. We made sure that we also did not compete against ourselves so as to keep prices high. In more recent times, however, we are recognizing the beneficial role that external competition can play. Our fruit is gradually being squeezed out of Hong Kong markets by fruit from Southeast Asia. Even our vegetable sales to Hong Kong are being threatened by Southeast Asia. We must rally our forces and try to retake lost market share. To do that, we must change our operating methods. We cannot rely on the State imposing quantitative limits as the way to keep prices high. Instead, we must broaden the decision-making authority of enterprises themselves. We must increase the autonomy of our microeconomic units if we intend to improve their competitiveness. Changes in our export system have a direct impact on how we price export products. They also, however, have a huge indirect impact on our entire domestic pricing structure.

There is another way in which a "passive style of price change" comes about. We used to provide subsidies for things on which we mandated low prices. As conditions changed and subsidies unavoidably were reduced, this then morphed into a "passive evolution" of price changes. Yet another consideration is that local governments and enterprises often violate price regulations as set by the central government and its pricing departments. They start to revise certain prices on their own which then leads to changes in the overall price structure. This too can be defined as a "passive style of price evolution."

Naturally, it is not so easy to differentiate clearly between "passive" and "active" types of price evolution. Many prices lie in between these two. A general way to distinguish them, however, is the degree to which active steps are taken to reduce price distortions. If it is felt that the price system is highly unreasonable, and steps are taken voluntarily to reduce obstructions in other areas that will facilitate more rational price structures, in other words, if we feel that the risk of price reform is worthwhile, we undertake what could be termed "voluntary price reform." If, on the other hand, other factors simply cannot go on as they were before and we are unwillingly forced to accept new price structures, then this belongs to the category of "involuntary change."

This distinction is important. The reason lies in the timing of the process, the effect it has on income distribution, and the effect it has on changing our ranks of cadres. Even if the end results might be the same in terms of prices, the process and end results are different in these three categories. If we differentiate between the two types of price changes, we can better understand how we arrived at our current pricing situation and we can compare the two options more easily and make better choices.

Note

1 This article was originally published in the book *Towards an Open Economy*, by Zhou Xiaochuan and Ma Jianchun (Tianjin People's Publishing House, 1993). It was included in Section 4 of Chapter III.

7 Social security

Economic analysis and systems
engineering[1]

(1994)

Conceptual distinctions among types of social security systems

Research into social security systems has been a "weak link" in both economic and administrative circles. Some basic concepts are misunderstood, which leads to the inability to discuss the subject intelligently. In the past, China's social security structures and concepts were in fact determined by the department in charge— each system was different depending on the sector of the economy. We now have a new understanding of this subject, as a result of the Decision (the "*Decision on Major Issues concerning the establishment of a socialist market economy*") as approved by the Third Plenary Session of the 14th Central Committee of the Communist Party of China (1993). This includes a new approach to determining sources of funds and methods of guaranteeing benefits depending on the different types of social security. For the first time, the Decision also proposed the idea of setting up individual accounts for social security.

From an economic standpoint, the issue now is to evaluate different types of social security systems and understand their basic theoretical approaches.

Social security system that works on a "contributions basis"

Social security that works on a contributions basis means that the benefits provided to each individual beneficiary are determined by how much that person paid in to the social security fund in the past. One of the basic features of this system is that it involves accumulation of funds in advance, that is, it is "pre-funded." Over a period of many years, the person paying into the account pays in a specific percentage of his income every month and every year. These funds do not remain static, however, since they in turn are invested and therefore accumulate additional funds. The advantage of this kind of system is that it ensures there will be a reliable source of funding for social security. The system does not have the problem of "eating the seed corn" and having nothing to grow in the future.

Another basic feature of this system is that the person who accumulates funds is the one who benefits from them in the end. Benefits are correlated to the accumulated amount. The specific means by which this is done is called "individual accounts." This therefore creates an incentive mechanism for paying into the account, since the property rights over each individual's account are clearly defined. This motivates people to want to work and accumulate more, and it avoids the problems of a "one big pot of rice" system.

The social security system that works on a contributions basis can be further subdivided into two categories depending on how each is handled.

One kind handles the organization of the system and management of the funds via a public institution. Singapore's system is the classic example of this. Each link in the process of social security is the responsibility of the Central Provident Fund Board. Certain requirements must be met for this kind of system to work, however. One is that the population is small. Another is that there is little tradition of a free-market system, and a third is that the State and public institutions are relatively "clean" and effective.

The second kind handles the organization through private institutions in a more "free" way. The pension systems of the United States are an example of this category. Pensions in the US are basically run according to the rules and operating procedures of private institutions. The United States has a strong tradition of free-market economics, plus its capital markets are well developed and consumers have a strong tradition of making decisions for themselves.

If we analyze further, however, we see that there is not an absolutely clear-cut distinction between the two types as described above. First, we can divide the process of implementing social security into several segments. These include formulating rules and regulations, handling information systems that relate to investments and return on investments (this includes managing personal accounts), and also benefits distribution. Each of these steps in the process can be handled in different ways. Each of these many ways of handling things can have various combinations and permutations which then form finer categories of the system.

First, formulating rules and regulations. There are various options for how to formulate the specific rules that relate to implementing a contributions system. The rules can be created by a public institution or by private institutions. They can include, for example, the percentage of a person's salary that goes toward his social security contribution, the percentages paid by the employee and the employer, the standards that apply when pension funds are being distributed—if a person's balance is sufficient, he is allowed to take those pension funds and put them to some other use. There are also different options in deciding on whether public or private institutions should decide on such things as how much overlapping use of the funds can be allowed.

Second, managing information systems. When a private accounts method is used, and funds are accumulated in advance, this necessarily generates a large amount of information requiring massive information systems. Such information systems management can be handled by the public or it can be handled by private institutions on a competitive basis. For example, Singapore's personal account information system is managed by the Central Provident Fund Board through computerized operations. Given its modest population, the size of Singapore's information system is relatively small and Singapore's monetary authorities can handle it. The practicalities of the situation mean that this is effective. However, if the country has a large population, the information systems required can potentially be enormous. How to manage such a massive information system needs to be addressed by plans devised from a management sciences perspective. Under such conditions, it may not be appropriate to use a public institution to handle centralized data. It may be more appropriate to have distributed management that is conducted at different levels. The question then arises of whether or not it should be done by private institutions. Naturally, this would generate a whole new set of issues that include, for example, efficiency considerations and dispute resolution.

Third, investment and return on investment. A pre-funded system with accumulating funds means that the funds constantly have to be invested. There are two potential methods for carrying out such investing. Singapore uses a public institution as the responsible party, namely the Central Provident Fund. The other method is adopted by countries with a strong tradition of market economies. People in such countries are not inclined to have public institutions handling the investment—they would rather trust the investment efficiencies of private investment institutions. Carrying out investment activities requires dealing with several considerations. The first is being able to measure and also bear investment risk. The second is achieving fairly high returns on investment. The third is the ability to provide investment groupings that are in line with the preferences of the investor. The fourth is earning returns that are in line with different kinds of investments. This involves accurate choice of investment vehicles, and balancing the pros and cons of each depending on its features and overall considerations.

In fact, there are many more combinations that can result from different approaches to handling social security funds. For example, the government or public institutions may set the rules while private organizations are responsible for information management systems, organizing investments, and distributing benefits. The country Chile practices a system of this nature. Another example, public institutions may be responsible for formulating rules and managing information systems, while private institutions are responsible for making investment decisions. Further rules can apply to investments made by private institutions that require reinsurance of either the private institution or its investments. Such rules can specify whether the reinsurance organization is to be a publicly-operated entity or a governmental institution.

Social security systems that are benefits-based

"Benefits-based" means that the welfare (security) measures provided to each beneficiary depend on a specified set of criteria and whether or not the beneficiary meets that set of criteria (or "formula").

First, the distribution of benefits is determined by a formula that takes the current conditions of the beneficiary into account. Criteria include age, health, and employment. This distribution method focuses on equality rather than on the past contributions made into the system by the beneficiary.

Second, the benefits-based model is a pay-as-you-go system. Current receipts fund current benefits.

Fairness is meant to be ensured by this system since the ultimate benefits are determined by pre-established conditions, and everyone stands in an equal position. The system therefore appears to equalize income distribution. In another sense, however, this way of equalizing income may actually restore the egalitarian problems of a "one big pot of rice" approach. Benefits are not determined by how much one contributes into the system. This therefore provides a disincentive to work hard, while it frustrates those who do work hard. In order to compensate for the lack of incentives, we are currently trying to figure out how to add alternative ways of calculating "labor contribution," so as to allow for greater benefits to those who pay in more in labor.

The tax base provides the source of funding for the pay-as-you-go system. It is therefore easier to manage. There is no need for a massive information management system. There is no need to worry about investing and return on investments. Administrative costs are therefore also lower. An effective pay-as-you-go system needs a stable environment. It needs stable economic growth and the tax-revenue stream that comes from stable growth. The amount that the system pays out in benefits needs to be steady or at least change only a little. Therefore, the aggregate income level that feeds this system also has to be steady. If revenue is volatile, the system will have problems paying benefits and the benefit formula may need to change.

In addition, the pay-as-you-go system requires demographic stability. The social security taxes paid out by today's workers pay for the benefit of current retirees. In the event of drastic demographic change, such as when a population ages quickly, there are fewer of today's workers to pay for the retirees and this again leads to problems in paying out for benefits. Workers may become so over-taxed that they feel a negative incentive to work.

In recent years, people have begun to recognize the problems of the benefits-based model. Changes are being made as a result, such as changing the formula for paying out for benefits. This formula used to be rather simple (including an expression and algorithms). It is now more complex, with more variables added that relate to the contributions being made into the system. As a result of these changes, the benefits-based social security model is increasingly able to combine the advantages of the contributions-based model to come up with an improved version that makes up for shortcomings in the benefits-based model.

In a pay-as-you-go "benefits-based" system, funds are mainly raised via taxes. If finance departments are able to make plans using science-based dynamic projections, they can deal with fluctuations caused by economic cycles or structural changes in demographics. They can make long-term investments which allow for capital accumulation when tax receipts are higher or social security spending is lower. These then help cover costs when needed. For example, when the population as a whole is younger and the economy is growing more rapidly, tax revenues are high. A portion of those revenues may be used to invest in infrastructure as a way to ensure adequate spending on social security in the future. To a degree, this is similar to a pre-funded system. It helps smooth out the effects of economic slumps and helps filter out the effects of an aging population.

A "mixed" social security system

As described above, the contributions-based model and the benefits-based model of social security are different in a number of ways, including how they are funded and how benefits are distributed. Each therefore has its advantages and disadvantages. Moreover, each type can be further subdivided into categories. This then allows policy makers a greater number of options. People prefer not to see only the extreme-case options but rather a range of options that are of a "mixed" nature. That is, instead of choosing from only two possibilities, one or zero, policy makers would like to choose options that range from one to zero. Fortunately, the contributions-based model and the benefits-based model can indeed be combined using different proportions of each.

It is possible for a mixed type of system to provide different kinds of benefits to different people. A benefits-based system can have universal application in providing the most basic social security. A contributions-based system can provide supplementary benefits to certain individuals. That is, under the benefits-based model, a relatively low payroll tax can provide public revenues that then become a part of funding social security. Pensions, healthcare, unemployment, disability, and accident insurance can be paid according to formulas that apply to beneficiaries. Such security can focus on equal treatment for everyone and serve as a kind of safety net for society at large. The great majority of people, however, will not be content with the low levels of pensions and security provided by such treatment. They will want to pay in to a contribution system that enables them to receive more benefits. This then is a system that is pre-funded and has clear incentives. People pay in to their own private accounts that are for their own eventual use. The relative percentages of these two systems depend on the specific desires of people as well as economic and social conditions. If the economy is going well and preferences are able to favor equality and social stability, then it may be that a benefits-based model plays a stronger role. If the economy is not strong enough to support adequate benefits, and it is more important to incentivize economic growth, then a contributions-based model may play a stronger role.

It is possible to have policy options that lie anywhere between the spectrum of one and zero in terms of determining the percentages of the two systems. It should be noted, however, that it will never be possible to have all the advantages of both systems and none of the disadvantages. It may be that social costs are increased by combining the two systems. Payroll taxes will be collected from a group of people and then redistributed according to certain formulas. In addition, one group of people will have to manage personal accounts and deal with the business of investing those accounts. For society as a whole, this will undoubtedly consume more resources in order to realize social security objectives that are at a certain level.

China in fact has a rather strange kind of mixed system already. In our current system, government employees and the staff and workers of State-Owned

Enterprises have a benefits-based system of social security. Collectively-owned enterprises and *ge-ti* or individual business owners may rely more on what they themselves put into a contributions-based system. Meanwhile, rural people rely on their own household savings to provide for old age and healthcare. This system is inherently hierarchical (or class-oriented). It makes a distinction between "rural" and "urban" status (depending on a person's household registration). It is not only unreasonable but cannot be kept up for long. Naturally, if we recognize that to a degree this kind of mixed system is transitional, and that we cannot discard the former class-oriented system all at once, then for the short term there is some logic to changing it gradually.

Finally, in discussing basic concepts we should also address the question of insurance and we should be explicit about the rule that insurance and the insurance industry plays in all this. The reason is that some people do not make the distinction between "social security" and "social insurance." Insurance refers to specific circumstances where a person pays premiums and is insured under defined rules. The insuring agent bears the cost of paying the beneficiary for uncertain contingencies. A formula is applied to what benefits might be. The premiums paid out are somewhat similar to taxes. In that sense, the benefits-based kind of social security is also a kind of social insurance and the two terms can be used interchangeably. However, the benefits-based system is not the only form of social security. A contributions-based system is not insurance, or is only similar to a limited degree. If an individual's contributions to his individual account are insufficient, he cannot use the contributions in someone else's account to cover his needs. This goes for whether his needs are for uncertain contingencies or not. In this case, the two concepts should not be confused with one another.

The extent to which a social security system serves as insurance is also a measure of the system's performance. The contributions-based model can also offer a certain level of guarantees, as according to the design of the system. Singapore's Central Provident Fund was initially a non-insurance type system. As it evolved, however, its insurance nature increased but still remained quite low. This has had to do with the way Singapore emphasizes incentives in its system.

The benefits-based system of social security is already a form of insurance. It therefore need not adopt the commercial sort of supplementary services that go along with the insurance industry. This is not true of the contributions-based system. In principle, the contributions-based system is distinct from insurance and therefore often should adopt insurance industry methods in order to improve the safety net aspect and deal with all kinds of uncertainty. China's insurance industry should therefore be able to play a greater role in the contributions-based system.

First, this role can be performed in the arena of life insurance. As organizations in the private sector, life insurance companies can provide products that are outside the scope of officially mandated social security. They are responsible for setting up and managing information systems that relate to beneficiaries and they can be responsible for the task of distributing benefits to beneficiaries. All of these duties can make use of their professional expertise. Through the introduction of competition, they can also be done at lower costs.

Second, this role can be expressed in the form of reinsurance. In order to guarantee the interests of beneficiaries, investment fund activity that is carried on by entities in the private sector can be used for "reinsurance" via either government, quasi-government, or commercial-type insurance institutions. Reinsurance itself thereby becomes an internal component of social security.

Third, this role can help reduce uncertainties via the use of annuities. Social security incorporates three different qualities, including provision for old age pensions, for disability and injury, and for healthcare. These are suited to methods used in insurance. For example, disability and injury carries with it a high degree of uncertainty. There are uncertainties related to how much medical treatment, medicines, and time is needed. Because of this, the functions provided by insurance should be adopted. As for old-age pensions, the age at which a person enters "old age" can be defined, but not exactly how long that person is going to live. Once a person who is on a contributions-based system enters retirement, it should be determined whether or not he can draw out the entire amount in his personal account. There are uncertainties relating to how he will be able to deal with his own lifespan and health issues, so one option may be to turn the entire amount of his personal account, or a portion of it, into an annuity. That way, he can draw on the annuity no matter how long he lives. This again is where the insurance industry can play a role.

Different kinds of evaluation systems that can be applied to the social security system

The most intuitively obvious manifestation of the social security system is the "safety net" that it provides to society. This is looking at the system in the simplest way. In addition, however, the system serves a variety of economic objectives. It provides basic social security for members of society and should accomplish that one objective fairly well, which then involves issues of fairness (social equity), redistribution of income between generations, and incentive considerations. When evaluating a social security system, therefore, one cannot use an overly simplified measure. One should see how much it meets various objectives by conducting a comprehensive evaluation. We want to avoid bias and also omissions when we redesign and reform our social security system.

Based on this understanding, we recommend designing an evaluation system that is multi-faceted. Such a system would include the following criteria.

How well it creates a sense of security in society at large

The need to feel secure is one of man's most basic requirements. In real life, people may confront a whole host of unsettling events that include, for example, disease, death, mafia organizations, ethnic conflicts, robbery, and other forms of crime. Individuals and families have a limited ability to deal with these risks. Society itself needs to provide a certain degree of security. In a society with a fairly well functioning social security system, people have a fairly high sense of safety. Criminal activity that is undertaken for the purpose of dealing with a lack of security is greatly reduced. The basic yardstick for measuring how well we have set up a social security system relates to how much people feel they are living with an adequate social safety net.

Setting up such an adequate social safety net, and satisfying the desire of the public for a sense of security, should be our fundamental objective as we design and reform China's social security system. No matter what concrete methods we use, such as a uniform system for all, or individual accounts, we must make people feel there are real guarantees in such basic respects as provision for old age and for health care. We cannot infringe upon people's rights because of unforeseeable events. For example, if inflation occurs, or if there are political or economic problems in the transition of the country's leadership, we cannot allow that to affect the future of old-age security. There should be basic guarantees in economic terms no matter whether or not people get hit with major illness or unforeseen injury. In sum, people should have a certain expectation about the arrangements of the system. They should feel that prudent and solid arrangements allow them to expect a certain security in the future.

It should be pointed out that the formation of a sense of safety in society is not absolutely correlated to people's standard of living. In some countries, people may have low incomes but yet feel secure due to the establishment of an excellent safety net. In other countries, people may have high incomes but feel insecure due to a high crime rate and strained relationships among people.

How well it provides for society equity

A social security system is the product of social advancement. It is concerned with the basic security of the entire body of members of a society and it seeks to achieve security for the society at large. It therefore focuses on the fairness with which it is applied to each member of society. To a degree, it embodies a sense of equality. The extent of coverage is therefore highly important. For example, is one portion of society able to receive the benefits of a social security system and not another—another way of putting this is does one portion of society have to pay more for security than another? This kind of question focuses on the equity aspect of a system, and it puts more demands on the design of the system.

Naturally, the reality in many developing countries is that only a portion of citizens actually receives social security benefits. Generally speaking, those who receive benefits are those who draw a salary from the more modern parts of the economy. Coverage of all members of society is constrained by the level of economic development in the country, as one consideration. Another consideration, however, is choices made in designing the social security system.

In the specific case of China, we mainly have two different kinds of disparities. One relates to the difference between rural residents and urban residents (by "urban," we mean employees of modern industrial sectors; by "rural," we mean traditional agricultural sectors). The differential in the benefits received by these two groups of people is large. The second relates to the disparities in benefits that accrue to employees of different kinds of ownership systems.

The first type of disparity is unavoidable right now, but in the future we must do all we can to lessen the benefits gap. The second type is related in large part to the former traditional economic system, which is something we can and are in the process of reforming. Just because the means are different does not mean that the end results must necessarily be different. There are many ways to achieve a given objective. In the end, our goal is social equity.

How well it creates incentives for individuals

Social security can ensure that people have a basic sense of safety, and social security provides such a safety net with a certain degree of equity. This is its good side. At the same time, the question remains as to whether or not a sense of security serves to make people work hard enough to drive forward economic growth. Two types of problems can emerge if a system is not well designed. One kind relates to the enthusiasm with which people work. In some European countries, unemployment relief benefits are so great that there is little difference between working and not working. Retirement benefits are the same for all, and all are born by public finance. Not only does this provide a disincentive to work, but the burden on public finance is so great that taxes have to be raised to cover costs. If the marginal tax on people's incomes is too high, this provides an even greater incentive not to work.

Another kind of problem relates to people's consumption and the difference between saving too much and saving too little. (I discuss this in the next section.) If personal savings do not figure into how much one gets from social security, this damages the enthusiasm with which people save. Under the centrally-planned economies of traditional socialism (and particularly under the former Soviet Union and eastern European countries), social security was a benefits-based system that provided fairly high levels of security. The system featured such things as publicly-funded healthcare, low-rent housing, zero unemployment and so on. All of these were one reason there was little motivation to work.

How well it serves savings as a contributor to economic growth

From the perspective of savings, a critique of the social security system would look at how well it encourages society to arrive at an appropriate rate of savings, and thereby stimulate economic growth. Economic growth depends on the hard work of each member of society, but at the same time it depends on how savings are constantly being transformed into new investment. From the Harrod-Domar model, we know that savings are the greatest factor in economic growth. Among Asian countries and regions that have experienced relatively fast economic growth, the savings rate has also been high. The social security system and its various considerations play a major role in determining the formation of aggregate savings or "accumulation." Table 7.1 presents the amount of social security funds that are derived from savings in various countries.

Table 7.1 displays the aggregate savings of various countries and social security as a percentage of a country's aggregate savings. As some economists point out, it is not necessarily true that the more savings the better. Savings should be matched appropriately to the structure of supply and demand. Sometimes one even needs to encourage greater consumption. Because of this, policy options with respect to social security systems also relate to the optimum model for consumption. The issue is fairly complex and we should research it in more depth.

First, which kind of social security method will play the most active role in stimulating accumulation (savings)? The benefits-based system employs the pay-as-you-go approach which does not require accumulating savings. It does not, therefore, play that much of a role in generating savings. This is fairly clear. Naturally, society as a whole still has "accumulation" (or savings). This is formed through the action of voluntary individual saving, money in public finance departments from tax collections, and the retained earnings of enterprises. This kind of accumulation has no direct relationship to social security.

The contributions-based system is different since its savings come directly from money put aside in advance. Whether or not this can lead to the creation of

Table 7.1 Savings from social security of 15 countries in 1977

Country	Gross national savings (A million monetary units of the currency of respective country)	Savings from social security A million monetary units of the currency of respective country)	Percentage share in gross national savings (percent)
Morocco	6,166.00	249.87	4.1
Mauritius	1,020.00	32.61	3.2
Tunisia	255.10	56.73	22.2
Zambia	199.30	30.34	15.2
Brazil	345,137.00	1,904.80	0.6
Canada	21,569.00	3,774.70	17.5
Costa Rica	3,308.50	414.90	12.5
The United States	91,634.00	20,929.00	22.5
Panama	291.00	45.79	15.7
India	99,620.00	9,617.60	9.7
Japan	37,809,000.00	4,708,900.00	12.5
Belgium	353,695.00	3,507.20	1.0
France	205,968.00	6,841.70	3.3
Norway	12,555.00	2,163.90	17.2
Britain	9,508.00	1,786.00	18.8

Source: Social Security Department, International Labor Organization, *Introduction to Social Security*, Labor and Personnel Press (Beijing), 1987, 152

an appropriate "savings rate," depends on specific policy mandates and quantitative quotas. If the contribution amount is not great, the savings (accumulation) will be quite limited. If we want to accumulate an appropriate amount of savings, then we have to mandate an appropriate amount for contributions.

The "pre-funding" method of the contributions-based system is in fact a kind of mandatory or semi-mandatory system of requiring savings. Why should we use a method that smacks of being mandatory? The theoretical answer to this is that people do not act rationally when they plan for the future. That is, people do not necessarily all have the foresight to act in accord with rational expectations. When young, they generally make arrangements that are insufficient for later needs. They use more for current consumption and do not put enough away for the future. We therefore require mandatory measures to help them save and accumulate for the future.

Is the use of mandatory measures an effective way to ensure that aggregate savings of society as a whole are sufficient? One view says no. This view holds that mandatory savings offset voluntary savings, and so are ineffective when it comes to the society at large. From actual experience, we can see that there is no evidence for this view, however. Voluntary savings do not drop at an equivalent rate once mandatory savings are introduced. Aggregate savings do indeed rise to a degree. It is beneficial to do pre-funding prior to when a youthful demographic structure becomes an older demographic structure. Mandatory savings can therefore help prepare for when an older population experiences a dramatic increase. Naturally, if planning for tax revenues takes a long-term view, then public-finance savings can also prepare for this to a degree. For example, such long-term thinking would include ensuring adequate tax revenues, using a portion for current spending and the remainder for funds, basic infrastructure, such as building roads, highways, urban facilities and so on. What this does in fact is institute a material form of savings. By the time a population ages, public finance will be able to reduce the amount it needs to spend on basic infrastructure. Meanwhile, the amount saved can be put to old-age spending. There remains the question of precisely how to carry out "accumulation" or public saving, which is disputed.

Is it in fact beneficial to encourage a higher savings rate through the use of social security measures? There are also different points of view on this subject. One consideration is the "appropriate" rate of savings, together with choice of the optimum consumption model. Generally speaking, an excessively low rate of savings is not good for economic growth and also not good for social security for the elderly. An excessively high rate is also not necessarily a good thing, however. In the past, much of our analysis felt that an overly high savings rate would incur various problems. First, it would influence consumption and create overstocked inventories of consumer items. This in turn would affect the growth of consumer industries. Second, it would greatly increase investment demand, which would lead to an inadequate supply of capital goods and uncoordinated growth. Third, if mandatory savings were too high, this would affect the positive enthusiasm of producers. Fourth, if mandatory savings were too high, this would also increase the cost of labor. Not only would we lose the advantage of cheap manpower, but it would also affect foreign investment, and so on.

What these kinds of analysis indicate is that there is indeed a policy determination to be made about the appropriate rate of savings and the optimum model of consumption. That is, how large should consumption be as a percentage of GDP in order to be "optimum?" How large a percentage should consumption be in order to meet the needs of the population structure and production capacity at a given time? (The structure of a population has a direct impact on product structure.) How large should the percentage be in order to fuel economic growth? We can analyze how to optimize results based on static or dynamic models. The conclusions are different depending on whether we use an optimization model or the Harrod-Domar model.

No matter what kind of analysis we use, however, there is only a certain range within which savings and consumption are reasonable. Anything higher or lower than this limit will require adjustments. This then involves the whole issue of the capacities of our macroeconomic regulation. If we do indeed have mandatory savings, adjusting that percentage will mean carrying out measures that adjust the percentage-relationship of savings and consumption. In those economies where it is not possible to make adjustments, especially when interest rates cannot be modified with any degree of success, it becomes more important to make use of the role that this kind of adjustment to mandatory savings can play. For example, when Singapore was faced with a recession, the Central Provident Fund lowered the contribution rate in order to increase consumption and stimulate the recovery of the economy. Naturally, this method is also controversial. Nevertheless, it is indeed one way to make macroeconomic adjustments. Meanwhile, the design of the social security system has an effect on this kind of macroeconomic measure.

Another thing that the social security system has an effect on is taxes, given the important effect that the system has on accumulation (or savings). Under a progressive individual income tax, the question becomes the effect that the highest marginal tax rate has on investment. If investment can be deducted from the taxable income, then this is a measure that encourages investment. In similar fashion, tax policies specifically aimed at social security will affect accumulation. Basically, the percentage of a person's income that he sets aside for contributions to his own pension can be tax free. The part paid in by enterprises can be accounted for as a part of labor costs. This tax treatment can play the role of encouraging savings as well as facilitating the creation of the social security system.

How well the social security system meets the needs of management costs

Implementing a social security system necessarily involves human, financial, and material costs but particularly costs that relate to information systems. The problem therefore arises of how to handle all of the management costs associated with such information systems. If we adopt a contributions-based system, we face the issue of managing individual accounts and the costs of managing those accounts.

This includes the costs of managing all kinds of information on each account. That means that person's ongoing work history, whether or not he was unemployed, how much he paid in to his account and how that changed. When the pre-funded amount was then invested, the information must include such things as return on investment and how the funds were managed. The ultimate link in the process is information on the beneficiary so as to determine pension payments according to his specifics, and so on.

If we use a benefits-based system, we still have this issue of management costs. We must collect information on each person so as to determine the formulas for how much each is to receive. As formulas get complex, the sheer volume of information that needs to be managed will further increase. Whether it is the responsibility of public institutions or is managed by private institutions, the spending of a considerable sum will be necessary. That is, a portion of resources in the country's GDP will be used for this task, which is unavoidable and necessary. However, as we study how to design China's social security system, we should take into consideration how to make management costs as reasonable as possible. This is what is meant by "how well a system meets the needs of management costs."

Both economics and management sciences seem to indicate that there is always a way to make management costs more rational, under certain specified systems. This is not necessarily so, however, in the actual practice of management. That is, it is not possible to find a way of lowering costs that is independent of the choices one makes about what system to choose. Different systems and policies can often lead to enormous differences in costs. Management costs can be lowered to a fairly low level in implementing the benefits-based social security system, if the government uses tax revenues to collect funds and then distributes benefits according to formulas.

For example, the management component of administering the benefits-based system in the United States comes to not quite 3 percent of the total sum of contributions. However, a contributions-based system that uses individual accounts can have management costs that are much higher, if a number of entities are encouraged to compete for the business and to promote similar types of services. Chile, for example, has adopted this method. Its costs come to around 30 percent of the total collected amount. Although this portion of costs is paid out after the value-added return from investments is figured, from the perspective of those who paid in to the system, their returns on their investment have been reduced. In terms of society at large, the efficiency with which total resources have been used has also been reduced.

The above two examples show that it is possible to find ways to design a system that uses less in the way of society's manpower, materials, and financial resources but that can still produce effective social security. A poorly designed system, on the other hand, can use considerable resources and not produce results that match the costs. This is very similar to the price/performance ratio of a product. It shows the crucial importance of choosing the right policy options and designing a good system.

Several considerations should be mentioned in this regard. First, is there perhaps any room for improving what we have already planned? For example, is it possible to discuss the idea of introducing competition into the process when we implement the contributions-based system? When a number of organizations are marketing various kinds of long-term social security services, each one must spend an enormous amount on marketing costs. Meanwhile, the reality is that most people are quite unclear about the future even though they must make decisions now that anticipate what might happen. Although competitive marketing of different products gives people more options, they actually cannot decide. A great deal of cost therefore goes into limited results. We can deal with this by setting forth overall guidelines for social security services and therefore reduce unnecessary costs of competitive marketing.

Second, the question arises of how to improve investment efficiency by choosing methods for deciding on investments with relatively low cost. This relates to a number of other economic measurement issues. For example, one can imagine that a number of investment portfolios can be offered when there is a highly developed stock market. This lowers the investment risk, and both investing and recouping one's investment are much easier. If there is no stock market, however, and one must invest in such things as government treasuries, less manpower is necessary which saves on costs but which also increases risk. Changes in the political situation or in macroeconomic policy can have an impact on returns.

Finally, another thing must be pointed out which is that management costs are only one way of measuring the social security system among a number of other yardsticks one might use. Under some systems, costs may be a bit higher but the results are more feasible. Such systems should also be considered.

How well a system handles the issue of income redistribution among generations

In and of itself, a social security system has a very clear redistributive nature to it. In evaluating options for social security systems, therefore, we should apply methodology used in the field of economics to examine the whole issue of redistribution of income. We particularly want to avoid the appearance of unfair distribution of income between generations. What this refers to is redistribution of income to specific demographic cohorts or generations within an entire society. For example, the contribution of an older generation to economic growth may be substantial yet these people are unable to receive an appropriate level of pension benefits—the result is equivalent to taxing the older generation and passing the benefits on to the younger generation.

In a benefits-based system, redistribution is carried out according to a certain predetermined formula. This clearly has a redistributing effect in society. In theory, the contributions-based system can avoid being excessively redistributive but this system too has a certain redistributing function. This is more apparent in such things as unemployment, injury, disability, and other such forms of social security. Just how a society determines what its redistributive effect should be for old-age pensions depends on the specific policy choices made with respect to social security.

If we do not take into consideration the generational income redistribution, or we ignore it, we are likely to provide a certain generation of people, whether younger or older, with benefits that exceed what they have paid in to the system. They get more than they have contributed to society's wealth. This conflict can easily become more acute when the society is undergoing rapid demographic change. Not only is this a socio-economic problem, but it is a major socio-political problem. It relates to political feasibility and the choices made for different groups of people. As we design our social security system, we should give full attention to this problem and seek to find solutions that are as objective and as fair as possible.

The influence of political choices

The design of a social security system should avoid the influence of political objectives and political choices to the degree possible. This is to ensure the stability and reliability of the system. This includes two different considerations.

First, a social security system should be able to carry on despite institutional and political changes. Such changes must not affect social stability. If institutional and political changes cancel out former promises that were made regarding social security, not only will this destroy people's safety net but it will also damage their sense of security. They will feel both insecure and discontent. The design of a social security system must take into consideration how to withstand political turbulence and crises. Even if political change does occur, the system must maintain its ongoing functions and overall stability.

Second, a system should avoid any arbitrary arrangements that are the result of short-term or narrow thinking due to political considerations. It is altogether possible that some politicians may make fairly arbitrary promises to people out of a desire to win their support. For example, they may promise to increase benefits to the older generation, or to reduce the burden on the younger generation. This has the effect of changing the income distribution between generations and is irrational in economic terms even though it can be used by politicians to manipulate public opinion. In some countries and at some times, social security policies can become highly sensitive and can serve as a weapon in political contests. From the perspective of design, it is best to limit the degree to which politics can use the system as much as possible. Design should stem from economic, social, and demographic factors, and should not be subject to short-term political considerations. Design of our system should not serve the arbitrary interests of one or another political faction.

The costs to be paid in the transition process

A social security system is a long-range dynamic system in that it makes promises in the present but realizes them only in the future. Because of this, there is necessarily a transition process when a society goes from one type of system to another. This is particularly true if a country institutes reforms that move from a benefits-based system to a contributions-based system. If the transition is not conducted properly, extremely severe problems of income redistribution between generations can result. For example, the former Soviet Union and eastern European countries all had universal retirement and healthcare security. They are now instituting revisions of their former systems so that former promises with respect to social security are not in fact being met. The situation of older people is extremely grave. Naturally, there are many other reasons for this, such as a poor economy during the transition period, which has led to a drop in living standards for the entire body of people, and the fact that long-range systems are more susceptible to the eroding force of inflation. Nevertheless, in overall terms the situation in the former Soviet Union and eastern European countries demonstrates the difficulty of coming up with the right transitional policy choices.

Because of this, how a social security system deals with transitional issues is one of the criteria for measuring its value. This includes evaluating the degree to which fairness is maintained and the extent to which social turbulence is avoided. It includes evaluating whether or not society can withstand the costs to be paid by the transition.

Influence on ownership

A system that involves funds for pensions necessarily involves the question of accumulation or savings, whether that connection is explicit or implicit. Meanwhile, investment is the way in which savings are expressed, and investment is linked to the whole subject of property rights. Because of this, our choices with respect to social security systems are related to our policy determinations with respect to property rights. For example, if we decide to implement personal accounts, the aggregate amount in these accounts will constitute a very large fund that can be invested. It is therefore necessary to have effective mechanisms that ensure that the individual has returns from and can recoup his investment. Ownership of the funds accounts for a substantial percentage of all ownership. As we design our social security system, therefore, we should think of it in terms of a comprehensive system. We should take into consideration the property rights over the assets that are formed through investment, how effectively those assets are managed and whether or not management can provide an appropriate return on assets.

Taking this a step further, given that our former property rights relationships are ineffective, we should think of whether or not the investment system relating to social security can serve to improve ownership reform. I believe that these two things can be linked and considered in tandem. Reform of the social security system should be able to play a certain role in spurring change in the ownership of enterprises. This is an aspect we should make use of as we design our social security system.

The role a potential social security system can play with respect to capital markets

Given the accumulation aspect of a social security system, such a system can be linked to the development of capital markets. The degree to which the system can propel advances in capital markets should serve as one measurement of the system's value.

Precisely how this works is related to the specifics of the policy choices we make for social security systems. A benefits-based system is basically unrelated to capital markets. For years, the Soviet Union and eastern European countries lacked capital markets and yet carried out a benefits-based social security system without any problem. A contributions-based system can play different roles with respect to capital markets. In Singapore, the Central Provident Fund is handled by an institution and does not play a particularly important role in spurring the formation and development of capital markets. In Chile, the situation has been different. Chile adopted a system of a number of different pension fund managers who carry out investments, and this has had a powerful effect on developing the country's capital markets. One reason is that a number of competing entities participate in capital markets, which makes them very dynamic. Another is that a large sum of capital is injected into the markets every year, which has led to a swift increase in their size.

The above examples indicate that different policy choices can lead to different results. In choosing the proper social security system for China, we should take into consideration the degree to which we need to foster capital markets given our current stage of economic and social development. We should take into consideration how our choice of system will play a role in developing our capital markets.

Avoiding bias in our thinking

In discussions on policy options for social security systems, various kinds of bias crop up in people's thinking. This may be intentional or not, but it presupposes certain things that still need to be discussed and demonstrated.

We can frequently discern the following two main kinds of biased thinking.

The first kind is related to traditional concepts of social security as held in socialist economies under a Soviet model system. It exaggerates the fairness and equity aspect of social security insofar as these relate to "all the people." At the same time, it emphasizes the role of government, and overlooks incentive mechanisms as per the standard way that centrally-planned economies function. Because of this, it refuses to accommodate any discussion of "incentives" as they apply to a social security system. As reform moves forward and impacts deeper levels, this kind of thinking is not unwilling to take in new concepts, but it feels that the new concepts should be applied to other things and not the sphere of social security.

The second kind is related to the influence of the economic ideas known as Reaganomics and Thatcherism, which have been popular over this past decade. Many Chinese have learned what they know about economics from the newspapers and magazines over these years of reform, so the media has contributed to the spread of such ideas within China. In simplified terms, they espouse lower taxes, reduced government, privatization, and reduced responsibility of public finance in the overall economy. By now, this approach has been met with growing doubts. At the very least, people are not quite so willing to show their enthusiasm for it. In terms of social security, however, the moment some people hear that the government may take responsibility for some aspect of social security through the use of taxes, they are against it. They make no distinction at all when it comes to level or scope of involvement. Without any analysis whatsoever, they lean in the direction of having private institutions handle all social security functions.

As noted above, such biased forms of thinking are often involuntary. In what follows, I therefore attempt to bring them into the open to discuss them. (Note that this section was abbreviated due to space so does not carry the full discussion.) Economic thinking often moves in cycles that last a decade or even several decades. It shifts back and forth, from right to left. In contrast, social security is something that needs to be designed for long-term operations. It becomes even more imperative, therefore, that we avoid any influence from short-term economic and social trends. Our analysis and our design of the system must be based on very firm economic theory and management science.

Initial thoughts on China's current social security reform

The orientation of China's social security choices

China's ongoing economic reform currently faces the need to make choices with respect to social security. The basis on which we make decisions can only be China's very real national circumstances. China is a developing country with a low per capita level of GDP and economic growth that is only reaching the take-off stage. The main goal of society at large is to realize greater economic growth, and as fast as possible. If we weigh efficiency against fairness, therefore, people are more inclined to want efficiency. They would like for a fairly high degree of economic prosperity to be realized on a widespread basis. This basic premise determines the basic orientation of our social security system, as we carry out policy decisions. First, we need to focus on the effectiveness of incentives in encouraging people to work. While we hope to achieve basic security with our social security system, we also hope that it provides incentive mechanisms that abide by the rule "the more you work the more you get." We want to encourage people to work hard, improve their incomes, and thereby enjoy a higher level of security, and we want to avoid the drawbacks of the "one big pot of rice" system.

Second, we should stress the need to maintain a fairly high rate of individual savings and social accumulation. We do not want our social security to become a "burden on the treasury," as in some western welfare countries. Rather, it should serve the role of encouraging greater accumulation by all of society. It should encourage people to work more, and save more out of higher incomes, so as to achieve a fairly high speed of economic growth. Our orientation must be different from post-industrial countries that provide high levels of benefits as well as equal treatment for all. We must adopt a model that fits our initial stage of development.

Third, we should make sure that our social security system plays a coordinating role among other social and economic reforms. We hope that it can generate positive responses from other aspects of reform. For example, it should be helpful in reorganizing and adjusting the structure of ownership rights, and it should help in fostering capital markets.

Given these factors, which have a very clear orientation, we feel that China should adopt a social security system that uses the contributions-model as its primary component. This system can still allow for a mixed form of operations, that is, the integration of a contributions-based system with a benefits-based system, but the guiding role must be played by the former. This should be the primary orientation of our social security choices.

The transition from old to new in the course of transforming our social security system

If we decide to set up a social security system in which the contributions model is dominant, we face the issue of how to transition from the former benefits-based model. The key issue here, and the hardest part, is how to adjust interests between one generation and the next. For younger people, the issue is fairly simple. From the day they start working, they can enter into the new social security system. They can set up a personal account, begin to accumulate savings, and later draw benefits according to the new rules. The problem is more complex for older people. In the past, they were covered completely by a benefits-based system. Once the system changes, we must find ways to ensure that their interests are being met.

A broadly held popular opinion in China addresses this issue of transition with the catchphrase, "old ways for older people, new ways for newer people." In fact, this is quite hard. If we think about changing the benefits-based model to a contributions model, the "old ways for older people" method dictates that we continue with a pay-as-you-go method, with current receipts paying out for current expenditures. These older people have no personal accounts and no accumulated funds, however, so payment into their retirement funds relies on the contributions of younger people who are currently working. That is one thing. Another is that the "new ways for new people" method means young people are making cumulative payments into their own accounts for their own future needs. They are not paying to fund the needs of the elderly of the next generation. The source of funding therefore becomes a dilemma. If we simply add on taxes and try to deal with funding that way, this will add to the tax burden. It is truly difficult to make the proper arrangements for transitioning from old to new.

One approach is provided by Chile's experience as it reformed its social security system. Prior to reform, Chile practiced a benefits-based system that covered some civil servants and the employees of State-Owned Enterprises. As the system transitioned, the government provided those who were under the former benefits-based system with bond certificates that acknowledged the government's debt to them. Depending on the contribution of the former employee (using a combination of years in service and pay scale), the government calculated a quantity. This was then similar to having funds that had built up in a personal account. By the time of retirement, employees could receive retirement benefits up to this amount.

To resolve the issue of funding this new kind of debt, the Chilean government practiced surplus fiscal policies that enabled it to accumulate a certain amount prior to the reform. Chile's example can illustrate a path for us to follow, that is, we can convert the past contributions of people into a certain estimated sum and regard that as the amount the person has already accumulated, then later convert that into a private account. The problem, however, comes when China does not have enough of a fiscal surplus to cover the costs. In fact, this method would then use nominal or phony bonds and would put the government in the hole. Since China's population is so massive, the extent of the government's deficit would be huge. It could be hard for our public finance to bear the burden.

We feel that we should take China's actual situation into account as we devise solutions. As we consider adopting Chile's "conversion method," we should also think of linking it to how we handle the property rights of State-Owned Enterprises. We might consider converting a contribution that was made by employees of enterprises in the past into a renewed transfer of assets back to them in the present. We can organize pension funds that resolve the issue in this manner.

An analysis of our "actual situation" indicates that older workers in State-Owned Enterprises, as well as people in their thirties and forties, have no savings in personal accounts but they have made contributions nevertheless. Those contributions were made in the form of low wages, with the amount of contribution over and above the wages going into funds that were already absorbed either by State finance or by the State-Owned Enterprise itself to be reinvested in new assets for the corporation or new basic infrastructure for the country at large. Some may have been collected by local governments and departments in various ways and invested in other things. At the same time, some enterprises were forced to accept distorted pricing that meant it did not actually show profits. The enterprise itself never accumulated funds, therefore, but this did not mean that its employees did not make a contribution to society at large. Some of society's accumulated wealth in fact incorporates the work of these people.

Due to the various historical reasons noted above, China's existing State-owned assets include a substantial portion that actually represents a debt to employees. We feel, therefore, that it should be possible to convert people's former contributions into their own personal accounts. We also feel there is every reason to do so. We would again take a portion of State-owned assets out, in the appropriate amount, and allocate it to social security funds such as retirement funds. In this way, we would resolve the problem of how to transition our reform and still meet the former promises made by our social security to an older generation.

As we see it, the catchphrase of "old ways for old people and new ways for new people" is an insufficient improvisation. Instead, old people should also be allowed to participate in new ways. Simply evading this problem is going to put us in a passive position in which we become subject to further problems. First, an improvised way of doing things easily hurts the interests of older people and aggravates the problem of unequal treatment between generations. If it leads to too great a degree of social turbulence, it will also block smooth implementation of further reforms. Second, this way of doing things may put the contribution rate at too low a level when we first start out, as an attempt to mitigate the difference between the older and younger population. If the rate is too low, however, accumulation will be insufficient and this will hinder the effectiveness of social security. This holds particularly in the case when a population is aging very rapidly. From either a short-term or long-term point of view, therefore, we must not evade the problems of transition. Instead, we must find proper ways to resolve them.

Advancing social security reform in the course of "corporatization"

The above solution to problems of transition is actually part of a comprehensive plan that puts social security in the context of overall economic reform. This comprehensive plan links social security to reform of the corporate sector.

From the perspective of social security, this solution aims to address problems of transition. From the perspective of State-Owned Enterprise reform, it aims to ease the burden of social responsibilities of these entities while also delineating property rights. This solution therefore impacts a range of considerations and means that social security reform must keep up with the pace of State-Owned Enterprise reform. Putting it more concretely, the transitioning of our social security system needs to be expressed (or realized) through the process of turning State-Owned Enterprises into corporations.

Turning large- and medium-sized State-Owned Enterprises into corporations is one important aspect of enterprise reform. The general framework of this process includes restructuring ownership rights to State-owned property via both multiple levels of shareholding and cross shareholdings among entities. For this purpose, State-owned holding companies can be divided into top-tier holding companies and the second-tier holding companies that are their subsidiaries. Each of these has independent legal-person standing. Companies that primarily engage in investing include three main types. The first includes holding companies that were formerly State-owned financial institutions. The second includes legal-person shareholding companies that are newly established social security funds. The third includes the parent companies of industrial sectors that are either natural monopolies or in the public sector.

Among these, the second type, relating to social-security funds, is what I would like to address here. As noted above, people who have already retired or just retired, or will soon retire, have already contributed to the formation of already existing State-owned assets. Their contribution was converted into or paid into a form of social security, which the State then put to future investment in employee pensions and healthcare by investing it in a certain amount of assets. Although this portion of assets appears to be "State-owned," in fact the State itself cannot use the returns off these assets for its own purposes. As we carry out "corporatization" of State-Owned Enterprises, we need to clearly demarcate the amount of retirement funds and healthcare funds that should be allocated to "the older generation" of previous employees. This portion should be deducted from the existing corporate assets of the relevant department. It should then belong to (or come under the jurisdiction of) the legal-person shareholding institution that handles social security-type funds.

The specific way to achieve this transition is as follows. First, we set up pension funds and healthcare funds within the top-tier holding companies. When second-tier holding entities bid for the purchase of State-Owned Enterprises (which can be virtual), they must incorporate the burden of the pension funds and healthcare funds that have been assumed by those enterprises. These costs have to be incorporated within their bid. As State-owned assets are transmitted/transferred into the hands of second-tier holding entities, the social security rights of existing employees can be transferred on into the pension funds and healthcare funds set up by the top-tier holding institutions. Each individual employee will be able to receive social security benefits that correspond to the number of years he worked and the amount of his original salary that was paid in.

This way of handling things also has to do with how former State-owned property rights are reorganized into a new form of property rights (or ownership). The property rights as represented by the new pension funds are different from those that applied to our former concept of ownership. On the one hand, they have specifically articulated property rights relationships, and these belong directly to each individual retiree. Management of these is granted to an authorized pension fund manager. From this perspective, the property rights are no longer "owned" by an enterprise that is under a system called "owned by all the people." They are no longer subject to the drawbacks of unclear ownership. They are more akin to direct private property rights. On the other hand, the pension funds still have the "nature" of public ownership. Their capital comes from large-scale public participation. This then is more akin to an ideal form of quasi-public ownership. We must therefore change our traditional notions of "public ownership." Public ownership is not limited to just one form, namely "ownership by all the people." It should not be judged on the basis of how "purely" public it is.

Choices with respect to management systems

As we design our social security system, we should pay close attention to the issue of creating a management system that achieves the best results at the lowest cost. Our approach must be quite rigorous and also flexible. It must abide by the fundamental principle of taking China's specific circumstances into full account. First, China has an enormous population. The scale of its social security system is beyond that of any other country. The requirements are massive, whether in terms of information management or investment practices. Second,

China's economic development is highly uneven given the physical size of the country. The regional nature of its social security management must therefore be different from that of most countries. Different regions may well have differing social security benefits, which is one problem. The transient population that moves among regions is another, in terms of how to manage their social security benefits. In addition to this regional problem, China manages its overall population via a household registration system, by which people's urban or rural status is defined. At the same time, we have not yet set up a "security numbering system" by which each person is allocated a number. We therefore lack the basis for a comprehensive management system. Given these basic preconditions, there are several things we should consider as we set up a system for managing our social security.

First, should the system be centralized or decentralized at different levels, in terms of management? Right now, one view on this feels that we should set up a comprehensive system that operates on a nationwide basis, under one institution that manages all of social security. We feel, however, that this approach does not take China's circumstances under adequate consideration. China's has more than 1.1 billion people, and within this figure the working population approaches 600 million. Handling the information volume for this number of people presents formidable problems to any kind of centralized institution. Our situation is wholly different from small countries in this regard, so we cannot simply copy over their way of doing things. We feel that we simply cannot use a highly centralized system for information management. We must operate under a principle of distributed management. We should set up information management systems at different levels that can handle appropriate volumes of information, so as to carry out more effective management.

Second, should the system be managed by a small number of government institutions, or should it be managed by a number of investment institutions that are in business and that compete with one another? If we were to operate as Singapore does, with one centralized public institution handling everything on a uniform basis, not only would the information be too hard to handle but the enormous sum of invested money handled by one organization would easily imbalance the structure of the investments market and would increase investment risk. If we were to operate as Chile does, with many private institutions handling investments, this could easily raise costs to an unacceptable level.

To deal with these problems, to lower costs and preserve investment stability, we feel we should choose a variety of arrangements. The tasks involved in handling information management systems and investment management systems are different. We can separate them and handle them via two different methods. Information management mainly involves handling the private account information of social security participants. This includes such things as length of career, wage level, monthly and annual contributions, amount of pension that should be paid out on retirement, and so on. Pension benefits that are to be paid are based on these criteria. The payment system must therefore be put together with the information system.

Investment management mainly involves utilizing capital in a safe and effective way within the environment of the investments community. The objective is to maximize returns within the constraints of ensuring safety of the invested funds. We can therefore separate out investment management of pension funds and consider it separately.

In terms of information management, having the government or a quasi-government institution handle things provides the public with a greater sense of security. At the same time, it does not require that there be competitive relationships, which helps to reduce unnecessary marketing costs and fees to lower the overall costs of management. In terms of managing the investments themselves, having a number of entities participate and keeping a degree of competitiveness has its advantages. Not only can we use the capacities of our existing financial institutions, and thereby stimulate the development of our capital markets, but we can reduce the amount of "bureaucratism" and the likelihood of major mistakes. This will help ensure the safety of investments, while also raising economic efficiency through the use of competitive practices. In instances where investment institutions are fairly small or have inadequate credit, we can use government or quasi-government entities to provide reinsurance so as to guarantee recovery of the investment. This is to ensure that the interests of beneficiaries are safe and sound.

Given the above analysis, we can be more specific as follows. Appropriate levels of government, or quasi-government institutions, may formulate rules and regulations regarding social security, including the rate of contributions, ways in which benefits are paid out, and they can provide beneficiaries with a limited number of services. Such "service products" can be relatively simple but they will provide beneficiaries with a range of options, depending on their preferences and particularly investment preferences. The information management system will be a unified system. Once funds are collected on a unified basis, authorized investment institutions will be responsible for investing them and providing returns. Such institutions will be in business and will operate on a competitive basis, and they will include State-owned as well as privately-owned entities. Payments that are made with investment returns will still be handled by the above-mentioned government institution (or quasi-government institution). It will be responsible for issuing pensions and similar funds. Different regions may have different ways of handling things, and differences in terms of rules and regulations, investment returns, level of pensions, and so on. When people move from one region to another, their personal account and all the accumulated funds in that account will follow them to the new social security management institution. They will then follow the rules and regulations of the new jurisdiction.

The issue of how to come up with appropriate methods of combining social security objectives

Reform of our social security system must take into account the legacy we have inherited of different kinds of systems. These include the difference between urban and rural systems, and the difference among entities that fall under different types of ownership. We should try to make as smooth a transition as possible. To do this, it might be possible to consider a mixed form of social security system. What that means is we use primarily a contributions-based system while we also partially have a benefits-based system. The individual's pensions will primarily make use of the contributions-based system, which will be achieved by the use of personal accounts. Such things as healthcare, unemployment insurance, and so on can to a degree rely on the benefits-based system. That will be achieved by a social security tax on wages. From an overall perspective, this will enable the system to have continuity, while it also facilitates transition. We can implement this system in urban areas at the start and then extend it to rural areas over the course of a number of years.

The situation in rural areas is different from urban areas in that rural areas never had a benefits-based system to begin with. Only certain areas organized a limited amount of centralized funding plans, and such differences were due to how history unfolded.

We have looked at the issues surrounding transition to a contributions-based system for pensions that uses personal accounts. I do not discuss any further details here, but now want to move to the subject of transitional issues surrounding healthcare and unemployment insurance.

China's previous system had healthcare that was covered at public expense, while unemployment did not exist. In our social security reform, it is therefore going to be best to use transitional measures—this goes for reform of publicly-funded healthcare as well as the newly appearing problem of unemployment. We therefore recommend using a partial benefits-based system in this arena as well. For example, some of the healthcare costs of employees can be paid for by the individual, while another portion (such as for serious illness and costs that exceed a certain specified amount) can be covered by a benefits-based system. This method, which is publicly funded to a degree, can mitigate the shock of reforms. It can keep people from feeling that all of a sudden they have burdens that they cannot handle. At the same time, it will lessen resistance to reform of State-Owned Enterprises, since these enterprises promised lifelong employment to people. It has been somewhat of a tricky issue to tell employees that they now have to handle their own unemployment problems and this has put enterprise reform in a difficult position. The practical solution to this is going to be setting up an unemployment insurance system while at the same time having the State cover a portion of the spending for that system.

Premiums for both unemployment insurance and healthcare insurance have to be gathered through the mechanism of a tax on wages. To a degree, the payroll tax for social security and the contributions for healthcare and unemployment can be combined and collected together. For example, tax-collecting authorities can collect them on a unified basis by having a certain percentage of a person's pay deducted out and put into that person's individual account. Meanwhile, a certain percentage would be collected as a payroll tax going into public-finance type social security schemes to cover healthcare and unemployment relief.

We could also handle this in a different way, however. We could have both payroll taxes and contributions deposited into personal accounts. We then lower the yields that those accounts pay out to the beneficiary, and we take out a portion of total returns to cover the costs of healthcare and unemployment insurance. Naturally, whichever method we use, we still have to figure wages at the real cost (make wages "real" as opposed to very low, with subsidies covering the bulk of a person's living needs). Once we incorporate all costs into wages, the revisions will increase the cost of wages to an enterprise which in turn will increase the indirect tax base. Ultimately that will be added into the price of products and lead to higher overall price levels. The policy orientation of making the costs "real" is a correct one, but as we implement it we will want to make sure that we accompany it with appropriate macroeconomic measures.

It should be recognized that the above way of handling things is merely transitional. Because of this, we should be explicit in how we limit its scope and duration. For example, the State should not be involved in handling unemployment insurance for small-scale collective enterprises, or town-and-village enterprises, or foreign-invested entities. These should set up sources of unemployment insurance that correspond to their situations. In contrast, the State has to carry a greater responsibility for unemployment issues in State-Owned Enterprises, given the historical legacy of these problems. Some people believe that the State should not in fact bear any responsibility for unemployment during transition. Given China's actual situation, however, bearing some responsibility is in fact simply necessary.

In terms of healthcare insurance, we should set up mechanisms that allow for contributions by both individuals and society at large. The portion funded by individuals could come out of the increased portion of wages that comes about when wages are "made real." That is one idea, since it enables individuals to actually pay it. If payments need to be made for major illnesses or other things that exceed the individual-account standards, then social security would pay for this according to insurance methods. This manner of handling things could achieve transition in a fairly stable way. In looking at this policy option, however, we should be careful to set rules regarding sequence of payments. That is, under what conditions would the individual be responsible for paying all medical and pharmaceutical costs, and under what conditions would social security pay? Under what special circumstances would we allow advance withdrawals from a personal account in order to pay for medical costs, and so on.

A variety of viable options could be considered. For minor illnesses, medical costs would be paid for initially out of the personal account. Once illnesses are major enough to exceed a certain cost figure, that portion could be paid for via medical insurance. We could set up a separate private-account insurance fund and could then put the private-account pension funds and medical insurance funds together. (Singapore adopted a method of first setting up pension accounts and then later setting up healthcare fund accounts.) Or we could use reinsurance mechanisms—for example, using a portion of the personal account to cover medical insurance for major illnesses, and so on. It should be pointed out that whatever specific measures we adopt, we must first have institutional arrangements that allow for payments to proceed in proper sequence through institutional arrangements that allow for different tiers of payment procedures. We must ultimately come up with a mechanism that protects incentives within individual accounts. That is, we do not want to foster the practice of turning "minor illnesses" into major illnesses when it comes to their treatment costs. At the same time, when people do indeed run up against a major illness, we want to make sure the funds are there to pay for treatment. We should also take note of the fact that this whole endeavor is operating within a limited scope. In the past, rural people did not enjoy publicly-funded healthcare at all. Arrangements for their healthcare as we move forward will be different from the healthcare received by urban employees, for now. The long-term orientation of social security reform is to move gradually toward equal treatment.

If China's new social security system does indeed adopt a mixed approach, that is, with a dominant contributions-based system and a smaller portion coming from a benefits-based system, then we will need to cover the costs of these two systems concurrently. From a cost perspective, that of the contributions-based system is fairly high—setting up individual accounts and organizing investment of the funds. The methods relating to the benefits-based system are different but they too require a certain level of costs. From a cost perspective, therefore, a mixed system may involve a greater outlay than adopting just one system or the other. However, we are already seeing a dramatic reduction in the costs of information management and we are actively seeking to reduce costs through making use of tax-collection institutions.

The issue of "making costs real"

Whatever methods we choose to adopt, all will involve this whole issue of turning enterprise costs into "real" or actualized costs. If we collect fees related to social security and add those into the cost of labor, we will *de facto* increase the existing cost of labor. That will increase indirect taxes, which might very well increase the cost of the products that an enterprise produces. In fact, this will be unavoidable as we turn enterprise costs into real costs.

Our cost structures were distorted under our traditional system, simply not in line with reality. Some items that should have been included in costs were not. From the perspective of an enterprise's discrete finances, the cost of labor was therefore relatively low, but the situation was quite different if one looked at the total cost of running the enterprise. For example, pension funds were accounted for "outside the business" of the enterprise, as non-operating expenditures. Major subsidies lay behind low-cost housing for employees. Healthcare fees paid for at public expense were covered by either public finance or an enterprise. None of these were directly entered into labor costs.

Now, as we add in social security payments, it is normal that labor costs will rise. From the perspective of society in general, this is merely a kind of change in financial accounting. Meanwhile, from the perspective of developing a market economy, making labor costs "real" is going to be helpful in making product costs real as well. The process will help straighten out distortions and will make costs and profits conform more accurately to one another.

The revision of financial accounting rules and enterprise accounting standards that we began in 1993 is a reflection of this orientation of reform. We should not only adhere to this orientation but we should take it even further.

Naturally, a rise in labor costs may indeed lead to an increase or at least an adjustment in the prices of products. Will this serve to push the existing wave of our current inflation even higher? Given this consideration, we feel that our social security reform measures should be coordinated with macroeconomic measures as called for by the situation, in order to reduce any unfavorable results.

Social security arrangements in large enterprises

The situation among very large enterprises is clearly different from that among the usual type of enterprise. One example would be the Anshan Iron and Steel Corporation. Enterprises of that size essentially cover the population of an entire region. They are themselves the community, with employees that number in the tens of thousands—to a certain extent, these enterprises are a society unto themselves. Given this, we should handle their social security arrangements in a different way. In terms of how we determine the unit handling social security, we could, for example, say that enterprises of this size are under the "top tier" of government management, or top-tier municipalities. Enterprises that are super-large could also be defined as a social security unit unto themselves.

The general principle with respect to large enterprises should be that social security is handled on a separate and professional basis. Enterprises are responsible for the social security of their own employees, but they cannot mix their business operations with their social security and welfare benefits operations. As for how they go about setting up professional management of social security, the answer will depend on the specific conditions of each enterprise. Generally speaking, enterprises that have a relatively small number of employees can authorize specialized institutions to handle their social security. Those that have large numbers of employees can consider managing the social security themselves, either under separate management or combined with the work of the labor union.

When enterprises manage their own social security, and cover the costs of public services in the area, those costs should be defined as public-finance spending on public services. To cover those costs, we should either extend transfer payments to the enterprises or extend tax exemptions (or refunds) from the national budget.

A number of benefits can come from having large enterprises perform this task of handling their own social security, if they perform it well. Among those are the following three considerations.

First, large enterprises can determine different levels of social security depending on their own circumstances. Their benefits may well be higher than those of a medium- or small-sized enterprise. The provision of preferential social security will help motivate employees and strengthen the cohesion of the enterprise. This is a way to create competition among human resources and is helpful in drawing in qualified people as well as retaining the good people already in an enterprise.

Second, having large enterprises handle their own social security issues helps invest in the manpower resources of the enterprise. Since large enterprises will have preferential social security treatment, employees will leave them at a lower rate and the enterprise can put more effort into training and other kinds of human resource investment. This will provide constant upgrading of the technical and knowledge levels of employees. This all-round employee improvement will be the most effective source of the future competitiveness of the enterprise. An enterprise tends not to put much effort into such cultivation of its employees if its turnover is too high.

Third, if an enterprise invests the pension funds of employees in its own operations, to a degree that makes the employees shareowners of the enterprise. To a degree, employees can also participate in the decision-making of the enterprise. This in turn is an effective component of improving the corporate governance structures of the enterprise. Generally speaking, the property rights (ownership) of large enterprises are more fragmented and it is not an easy task to have the policy decisions of a board truly represent the owners. As shareholders, employee representatives may be able to carry more responsibility within the enterprise. Naturally, there should be a limit to the percentage of shares that are held by the retirement funds of employees. For example, it might not exceed 25 percent, since otherwise there might be other kinds of problems. There is also the problem of placing pension funds in too risky a position by having them invested in the enterprise itself. If the enterprise runs into problems in the future, there will be no financial source for the funding of either employee wages or pensions. To deal with this, we might adopt the practice used in Germany. That is, while pension funds are invested in the enterprise, a government or quasi-government reinsurance company also reinsures the funds. This means that funds can contribute to the growth of the enterprise while still remaining a reliable source of income for beneficiaries. In short, we should explore this and similar solutions.

Conclusion

This article has tried to put forth an initial exploration of the major issues surrounding policy options for China's social security system. One thing I want to make clear is that its purpose has not been to present specific recommendations for policies or systems. I have tried to put forth basic concepts and a framework for analysis with respect to setting up a new social security system in general. The framework itself must be very flexible. We should be able to opt for a mixed form of system that combines the contributions-based system with a benefits-based system, and we should be quite flexible in how we coordinate those. The framework therefore gives considerable room for various policy choices in designing social security systems.

To implement objectives, we first are attempting to set up fundamental concepts that are universally acceptable and that are in line with economic and management sciences. The goal is to come up with a consensus on overall concepts and terminology so that discussions can move forward among people with different points of view. We have taken advantage of international experience in creating this basic foundation, and hope that China can look for further successful models abroad so that we take a less circuitous path as we move ahead. We hope that we can elevate our own experience to the level of theory that is applicable to China.

Based on empirical analysis, we have put forth ten specific standards by which to measure a social security system. We do this in order to look at policy choices from a more comprehensive perspective. The aim is to avoid involuntary biases in our thinking, as well as to incorporate aspects that may have been overlooked in the past. Given this, our evaluation of the objectives for our social security system, and our policy choices going forward, must also be determined by China's specific circumstances. We will be able to make more rational policy decisions if we base them on a correct evaluation at the outset.

In this article, our views on various issues to do with reforming China's social security system should be viewed as material for use in further study and discussion. At the same time, we have reason to believe that the framework presented here is sufficiently flexible to accommodate different opinions and still provide room for moving forward with a variety of policy options.

Note

1 This article was originally published in the magazine *Reform*, 1994, Vols. 3 and 4 (excerpts in each). Wang Lin was the co-author.

8 Microeconomic concepts within the field of economics[1]

(March 1999)

Some of China's large enterprises have run into problems recently, and particularly large State-Owned Enterprises. The State Council asked specially designated inspectors to look into the problems, and they discovered certain universal features. As a result, everybody is now talking about the leadership system in enterprises, external supervision, preventing abuse of power, "each taking care of its own children" (self-rule), and so on. I believe that a number of economic concepts might be useful to our reform at this point, particularly with respect to corporate governance.

Differentiating between regulation (*jian guan*) and supervisory guidance or "corporate governance" (*du dao*)

Who is to blame when companies are found to be operating "out of control," and when behavior has "jumped the tracks" and is abusing power? Who exactly has neglected his duties in overseeing and handling such situations? We need to differentiate here between regulatory authority of specific industries and the type of supervisory governance that comes from owners. A market-economy system is one that enables enterprises to operate freely on their own. Other than certain unique industries and markets, most industrial and commercial entities have no specific regulatory body (department) overseeing them. Companies are not obliged to operate within a certain scope of business activities. Of course, certain industries do require regulation. The classic cases are the banking industry (regulated by the central bank or financial regulatory departments), capital markets (regulated by the China Securities Regulatory Commission), pharmaceuticals, and so on. Some industries and markets have self-governing organizations. The scope and degree to which these are internally regulated varies, but mostly the regulation is quite limited.

The type of supervisory control that derives from the owners of a company is known as "governance." (More specifically, owners include both those who put up the capital, or the "shareholders," and those who have interests that are involved, or the "stakeholders," as described below). Governance generally refers to how the shareholders' meetings and the board of directors regulate, supervise, and control the executives in the company.

Some people define "governance" as "corporate governance structures," or "legal-person governance structures" (the term for governance here is *zhi-li*, which also means control), while others use a different term to translate "governance" (*du-dao*), which combines the meanings of supervision (*jian-du*) and guidance (*dao-xiang*). I prefer the latter way of defining governance, the way that combines supervision with guidance, so I use it in this article.

The main tasks of governance are as follows: formulating the business objectives of the company, as well as major policies and management principles; selecting and appointing managers and being in charge of the compensation and bonuses of the managers; inspecting the operating activities of the company; coordinating or harmonizing the interests of the company and its shareholders, and the interests of the shareholders and the administrative departments (with which the companies are affiliated).

It should be pointed out that the executives of listed companies that have a highly fragmented share ownership, and of companies in the public sector, often show a tendency to violate the interests of shareholders. That is, their goal is not to maximize profits but rather to benefit themselves or their employees. Because of this, the board of directors must constantly clarify the business orientation of the company, and must redirect it. They must review the company's major strategic policies, and must arrange for audits of the company's finances.

The controlling force as represented by "governance" is different from that of "internal controls." The two are two separate concepts. The latter typically refers to procedures within a company, including authorizing or delegating authority, the investigation and approvals process, accounting and confirmation of figures, inspections, bonuses for performance, and other elements of the systems by which management runs the company.

In contrast to governance, government departments that carry out "regulatory supervision" tend to focus on four different things: compliance in operations, prudent financial decisions, qualifications for responsible persons and professional persons (such as traders), and whether or not the investors (shareholders) are qualified (such as whether or not they abide by legal terms of the industry). Naturally, sometimes supervision (*jian-guan*) and governance (*du-dao*) overlap and influence each other. Still, in conceptual terms it is important to make the distinction between the two. Table 8.1 presents the differences in principle.

Regulatory supervision is highly professional in its nature. Few people are qualified to undertake this kind of work. Governance, in contrast, is a kind of systemic structure. The role of governance in large companies is generally carried out through the board of directors, so these should be people with a high sense of responsibility. They should have some understanding of corporate law and finance. They should also ideally have knowledge about the markets, industries, technology, and customers of the enterprise. The board of directors is controlled by the shareholders, as expressed in shareholders' meetings.

Since the Asian financial crisis, a great deal of analysis has focused on China-specific reasons for the crisis from a variety of perspectives. They can be put into three main categories. First, supervision of exchange rates and foreign debt;

Table 8.1 The difference between supervision and governance

	Supervisory responsibilities	*Governance responsibilities*
Operating decisions	Compliance	Consistent with shareholders' interests
Auditing	Compliance and prudence	Whether actions infringe shareholders' interests or not
Persons in charge	Eligibility of qualifications	Appointment, dismissal, and incentives
Shareholders	Whether or not persons are eligible, responsible and authorized	Whether after-tax profits are used for dividends or not, increases in capital through new share issues, dissolution-related issues

second, the soundness of the financial system; and third, lack of corporate governance. In China, this last consideration has not been discussed much at all.

Fiduciary and agent relationships—authorizing people to serve in a fiduciary capacity or as an agent

After we increase the scale of companies, we will need to go further in clarifying the relationships among shareholders, the members of the board of directors, and the executive tier (general managers). First, the shareholders of large listed companies are dispersed. There are two situations then—one is that the shareholders, via shareholders' meetings, elect the board of directors. Directors may be elected to the board either because they have a large percentage of shares, or because they can represent others even though they hold few shares. In that sense, they are authorized to act on behalf of others in a fiduciary relationship. The other situation is to have external board members. These then do not own shares but shareholders nevertheless feel they can represent their interests and elect them at a shareholders' meeting. A fiduciary relationship is set up between the shareholders and the board of directors. When shareholders put forward board directors, the directors are authorized, through a fiduciary or "trust" relationship, to carry out fiduciary duties on their behalf.

The board can hire as well as dismiss the senior level of executives in a company, and it may hire executives at market rates. In large companies, the board then authorizes the senior executive (including the top tier of managers) to act on its behalf in a principal-agent relationship. Operations management becomes a professional skill. Such skills are uncommon and therefore can be highly compensated. A large company must hire highly competent businesspeople who are then in direct control of daily operations. They also may recommend strategic policies to the board, but these can only be executed with the permission of the board. The board therefore holds the power to constrain actions that management may want to take, and it is obliged to evaluate whether or not decisions are in the interests of shareholders.

This principal-agent type of relationship is highly marketized, which is to say that people are asked to undertake certain roles and those roles carry specific compensation. The operations of the company determine the future results of the company as expressed in the form of immediate profits and dividends. They also determine whether or not the company can continue to be competitive and maintain its ability to earn profits and pay out dividends, or its ability to increase its market price on a stock exchange. Because of this, a large part of the compensation that the board of directors of listed companies extends to senior managers is in the form of stocks and stock options. That is, in addition to earning immediate compensation, the greater part of managers' compensation is tied to the rise in share price in the future as an expression of the company's potential. This is a form of incentive.

In contrast, board members as well as the chairman of the board are not paid salaries by the company due to the fiduciary nature of their relationship. Board members and the chairman of the board are authorized to serve on behalf of others in a trust relationship due to their standing in society. They are not serving in order to make money. At the most, they can be compensated for travel expenses to the extent that this is allowed in the company bylaws. This mechanism is highly important. It shows that the board must stand on the side of the shareholders' interests and not that of senior management by whom they might be paid off. This is also somewhat similar to the system of corporate inspections that we arrived at only after years of exploration. That is, inspectors are not able to draw a salary from the company, or use the company car, or stay in company housing and so on.

State-Owned Enterprises and publicly-held companies have many similarities to large-scale listed companies in terms of their widely dispersed share ownership. They rely on fiduciary relationships to select and appoint external directors. Naturally, in theory the investors of State-Owned Enterprises are the Ministry of Finance and SASAC, those "putting up the funds." Those who are actually serving as directors on the board, however, are not themselves putting up funds—they are instead serving in a fiduciary capacity. This concept helps us clarify the relationships among various kinds of people as we create a modern enterprise system.

Some of China's State-Owned Enterprises do indeed pay salaries to the Chairman of the Board. The Guangdong International Trust and Investment Corporation is one example. At the outset, local governments may have appointed such people, but board members now are actually within the company itself. Meanwhile, many things are not clearly written into the bylaws of the company about such things as the board's supervisory duties and responsibilities. This has led to companies operating "out of control," and ultimately to the board infringing upon the interests of owners. This is the wrong way to do things.

Separating out ownership rights from operating authority, and the issue of insider control

Back in the 1930s, a famous economist in the United States named Gardiner Means took note of this issue of separating out ownership rights from operating rights. The reason was that as companies grew in size and their ownership became more dispersed, the owners themselves and particularly large shareholders were not capable of undertaking the role of corporate management. What was to be done? On the one hand, the answer was to hire professional managers. On the other hand, however, this very well could lead to senior management behaving in ways that harmed the interests of all owners. As Gardiner Means observed, senior managers might well inflate operating expenses which would give them more authority in allocating money but would also lower profits. This could even lead to what we ourselves have observed, which is that some companies make no profit at all. They merely break even—their expenditures pretty much equal their income.

If the labor union is strong, senior management may also have a tendency to placate them with higher wages. The resulting higher costs are beneficial to employees but not necessarily to owners. Meanwhile, some companies in China waste money on their board meetings by holding them in expensive hotels, wining and dining the board members so that they will be inclined to accept proposals put forward by senior management. Such proposals are not necessarily in the interests of shareholders.

In the 1930s, people were not sufficiently alert to such problems and bylaws were not sufficiently explicit about the "governance role" of a board. After this, most companies began to separate out management authority from ownership rights. They clarified that the shareholders maintain control over the General Manager (CEO) via the mechanism of the board, as a way to have ultimate control over management. They also clarified the role of the board, namely, that major strategic decisions have to be reviewed and decided upon by the board and particularly any that relate to capital. For example, if the company borrows money from a bank, this can be for two reasons. One is for cash flow. The board decides upon a certain overall amount, and within that amount the General Manager is authorized to draw funds from the bank. The other, however, involves taking out loans for new projects. For this second kind of bank borrowing, board approval is necessary. The reason is that borrowing money involves the interests of shareholders—if, for any reason, the loan is not repaid, this lowers the net asset value of the enterprise, which directly harms shareholders' interests. Such things as setting up subsidiaries, or putting up investment to engage in joint ventures with others also requires review and approval by the board. Using the assets of the company as collateral for loans, mortgaging the assets, allowing them to serve as the guaranty for other people's loans, and so on—all of these require board approval. When these things are mishandled, they directly impact shareholders' interests.

In addition to the above, board approval is required for changing the established production line of a company, and adjusting the orientation of its major products. The board must conscientiously examine the auditing reports on the company and often must ask in outside auditors. The board itself may select the outside auditors, or the owners may do so by voting in a shareholders' meeting. The great majority of large companies have a system whereby the board directly selects and appoints the chief financial officer. All of these are ways to prevent issues that might arise in the course of separating out operating authority from ownership rights. They serve to address such issues from the perspective of control.

A new term has emerged in recent years in the sphere of economics, namely "insider control." By all rights, control over a company's operations should be in the hands of the shareholders' meeting and the board of directors. Due to the dispersed nature of shareholdings, however, or the nominal existence of a real board, the board may not in fact carry out the fiduciary responsibilities as entrusted to it by owners. The result is that supervisory functions are non-existent and actual control of the company falls to people inside the company, that is, to insider control. Those who are running the company thereby infringe upon the rights of shareholders in order to serve their own interests.

This problem of insider control is often more pronounced in the public sector, that is, in companies owned "by the public." This is not to say that the private sector does not have the same problem, and indeed the issue was explicitly discussed in economics back in the 1930s.

In the public sector, two phenomena can occur. One is that the board of directors is nominal. Either it does nothing to manage affairs or it has been bought out by the senior management of the company. Its rear ends sit on the management side of the table. The result is that no real supervision of the company takes place and the company comes completely under the control of insiders. The other situation happens when those actually managing affairs, running the factories, are good at their job but more inclined to favor the interests of workers and staff. They issue more wages and bonuses, provide better benefits, help workers with housing and so on. This then cuts into the finances of the company and hurts its market price. This resembles the "workers autonomy" situation that occurred in Yugoslavia, and is another example of companies falling under insider control.

In China, this phenomenon of insider control is not limited to just making sure the company makes no profits. Insiders are also quite willing to have the company show a loss. Their own lives are easier when there are some losses to show, given all of the investigations they otherwise have to endure and the profit allocations they are forced to make.

In the early period of China's reform, the key issue we faced was how to deal with and reduce administrative interference in corporate affairs. The issue was how to ensure that the enterprise itself could make its own decisions—we tried to extricate senior management from interference by the government department that had authority over the enterprise. At that time, we brought forth the concept that operating rights should be separate and distinct from ownership rights (on a macro level), and this indicated that such a separation would also be launched within the enterprise itself. Although the department with authority over the enterprise could represent the owners, it had to stand to one side when it came to running the enterprise.

In fact, however, our understanding did not fully grasp the essential meaning of a separation between operating rights and ownership. One expression of this mistake was the way in which we allowed General Managers to be the legal-person representative of a company. Market economies generally do not take this approach. The board, as led by the chairman, handles determination of the legal-person representation. Naturally, sometimes the chairman is also the CEO, but at the end of the day the chairman himself cannot make ultimate decisions—the functions of corporate governance still lie with the board. In sum, China's enterprise reform started with the process of eliminating governmental (administrative) interference from companies, but at a certain stage it has to focus on what is happening inside them and has to prevent insiders from taking over control. It has to set up sound and effective corporate governance mechanisms.

The shareholders of an enterprise and the "stakeholders" in an enterprise

When a market economy is just getting started, its scarcest resource is capital. That means that the one putting up capital (investment) is the one with a right to vote. Later, capital is still scarce but not necessarily decisive—for instance, technical talent may be the scarcest resource in high-tech companies. Such people are then often given a say in the company, and often they get shares. They have not in fact paid out money for these shares, however. They are not capital contributors, but they have placed their own interests in line with the endeavors of the company itself. They have become this new thing called "stakeholders." Their energies and their futures are placed in the hands of the company. To a certain degree, employees, the local community, and enterprises affiliated with a given company are also stakeholders. New theoretical approaches to corporate governance believe that stakeholders should also have a voice and a vote when it comes to guiding company affairs. This is in the interests of the company. Members of the board therefore can also include stakeholders who have not actually put up investment in the form of capital.

In fact, Germany has long since had this dual-layered board system. A supervisory board sits on top, in the middle is a management board, and below that is the General Manager. One-third of the supervisory board is typically composed of employee representatives. External representatives are also included, including professional personnel and representatives of the community as well as investors.

In economic terms, this system has both advantages and drawbacks. One of its problems is that reallocating capital can be quite cumbersome. The attraction is that the existing deployment of a company's assets (or its asset portfolio) is quite stable and oriented toward long-term goals. Such stable and long-term deployment of assets is something that economics as well as management sciences accept as a good approach.

Holding companies (companies that hold control shares in other companies)

Two considerations apply to large-scale enterprises, or "holding companies." First, they need to carry out internal reallocations of capital as necessary. Second, they need to carry out corporate governance tasks with respect to their subsidiaries including appointing the chairman of the board and board directors and ensuring that they do not allow the company to "go out of control" or be taken over by insiders. Chairmen of the board and board directors that are appointed by the holding company are compensated by that company and should therefore also be scrutinized by the holding company. They should undergo performance evaluations and also comparison with the boards of other subsidiaries so that they are subject to horizontal pressures as well. They are not employees of the holding company nor are they the ultimate investors, but the leaders of the holding company will see quite clearly what is going on if their performance is not up to that of others.

Right now, China's State-Owned Enterprises are facing numerous problems with respect to corporate governance. A number of quite severe cases of insider control have come to the fore and, although this concept of a "holding company" is excellent in theory, it may not have been so good when it was applied to China's early period of reform. In the early period of our reform, we focused on separating out governmental authority from the autonomous operating rights of the enterprise. At that point, autonomous rights of the enterprise could not in fact be fully realized. In the past, administrative departments had direct control over enterprises. By slightly shifting their position, they could redefine themselves as holding companies and thereby hinder the process of separating out corporate and government authorities. They could prevent progress in realizing true autonomy of enterprises. By now, we have to admit that we see many State-Owned Enterprises with problems. Indeed, we have General Managers who have become accustomed to no supervision at all and have even sunk so low as to become corrupt. Now that we are at a different phase, however, it may be that holding companies can actually play a more positive role.

In market-economy countries, and particularly those with a fairly high percentage of State-Owned Enterprises such as Italy, Norway, Singapore, and France, holding companies are used to represent the country's ownership interests. Some are quite successful in this, whereas others are not. The successes mainly come from having holding companies pass on to subsidiaries the roles of proper allocation of capital and the functions of corporate governance.

Passive investors and active investors

In market economies, companies grow through a process of mergers and acquisitions and as that happens their share ownership becomes more and more dispersed. This is the way market economies resolve the problem raised by Marx of the contradiction between "socialized production" (production that is owned by society) and production that is owned by individuals.

We are in favor of improving corporate governance within large companies, but this also poses a new challenge. If share ownership is not so dispersed in a large company, if there is one major shareholder or just a few, is that a good thing or a bad thing? All our trends in recent years point to large companies wanting to have large qualified shareholders that play an active role in invest-ing and that participate actively in corporate governance. Such active investors need to be experienced as well as conscientious and responsible. They need to review and discuss major strategic decisions, oversee loan applications, the issuing of debt, use of collateral, setting up of (affiliated) institutions, and so on. They need to review and be responsible for auditing statements. If all this is truly achieved, the company will have sound enough mechanisms that it can prevent such things as insider control, insider corruption, and the overstepping of authority.

From the perspective of a General Manager who wants to expand his personal control, however, the more dispersed the shareholding is, the better. He hopes that shareholdings will be about equal so that nobody has a louder voice than others at shareholders' meetings or is overly concerned about what happens. Control can then more easily be concentrated in his own hands. In other words, he would prefer that people be "passive investors." Passive investors can easily lead to inef-fective corporate governance. In recent years, the supervisory institutions of many countries (including financial regulatory agencies) have explicitly said that they would like for qualified investors to hold a fairly large percentage of shares. As active investors, they can actively participate in corporate governance, which is good for the company.

From what we see in China, however, the situation is moving in the opposite direction. The reason is that our regulatory agencies have not properly distin-guished between the functions of "supervision" and the functions of "governance." To a large degree, they would like to substitute themselves in the role of "govern-ance." They themselves would like to be the ones that appoint General Managers and bank presidents. They would like to roll themselves into the formulation of major policy. This is in fact closely related to the influence of our former mode of operations in which government and corporation were one and the same. In reviewing and deciding upon permits for setting up insurance companies, securi-ties companies, and commercial banks, they (regulatory agencies) would rather have shareholders who are dispersed and uniform in their shareholdings. Ideally, for example, you might have ten investors, each holding 10 percent. Nobody can be chief and nobody can have more weight than others in decision-making. In such a situation, the authority for governance falls to the regulatory institution itself. As a result, shareholders themselves fail to take responsibility. In the end, when problems arise, the ones looking into the problems are the very same reg-ulatory agencies who caused the problems. Quite a few companies are already running into this kind of thing.

Revisiting the subject of supervision and governance

First, one should not think that "supervision" is omnipotent. After all, when a company runs into problems, who in fact should be held responsible? Naturally the generally manager may himself have problems. As a cadre, he may not be up to the performance requirements (of the Party), but still it should be clarified who above him has failed to exercise supervision or followed correct guidance procedures. In a market economy, the role of governance is highly important. If it is inadequate, then people place too much hope on "supervision," which in fact is hard to achieve. If "supervision" is concurrently "governance," relevant authorities who are doing both will focus on the wrong things. They will focus on the authority to appoint people and to bestow permits via the review and approval procedure, and not spend enough energy on regulatory supervision. This will distract their attention away from formulating reasonable rules and regulations and particularly from monitoring financial institutions according to established procedures. Relevant authorities will not improve their skills in this other important regard. In overall terms, the two sets of functions will be at odds with each other and will lead to a chaotic situation.

In the past, branches of the People's Bank of China authorized the establishment of credit cooperatives, small-scale financial institutions, and trust institutions. The leading cadres appointed to head these were themselves from the relevant branch of the bank. In fact, this allowed regulatory supervision to substitute for governance. When you appoint your own person, you may be more relaxed when it comes to credentials and performance reviews. If a problem comes up, then it is the other person's own fault and not yours.

If "governance" is to be established, we need to reflect further on the relationship between the right to appoint a General Manager and the "cadre management" exercised by the Communist Party of China, that is, the handling of senior personnel appointed by the Party. One possibility is to have the Party stand above "governance," doing its own final reviewing and approving. Another possibility is to have the role of the Party sit within governance structures.

Finally, I would like to touch on one last issue. Should "governance" as it is practiced in other companies also apply to such institutions as commercial banks, insurance companies, and pension funds? Each country has its own way of handling this matter.

The situation in the United States in the past was different from what it is today. In the past, the emphasis was on keeping lines of industry distinct. Commercial banks could not hold more than 2 percent of shares in an enterprise; insurance companies and pension funds could only be passive investors in companies as opposed to actively involved in the companies. They were not allowed to sit on boards of directors. Later, people gradually felt that this was not advantageous for governance and changes began to appear. Europe, in contrast, has always had a banking system that allowed it to engage in all lines of business. A bank has a seat on the board of directors of a corporation and even undertakes some governance functions. Banks also represent mutual funds and pension funds as their agent on boards, the reason being that banks are in a position to understand the internal situation of a company more thoroughly. The daily transactions of a company's business go through them. Germany has the institution of the "house bank," which processes all daily accounts. Japan has the system of a "primary" or head bank. This bank could originally hold 5 percent of the shares of an enterprise, but the figure was later expanded to 10 percent.

In terms of incentives, financial institutions hope that the finances of an enterprise are sound, since the financial institution is lending money to the enterprise. Similarly, from the perspective of incentives, it cannot be a conflict of interest to appoint a person to serve on its board of directors. Naturally, there are exceptions. For example, if credit is tight in any given period, the bank will tend to allocate credit in the direction of its own interests. A shortage of credit often has to do with intentional constraints on interest rates (i.e. those that are manmade or artificial as opposed to market-created). Given such a shortage, banks will reduce the scale of their loans and will allocate scarce funds to those companies in which they own shares. This will indeed lead to unreasonable situations. As we move forward with creating a market economy, however, and as there is more competition among the financial industry, we will gradually reduce our control over interest rates. Credit as a "scarce resource" will not be as apparent as it is now. Having a bank sit on corporate governance structures of an enterprise will gradually turn into something where the good outweighs the bad.

Why is governance such a hard thing to accomplish as we transform the public sector into the private sector? For one thing, it is not so easy to find trustworthy and reliable people who also have the requisite skills. For example, it is not easy to find eligible inspectors, and even then one has to train them. Not only do large enterprises need such people, but medium-sized enterprises need them as well. It may well be that we have to return to the idea of using holding companies, or to allowing financial institutions to play a small governance role in enterprises.

Note

1 This article is based on the handouts for a course that the author gave in the graduate school of the Chinese Academy of Social Sciences. It was initially published in the April 1999 issue of the journal *Comparative Economic and Social Systems*.

9 Resolving to deal with the nonperforming loans of banks, and some pitfalls along the way[1]

(July 23, 1999)

Conditions that must first be met in order to deal with nonperforming loans

Right now, one of the major issues being discussed among our economic community is that of how to deal with nonperforming loans. Specifically, how to strip them off the balance sheets of banks and pass them over to professional asset management companies that can get the highest results out of them, while allowing our four large State-owned banks to become excellent banks in their own right. I personally feel there are some preconditions to be met in how we deal with this. In other words, I feel a certain process should be followed. If preconditions are indeed met, then handling nonperforming loans should be manageable. In overall terms, disposing of nonperforming loans in order to create truly excellent banks will include the following considerations.

First, we have to eliminate all administrative interference in banks, or reduce it to a minimum, so that from now on our commercial banks can operate according to commercial banking principles.

Second, we have to put in place a two-tier banking system. The central bank should truly perform the functions of a central bank, which include monetary policy and regulation of the banking system, as well as necessary services. Commercial banks meanwhile should start making decisions according to the laws of commerce and not simply to comply with political objectives or to achieve any given macroeconomic goal.

Third, commercial banks are already beginning to have improved internal controls. This concept, however, should include not only internal auditing and internal systems that govern the authority to make loans. More importantly, it should refer to how the system of main offices and branch offices is coordinated in such a vast country. The question is whether or not the first-tier and second-tier branches as well as local offices of State-owned banks can comply with relevant policy decisions of the parent institution. Can they fully execute policies in a compliance system that is vertically oriented? This means that they are not subject to horizontal forces, such as the dictates of local governments or the commands of other local departments.

Fourth, are commercial banks truly being allowed autonomy in how they make operating and management decisions? This question relates to how we treat commercial banks as "corporatized" institutions.

Fifth, with respect to the corporate customers of banks and the debtors of assets management companies, in the past we resolved problems through the use of "soft constraints" that utilized public finance. Have such public-finance constraints now been stiffened up to the extent that we can call them "hard constraints"?

Sixth, has our accounting system reached the point that it can describe real financial figures, and is it at a level that is "prudent," "scientific," and "international"?

"Last but not least" is the customer base. This relates most particularly to State-Owned Enterprises as the primary customer base of State-owned banks. Have these implemented substantive real reforms, or are they in the process of carrying out such reforms?

The above considerations do not encompass all of the things that must be regarded as preconditions for dealing with nonperforming loans. Nevertheless, if we were to assume that the above things were all accomplished, then stripping off nonperforming loans from bank portfolios and establishing truly excellent banks would be quite a smooth process. In other words, we could be fairly confident of success if we basically met the above conditions, and reform of our State-owned banks could move forward with tremendous strides. I addressed all of this in a speech I presented at the August 1998 China International Capital Corporation (CICC) forum. That is, I noted that once all of our economic-system reforms were in place, we could begin to consider how to address the challenge of our fairly massive amount of nonperforming loans.

Given the situation as it now stands, things do not look extremely optimistic. The above preconditions have not in fact been met. Some people therefore say that it is premature to think about stripping off nonperforming loans, simply from an objective position. They say that even if nonperforming loans are stripped away, we will not be able to set up truly sound banks. Due to multiple layers of internal and external considerations, nonperforming loans will simply continue to mount up. Although a certain percentage of nonperforming loans may be necessary given the nature of market-oriented risk, a great deal more than that would result from ongoing failure to fix problems. This would compromise the credibility of our banking reform. After the first "stripping," we simply will have to strip again.

Meanwhile, with each ongoing stripping away of bad loans, we generate a tremendous amount of moral hazard for the banking industry as a whole. Given this, such people say, we should perhaps first consolidate all of the preconditions as noted above. In terms of the sequence of events, we should address the stripping away of nonperforming loans only when this has been achieved to an acceptable degree.

Nevertheless, from a different perspective, one could say that there has never been one so-called "ideal policy choice" when it comes to the sequencing of reform. The reason the whole issue of nonperforming loans has received such attention has been the Asian financial crisis. As the problem gets even worse, banks may well be reluctant to make loans, and this is highly unfavorable for our ability to make macroeconomic policy adjustments. Therefore, even though the situation is not yet truly ready and all conditions are not "in place," we feel that we have no choice but to seize the moment and move ahead. We must now deal with the problem. In other words, stripping off nonperforming loans from bank portfolios is now an urgent and necessary task. As for those conditions that have not been met, we would hope that pressure would be brought to bear on establishing these things after the fact.

Generally speaking, we are still quite a long way from realizing the necessary conditions as outlined above for stripping away nonperforming loans. In this regard, I would like to focus on four main issues. These may not yet have come to the attention of our economic circles or, perhaps, they are outside our economists' current field of vision. At the same time, they may be somewhat controversial.

The basic framework for a two-tiered banking system remains obscure

A two-tiered banking system has been mentioned above and much discussed. It means that the central bank and commercial banks have separate functions within the overall banking system. The central bank is "the banker for commercial banks." It focuses on monetary policy and banking regulation, while at the same time providing settlement services for commercial banks in ways that support monetary policy. The first thing to note, however, is that China began to set up the framework for such a two-tiered banking system back in late 1983 and early 1984. The central bank nevertheless continued to carry on its own direct loan business, indeed to a considerable extent. Second, our central bank is in fact not a not-for-profit entity. Since it has had to generate income to cover its own operations, it has actually been quite profit-oriented. Third, the relationship between the central bank and commercial banks is not purely one of regulated and regulator but rather more one of leader and those who are led. For a long time we have used this phrase, "China's banking system under the leadership of the People's Bank of China." This in fact describes the leadership relationship between the central bank and commercial banks. Fourth, in certain lines of business, the central bank has been in competition with commercial banks. The two conflict when it comes to commercial interests.

These problems carried on into the early 1990s, when they began to exhibit new problems. One that we need to focus on is the bank's regulatory capacities. Given the vast reaches of China, and regions that are distinctly separate from one another, how is a central bank to carry out its regulatory functions? This began to gather attention as a real problem in the early 1990s. Should each province set up its own branch of the central bank, which then regulates the local branches of commercial banks and non-financial institutions on its own? Naturally, this would mean that each branch would have to perform the functions of macroeconomic policy as well. Each would have to do all of the macroeconomic tasks required to regulate the entire financial industry.

The realities indicate that this is not possible. Instead, most branches of the central bank are inclined to side with the local government. This intensifies the problem that branches of commercial banks also stand on the side of local governments. When the headquarters of commercial banks attempt to strengthen internal controls, the fact of the matter is that they run into all kinds of problems since local branches use the excuse of the demands of local governments as well as local branches of the central bank to remain outside the control of headquarters.

What's more, in the early 1990s, commercial banks themselves still carried on a considerable amount of what is called "policy business." After the summer of 1993, the two-tiered banking system began to advance considerably after decisions to improve it were made. The central bank cancelled the authority of its branch banks to allocate funds and their ability to determine the size of loans. It gradually began to try to establish branches according to large geographic regions. It strengthened and improved the two-tiered system in very real ways. At the same time, the *Central Bank of China Act* and the *Law of the People's Republic of China on Commercial Banks* were gradually implemented.

All of the above notwithstanding, the framework of this two-tiered banking system remains unclear up to this very day. The central bank is still motivated to act as a commercial bank. It is still highly inclined to think in terms of profits and it is still performing functions that it should not be performing. On the commercial banking side, although most non-commercial type business has been reduced to an appropriate level, on occasion commercial banks are still pressured to make "policy-type" loans. The central bank is still not doing enough to ensure that commercial banks are protected from the need to engage in any type of policy-type business. The central bank is still a direct competitor to commercial banks when it comes to payment systems and credit card business.

From the above, it will be apparent that the two-tiered banking system is just as unclear now as it ever was. This serves as an obstacle to making our banks into truly sound banks. In addition, we need to reform our personnel and incentive systems in commercial banks, but the central bank has not been inclined to focus on this and give it the necessary support. Wage and personnel hiring systems and pension systems among others still need to be reformed.

A competitive environment and the rules of competition

The key consideration in building good commercial banks is to have a competitive environment in which to operate. In some of the speeches we have just heard, delegates (to this forum) have emphasized two issues. First, they feel that the State-owned system of commercial banks is not necessarily the best option. Second, they feel that we need more competition. My own opinion is that it is not very likely that we will see change in the State-owned system in the near future. Logically speaking, therefore, it becomes all the more important that we set up a competitive environment. With stronger competition, lateral pressures will put greater pressure on the management of commercial banks to achieve better results.

On a superficial level, competition already exists. In the 1980s, the diversification of the business lines of major banks and their regional expansion meant that competitive patterns intensified. The concrete expression of this could be seen in the overlapping business among banks, the way each began to penetrate the business sphere of others. Nevertheless, a distinction should be made between real competition and this kind of regional expansion and business diversification. Market competition is fundamentally not the same as simply expanding operations. Market competition presupposes that banks rely on their own profitability as they expand. Such expansion has to come from the improved ability to utilize capital and not through reliance on the State. It has to come from self-generated capital expansion through business operations.

In other words, the rules of competition that pertain to a market mean that the expansion of banks, and their ability to counter risk, must be constrained by capital adequacy ratios. One quantitative measure that can be applied to judging how "commercial" a bank is would therefore involve measuring the relationship between a bank's profitability and its rate of expansion. Naturally, we can quantify the correlation between a bank's capital and its rate of expansion, or measure other correlations. No matter what measures we use, however, the fact of the matter is that the banks that have expanded the fastest in the past two to three years have been precisely the ones that are least profitable. In other words, expansion is negatively correlated to profitability.

Such negative correlations can easily remind some of us of the old days, during the planned-economy period as well as the early period of transition. It can remind us of the problems brought on by expansion for its own sake without regard to economic benefits. In this regard, the State as "owner" is not yet performing its role in improving governance structures. From a regulatory perspective, it is not yet regulating the "blind" expansion of banks via the application of strict capital adequacy ratios. The result is that competition is not yet truly in place.

In point of fact, this problem has been present in our reform from the beginning. All kinds of (economic) distortions were the legacy of history during the early period of reform, including the burden of such things as "policy-type" loans. For quite a long time, everyone has hoped that we could "create an equal starting line" through our reform of State-Owned Enterprises. The idea has been to create that equal starting point for the race before asking enterprises to begin running the race. Reform is a dynamic process, however. Often, just as you are getting things organized on one front, new distortions and inequalities crop up on other fronts. The starting line again becomes different for different people. Should we try to "even up the line" yet again? Given that we have been pulling this way and that for more than a decade, perhaps we should think of a new approach?

The whole idea of creating an even starting line for all in fact means getting rid of the legacy of historical burdens altogether. Such burdens are, however, mixed in with historically accumulated profits. In easing historical burdens, we do not want to depreciate the former profitability and self-constraining ability of a given bank. We do not want to say that banks which expanded without regard for their capital were correct in doing so, that is, give credence to the idea that the fewer the self-constraints, the better.

China has a saying about "whipping the draft animal that is already pulling the hardest." Recently, our attempts to create an even starting line for all have meant replenishing capital in errant banks, helping out with their nonperforming loans, writing off their bad debts, and so on. I personally do not believe that we can create equal opportunity for all through such methods, since I do not feel it is possible from either a moral or a practical standpoint. Instead, we should create mechanisms that reward those who perform well and that punish those who do not. We should encourage the ones "pulling the hardest," and limit those who are behind. Otherwise we will not have instituted a competitive environment or created the rules for real competition.

Internal control systems in commercial banks

With respect to commercial banks, we must require that they set up internal control systems and then constantly work to improve those. The biggest headache in this regard is figuring out how to deal with the provincial branches of our largest banks—figuring out the degree to which the heads of those branches must obey the dictates of the head office. The corollary of this is figuring out the degree to which the second tier of bank branches must obey provincial branch dictates. This in fact is one of the ways in which we measure the effectiveness of internal controls in banks.

Roughly six years ago, when the heads of the provincial branches of our State-owned banks ran into an issue in which they differed from headquarters, some 60 to 70 percent sided with what the local (provincial) government wanted, or with what the local branch of the People's Bank of China wanted. At that time, the provincial branches of the People's Bank of China held considerable power. They had the authority to determine the size of banks and how capital should be allocated. They controlled the money markets of the province, and also had the power to decide on permits (review and approval procedures) for business outlets and banking networks. Because of this, the branches of commercial banks handled their relations with the People's Bank of China branches with considerable caution.

Meanwhile, provincial governments were also powerful at the time in their ability to control things directly, whether that was with respect to the local branch of the central bank (the People's Bank of China) or the branches of commercial banks. From my impressions of talking to officials of these provincial banks, at the time some 60 to 70 percent took their orders from the provincial government. Only 30 to 40 percent obeyed their headquarters.

Later, things gradually began to change, and particularly after the summer of 1993. Two years ago (in 1997) I asked my predecessor about the situation. He felt that by then it was roughly half and half. I am more optimistic. I believe that some 60 or 70 percent of provincial branch managers of commercial banks now respect the wishes of their head office. That means that quite a few still respect the authority of the provincial government, however, and I predict this will continue for some time to come.

In this regard, some people wonder if it is really necessary for China to have massive banks, given the size of the country. Could we not do better simply having a number of provincial banks? One can entertain all kinds of hypotheses, of course, but I do not think this is the real key to the matter. No matter what the scale of banking operations are, the government can always adopt measures to control the degree of concentration or monopoly power. The banking business is different, however. Due to its nature, it must be able to extend across administrative jurisdictions. We cannot have numerous small banks that do business on a strictly "regional" or provincial basis.

The fact of the matter is that there will always be provincial interference in the operations of banks but the internal systems of banks must be able to withstand this. The internal control systems of banks are critical. Banks must have effective internal vertical management so that they can deal with external interference when it occurs. Naturally, during the transition period, not only must banks have their own ability to counter interference, but they must be supported by the central bank, the Ministry of Finance, and the central government.

Regulation by the central bank, and self-governance by commercial banks

In Poland, State-owned banks dominated the banking system during a certain period of time. Because of this, the Ministry of Finance signed "governance contracts" with them that provided certain incentives to their senior management but that also placed controls on their strategic policy decisions and that regulated their finances. In China, however, this issue of governance structures in commercial banks is still highly chaotic and murky. The four large banks still take up around 70 percent of total banking business in the country. All four, moreover, are State-owned. In trying to create better banks, therefore, we not only need to have better management at the senior level but we need to have better competitive mechanisms and governance structures.

This poses a critical issue. In setting up "governance structures," should the interests of the State, as owner, be represented by the Ministry of Finance, or by the central bank, or by the Communist Party of China? To this day (1999), this is an unresolved issue. A number of considerations require further study.

Naturally, the situation extends not only to the banking industry but also to regulatory institutions covering the securities and insurance industries. I feel that a number of problems will be generated if we ask regulatory agencies to try to participate in governance structures. The end result may well be that there is poor enforcement of regulatory oversight.

Weak governance structures have been an endemic problem in all sectors of the economy since reform began. In trying to find ways to measure or quantify the strength of governance mechanisms, one possibility is to look at incentive mechanisms for bank executives. This would measure their performance both on profitability and their degree of prudence (including their ability to control the creation of nonperforming loans, and to ensure internal discipline and accurate accounting). In other words, we can look into whether or not there are incentive mechanisms that encourage profitability and prudent decision-making via the use of performance measures.

Seen from a broader perspective, the inadequacy of governance structures in State-Owned Enterprises leads to improper use of State-owned capital in general. It means that there are inadequate incentive mechanisms to control costs and improve profitability. This also applies to State-owned banks—at present, we have not yet set up truly effective incentive mechanisms. Looking at our four major banks, you cannot say that the one which is most profitable gets the most glory or encouragement, whether that is in financial terms or in terms of political support. It is also not the case that a bank with more nonperforming loans and less profits gets less kudos.

Whether in material terms or in psychological terms, we should provide signals that reward good governance, but right now even the most fundamental signals are not in sight. Bank executives have no reason to think that their responsibilities include living up to certain economic expectations. I take this as a serious problem. Instead, executives mainly rely on their own understanding and instincts, including their understanding of the "Party spirit." They lack any of the constraints as well as guidance that can come from governance structures.

The Construction Bank of China's current reforms, and issues they are facing

The inadequacies described above do not mean we should not proceed with reform. Instead, we should do our best to correct the problems and not simply sit and wait for better times. The Construction Bank of China is one example. It has already begun to strip nonperforming loans off its books and is considering how to retrieve the greatest amount of assets in terms of its own organizational framework and functions. At the same time, it is considering how to turn the bank into an exemplary bank once nonperforming loans are resolved. It is focusing on a whole series of internal reforms that can be grouped into three major areas this year (1999).

The first involves a new round of reforms regarding the credit system of the bank. This relates to separating out the two functions of credit operations and "review and approval procedures" for granting credit. It focuses on the independence of credit risk controls. It strengthens the ability to trace performance after a loan is made, and to evaluate performance, and thereby allows for direct pressure to be brought on decisions about making loans prior to the granting of a loan. It implements a professional system of reviewing and approving loans, as opposed to having the "chief" make the decisions on his own. It strengthens evaluation criteria and thereby improves the quality of credit.

The second involves a comprehensive strengthening of internal controls. In this regard, the bank has focused on internal auditing systems and has made internal audits the responsibility of the authority of the level above rather than being on the same level of authority and thereby subject to interference. It has greatly improved the "authorization system" (granting authority to act on one's behalf) of all lines of business and is strengthening management information systems.

The third involves the reform of incentive mechanisms for personnel. The system by which the bank hires people has been changed, and incentive mechanisms have been truly implemented whereby cadres, staff, and workers are incentivized to perform. A person can now be promoted and he can also be demoted. Cuts have been made in the branches that were making a loss. This has particularly applied to the redundant personnel at the grassroots level of the network. Personnel who have not been able to meet the demands of their jobs have been let go. Levels of wages and bonuses are being adjusted to allow for a wider distance between top and bottom. Consideration is being given to a system whereby housing, pensions, and healthcare will be incorporated into the incentives system of the enterprise.

The above reforms are being actively pushed forward, but we anticipate very real problems as we go into implementation. I believe the obstacles will come from the following three areas.

First, for quite a long time, State-owned banks have been viewed as State institutions. They have therefore been subject to the traditional way of thinking about personnel and incentive mechanisms. One of the hardest parts of reform is going to involve breaking through these traditional constraints.

Second, transforming banks into exemplary institutions requires two different kinds of considerations, one external and one internal. It requires reform of the system by which the entire industry is regulated, which mainly means policies and the external environment, and it requires reform within commercial banks themselves. Opinions differ on how these two things should relate to one another. Some cadres feel that banks cannot turn themselves into "good banks" until the context for their operations has improved. We, on the other hand, feel that this approach serves to weaken all of our current efforts. Inside (internal driving forces) and outside (external environment) should serve to propel one another forward.

Third, State-Owned Enterprises constitute a fairly large percentage of the customers of State-owned banks. Because of this, any improvement in the quality of State-owned banks will necessarily depend on the extent to which State-Owned Enterprises carry out substantive reform. In theory, without the pressure of administrative interference, State-owned banks should be able to select their customers directly. If reform of State-Owned Enterprises does not in fact proceed as desired, then State-owned banks can simply distance themselves from such enterprises. In reality, however, since the customer base of banks is so heavily dependent on State-owned entities, changes in that customer base cannot be all that great. One of the factors that constrain State-owned banks as they turn into "exemplary institutions," therefore, is reform of these banks' customer base.

The pitfalls involved in "incremental reform" and its costs

One of the defining characteristics of China's reform is its "incremental" nature. This contrasts it from reforms undertaken in the former Soviet Union and some East European countries, which adopted "shock therapy." There have been many reasons for adopting this kind of reform and there have also been different points of view with respect to each of the two approaches. I myself have expressed support for an incremental approach in the past, and the facts have shown that it indeed has had many advantages.

Nevertheless, I would like to go on record as clarifying that no one approach is perfect. Each has its advantages as well as its drawbacks. Because of this, we need to take timely steps to ensure that we enjoy the benefits and avoid the pitfalls of any particular course of action. If we are overly complacent, and think that we can always simply proceed "incrementally," take our time and be totally "steady," we will not necessary have the best possible grip on what might happen. What I am saying is that we do not necessarily have to keep an exquisite balance among the three considerations of "reform," "stability," and "economic growth."

As we wave the banner of "incremental" reform, therefore, I feel we also should be clear about the costs of this approach, and its shortcomings. At a certain stage of reform, an incremental approach may well run into one or even quite a few major pitfalls. Without having reached a certain speed and a certain momentum, it might be hard for us to get over these problems. The more we try to fix things, the deeper we may sink into them. Some people call this the "gradualism trap." Before we sink too deeply, therefore, we should do our best to extricate ourselves.

The first question we might pose is whether or not an incremental approach to reform has anything to do with nonperforming loans (assets). As everyone knows, and western economists say the same, nonperforming bank loans are unique to market economies. Examples would be the savings and loans institutions in the United States, and the nonperforming loan issues in northern Europe, Spain, and Japan. Planned economies basically did not have this problem. The term itself did not exist in the former Soviet Union, eastern European countries, or China prior to the time of reform, and we certainly did not have any concept of "invisible nonperforming assets."

In the course of economic transition (changing tracks) "nonperforming assets" necessarily appeared due to a whole series of issues including various economic distortions and immature institutions. Because of this, it is crucial that we now concentrate the problems in one discrete stage of reform and overcome them. After we have finished "changing tracks," the nonperforming loans of banks will decline in number and be at a level where banks can cope with them. They will reflect a normal level of risk in the market. Naturally, nonperforming loans can always pile up again to levels beyond the normal in the course of economic cycles or mistakes made by policy makers. This can happen in mature market economies as well as in emerging market countries. Nevertheless, one thing that all transitional economies have in common is this appearance of a large quantity of nonperforming loans. As past assets are reevaluated in the light of the market, some will necessarily be regarded as nonperforming.

Second, the necessary appearance of nonperforming assets in the process of transition is caused by many factors, but their accumulation relates to the time-table of reform. Their quantity will naturally depend on the speed with which "changing tracks" moves forward. If transition is carried out quickly, nonper-forming assets will not be generated on as large a scale after reaching a certain boundary. Since the extent of accumulated nonperforming assets is somewhat smaller, less effort needs to be expended in resolving the problems. Another possi-bility is that relatively high inflation can serve to dissolve a certain amount of the problem. If transition is carried out slowly, and a large quantity of nonperforming assets never reaches that certain boundary, then the so-called "accumulation" can be quite heavy indeed. This can happen even when policy options call for slow transition in other respects. While enjoying the advantages of incremental reform, therefore, we must also realize that there are costs to be paid. One of them is a large quantity of nonperforming loans.

Third, if we analyze the sources of nonperforming loans, we come up with two primary economic causes. One is the existence of economic distortions, which greatly increase nonperforming loans. Another is that institutions cannot transi-tion fast enough, which further distorts the operating plans of those institutions and creates even more nonperforming loans.

To be more specific: prices are the most distorted item among all the vari-ous distortions of our economic system. Price distortion can lead to investment mistakes, inefficient resource allocation, waste of resources, and low return on investment. It can lead to wasting public funds and not only the low efficiency with which funds are used but fairly sizeable fiscal deficits. If the funds are "bank funds," this then leads to large amounts of nonperforming loans. To give an exam-ple: at the end of the 1980s and in the early 1990s, countless small-scale ethylene projects were launched, producing in the neighborhood of 100,000 to 150,000 tons each per year. Nonperforming loans relating to these projects alone came to tens of billions of RMB. One of the more apparent reasons for this was the dif-ferential in pricing: the prices of crude oil and light diesel oil were relatively low while the price of ethylene was high.

At the time, everyone thought that these projects were profitable. One might have carried out feasibility studies or a return-on-investment analysis using theo-retical prices or comparative international prices, but people with the ability to do this and the desire to do it were few and far between. The great majority of investors and local government were not motivated to do so, but nor were they able to use price-corrected data to carry out investment decisions. As a result, fundamental mistakes were made. In the eyes of the departments conducting the review-and-approval process, however, the projects had been submitted by the State planning department (so should be all right). Yes, there might always be problems with inadequately qualified people doing the permitting process, but one cannot always assume that officials will be highly capable anyway. From the banks' perspective, the price levels at the time made it look as though the projects should pay back money. In brief, a large amount of our nonperforming loan problem can be attributed to distorted price signals.

Naturally, some people may point out that the problem also relates to China's State-owned system. After all, who cares about spending State money? One can also find a great number of similar cases that involve the non-State-owned sector, however. In the 1980s, a large number of town-and-village enterprises began making polyester fiber. This then generated nonperforming loans to the extent that enterprises closed down or reduced production lines given their problems. This was also related to distorted prices. Most of these enterprises imported polyester fragments, which was subject to the actual tariff protection rate. Since it is a "final product," polyester fiber was levied a higher import duty than the raw material of polyester fragments. The value-added was thereby exaggerated, while in fact this was a kind of price distortion.

Although this kind of protective duty seems to be related to policies regarding one industry or another, at a deeper level they are related to the speed at which we are "changing tracks." Distortions that are created by the process makes everyone want to do the same kind of project at the same time, since it looks as though it will be profitable. The result is a great deal of redundant construction. From what official organizations are saying, this kind of redundant construction is the cause of enormous losses. In the terminology of transition economics, redundant construction is actually wrong decisions in resource allocation that are caused by distorted signals. This is precisely the cost that we pay for an incremental style of reform.

In terms of institutional causes of nonperforming loans, if reform proceeded more quickly, institutions might be forced to reform somewhat faster. Banks that formerly just "dispersed funds" for public finance must now change tracks and become true commercial banks, or "policy banks," or a mixture of the two and existing in an in-between state. This all depends on the speed of reform. If reform can proceed quickly, then the timeframe for being "in-between and neither this nor that" can be shortened.

For example, we could declare that within three to five years, banks will change from being under a planned-economy system to being under a market-economy, and we will no longer be using them to make policy-oriented loans. Were we to do that, the internal affairs of banks would adjust themselves rather quickly. If, however, we transition slowly and the intermediate state of banks goes on for more than a decade, we naturally will generate a far larger amount of nonperforming loans. From actual observation, we can see that the managers of branch operations far prefer policy-oriented loans. They have a number of advantages. First, under the "flag" of being a policy-type bank, branch institutions can do all kinds of business. Second, when problems do emerge, the fact that they are a "policy bank" can be the ultimate excuse for poor performance. Many branches use this excuse to evade responsibility for the loans they have made.

Another situation often comes up, in which a bank says that a given project was initiated by a phone call from this or that provincial leader. It is impossible to find any physical evidence for such decisions, or investigate the causes, so in the end it is impossible to ascertain who should be responsible. In this intermediate stage of reform "transition," I personally feel it is almost impossible to control this kind of thing. Yes, it absolutely does exist. The key issue is how long we allow this period to carry on. If we prolong it, we must accept a considerable accumulation of non-performing loans. The longer we let such loans pile up, the harder it is going to be to get rid of the eventual burden. In our overall reform, as we choose to follow an incremental type of reform, we must therefore also choose to be willing to pay the cost. Objective laws would indicate, however, that we should resolutely push forward reform at a fast pace. The costs of not doing that will be extremely high.

Overall, the existence of and rapid increase in nonperforming loans is the necessary result of reform, of changing tracks from one system to another. At the same time, the actual volume of such nonperforming loans is quite strongly correlated to the pace of reform. We should note that nonperforming loans are a problem that is not unique to China, but also exists in the United States, Japan, and elsewhere. In all cases, the speed of addressing the problem, and dealing with it sooner rather than later, has a great deal to do with the results.

One can use the savings and loan problem in the United States as an example. People have pointed out that if the country had resolved the problems in the early part of the 1980s, the cost might have been no more than some 20 to 30 billion US dollars. In the end, the problems were allowed to fester into the 1990s, by which time the actual cost in public funds exceeded 100 to 200 billion US dollars. Japan's case is similar. When problems erupt within a financial system, the longer policy makers delay in resolving them, the tougher they become. The more they have to pay for salvaging the situation.

The lack of a sense of urgency behind reform may actually compromise our hope to create exemplary banks. Problems that may result include the following.

Problem one: an inability to face the problem of nonperforming loans squarely. We feel that the only way to deal with the problem is to face it head on and resolve to fix it. Unfortunately, such things as the way we categorize bank assets and account for them helps cover up issues. If we cannot see the problems clearly, and indeed even cover them up, our reforms will have insufficient vigor to do any good. Inside banks, people will not have the determination to change the situation. Outside banks, people will feel that the credibility of reform is compromised. What's more, we will not have viable systems to evaluate asset losses that have not yet been proven as such.

Problem two: an inability to carry through with the necessary framework of laws and regulations. In order to deal with nonperforming loans, and create banks that are truly good institutions, we will need the support of a legal framework. This then involves a whole series of things including a good bankruptcy law, a good law on contracts, and a good law on guarantees or collateral. Although we have some of these, we urgently need others and we also urgently need to revise the ones we have. It is beyond doubt that such a legal framework is essential if we are to resolve nonperforming loan problems and create good banks. We created the framework for a bankruptcy law over ten years ago, but given advances we have made with our reforms since then, it is now out of date. If we do not revise these laws in a timely manner, or if we take the attitude that we need not rush into things, retrieving any of the nonperforming assets will be tough.

Problem three: regulatory conditions. This relates to whether or not the government and its departments can recover nonperforming assets and set up real banks in terms of rules and regulations. Many things are involved, including the personnel system, incentive mechanisms, accounting, and tax revenues. We already have a basic consensus on the need to reform all of these things, or at least to adjust them, but we differ when it comes to the right pace. Some people think we should move more quickly and others more slowly. If we move slowly, however, we will hamper ourselves. Looking at the situation overall, people have an inadequate understanding of the urgency of the need to set up really good banks.

Use of the term "pitfall" implies a certain condition, namely that banks may be moving in the right direction but are moving at too slow a pace—they will keep sinking into the bog if they don't move more quickly. If there is no great force driving change, then it is possible we will face the same thing Japan ran into, namely an inability to restructure bank portfolios even as nonperforming loans continue to be exposed. The burden on public finance will then be ever greater. When banks recognize the problems internally, they will become ever more reluctant to make loans and will tighten credit. This will lead to long-term recession in the overall economy.

We should make every effort not to fall into the above pitfalls. The Finance Minister of Hungary addressed this problem, and I feel he made an important point: even though we might want to create excellent banks and deal with nonperforming loans, if the ultimate determination is not there then the treasury must come forth not once, but twice, even three times or more to take on the burden of the bad loans. This then creates a very serious problem of moral hazard. People refer to this problem as "cutting the tail." If a tail is unsightly on someone and you want to cut it off, the best way to go about it is to cut it at the base and have done with it. Otherwise you have to cut it bit by bit, and it hurts every time you cut. The analogy refers to how central finance must pump capital into banks. If the thing cannot be finished in one effort, and banks are allowed to request more in the future, then the treasury will constantly be drawn upon for supplementary capital. If nonperforming loans are not stripped off balance sheets and dealt with once and for all, then they must be stripped again and again and the eventual result must again be moral hazard.

Meanwhile, if a bank feels that the State must help it with a capital infusion whenever its own capital is insufficient, then that bank will never be strongly motivated to make a profit. It will not be driven to self-fund its capital base. If a bank recognizes that it can adopt this practice of "not stripping nonperforming loans all at once, but bit by bit," then it will not try to reform its credit system in earnest. It will not try to transform its whole credit culture. I personally feel that by adopting a policy of allowing banks to strip nonperforming loans off multiple times, each time replenishing their capital, we choose an option that must necessarily lead to substantial moral hazard and limited results.

Delegates to this meeting, and government officials who are attending, have commended the progress made by both the Cinda Asset Management Co., Ltd., and the Construction Bank of China in stripping nonperforming assets off their balance sheets. I hope, however, that people will not be too complacent about what is merely a pilot project at the very beginning stage of a long process. We still should be dissatisfied with many aspects. This reform may be a successful experience, but it may also teach us some major lessons. Right now, many successful examples of similar efforts are being broadcast around the world, but I have a feeling that some earlier failures also lie behind these more recent successes. Moreover, they may be successes that came after absorbing some lessons and deciding, in a more resolute fashion, to take action. Japan's case is somewhat like this. Both the Construction Bank of China and Cinda are moving in this direction, but they still may encounter pitfalls along the way. We may well still suffer losses, but we hope that we can contribute by blazing a trail. At this stage, we cannot afford to be too optimistic. We must face the immediate problems head-on, and we must keep strengthening our reforms.

Note

1 This article is from a speech made by the author at an international symposium that was jointly convened by the World Bank and the People's Bank of China, on the subject of, "How to dispose of bank's non-performing loans, in order to make China's commercial banks into sound banks."

10 Elevating our accounting standards[1]

(April 11, 2001)

There was a time when almost all Chinese banks were prohibited from listing shares on the market through an initial public offering (IPO). This was due to slow progress in the course of banking reform. In 1999, the Shanghai Pudong Development Bank was finally allowed to list on the Shanghai Exchange. In May of last year, we convened a meeting to discuss this specific question and we decided to eliminate all discrimination against specific industries in listing. All should now be allowed to raise funds on the market. At the same time, we agreed that the list of companies being listed should include a range of types of companies, including financial companies (banks, insurance companies, and securities companies), since we felt this would be beneficial to the structure of the market overall.

However, we also emphasized that listing should be done with the interests of investors in mind. They should be the main consideration, as per the cardinal principle of securities regulation in other countries. To protect investors' interests, we must first improve our accounting standards and disclosure standards so that investors can make accurate judgments about a company's finances and operating results. Otherwise, investors can easily be deceived. Our markets will fail to develop properly and we will be faced with an increasing chorus of doubts.

China's capital markets have been in existence for a mere ten years or so. During this period, both citizens and leaders have been calling for greater order in the markets. Putting order in the markets calls for investment decisions that are made on the basis of a company's operating results and future prospects and not on the basis of pure speculation. Such a market must be built on the basis of accounting standards that can reflect the real financial condition of a company and its operating results. Otherwise, investors will say, "How do you expect me to make rational decisions based on financial reports that you have woven out of accounting standards like these? They make it impossible for me to figure out whether the company is really profitable or not!"

As we see it, China's corporate accounting systems have made great progress in recent years and have implemented a whole series of courageous reforms. Progress has been fairly rapid but has concentrated on the areas of conventional industry and commerce. The coverage of systems is not comprehensive, particularly when it comes to financial entities—our existing accounting standards still cannot accurately reflect their financial status or their operating results.

Allowing financial corporations to list on the market is a major step in China's reform. The reason is that they amassed a fairly large quantity of nonperforming assets in the course of China's economic structural reform, so that that their capital adequacy ratios are inadequate and they are in dire need of an infusion from the capital markets. If we manage this affair properly, it will not affect just one or two banks, or securities companies, or insurance companies. It will be a major event for China's economy as a whole. It will be a move that galvanizes China's entire process of reform and opening up.

To a degree, China's banks became a kind of wastebasket for all of the costs of reform. The price that had to be paid for reform, all its many costs, were simply tossed into this basket. Absorbing, or "digesting," all of the nonperforming loans carried by banks will be a way of absorbing the whole string of costs that our reform has incurred. In light of this understanding, the China Securities Regulatory Commission feels that allowing banks and financial entities to list on the market will be highly significant in pushing forward banking and financial-industry reform.

Once we informed the financial community of the spirit of this new policy, and began to have meetings and further forums on the subject, some banks immediately applied for permission to list on the market. Last November, a moderate-sized bank called the China Minsheng Bank, which had been completely privatized, had a successful IPO and was able to raise more than RMB 4 billion on the market. In the process, however, we ran into quite a few problems with respect to financial accounting standards and disclosure standards. Our solution to this was to raise the disclosure requirements. Disclosure requirements were more stringent in fact than accounting standards. At the same time, we realized that it would be very advantageous to our overall endeavor to follow this up with improved accounting standards as fast as possible.

The first thing we confronted in this regard was how to account for accumulated nonperforming assets and the drawing down of capital reserves. In the course of China's switching tracks from one system to another, our banks amassed a very considerable amount of nonperforming loans. According to our regulations, banks are allowed to draw no more than 1 percent of total year-end loan amounts out of reserves to help cover. Most banks find this figure seriously inadequate. Not only does it not allow them to dispose of nonperforming loans, but it serves to exaggerate their (hypothetical) profits.

The second thing we confronted was how to account for overdue interest-receivables in financial statements. Our regulation at the time said that any interest receivable that was overdue by 180 days should be recorded into statements. Even though it had not been received, banks were required to pay tax on the amount. We have recently revised this and lowered the figure of 180 days down to 90 days. Two years ago, the figure was 360 days. This accounting standard therefore does not reflect the true state of a bank's profitability, and it also creates the false impression that the relevant tax has been paid.

The third thing we confronted was the whole issue of risk disclosure. Financial corporations have risk considerations that are more complex than those of other industries. These include risks that are outside the scope of regular loans, and they are risks that financial standards should reflect. Our current standards are too lenient in this regard and do not, in fact, reflect them accurately. Examples include risks involved in letters of credit, the risks involved in serving as guarantor of loans that are off-the-balance-sheet, risks involved in pricing the collateral for loans, risks involved in cross-loans made among banks and financial institutions, and risks involved in such payment vehicles as acceptance drafts.

It is hard for China's current accounting system to account for such risks to their fullest extent, while allowances or "readiness" for such risks are highly insufficient. We know the risk is there, but exactly how great is it? I'll take import/export letters of credit as one example. My understanding is that losses already incurred by just one fairly large bank on import letters of credit amount to over USD 1 billion. This is due to "money advanced for credit to be paid back later." This kind of thing may very well not be reported on financial statements if we go by our current financial accounting standards.

The following issue is related to the whole accounting system but is also distinct from it. It relates to how to classify loans. Speaking more broadly, this means how to account for the different kinds of assets of a bank. Our current method of defining categories uses the loan term or due dates of loans. Since loan terms are generally fairly long, the universal practice internationally is to classify loans according to risk probabilities. That is, irrespective of whether or not a loan has come due, it is evaluated and classified according to probabilities of repayment. At the same time, reserves can be drawn upon according to the probability of losses. Our current system does not follow this practice at all. The reason relates to the way the central bank classifies loans, as well as the requirements of our accounting system regarding withdrawals from loan loss reserves.

Generally speaking, the above considerations lead to overestimating a bank's profits. At the same time, they force a bank to pay more in taxes, and make it harder for the bank to dispose of nonperforming loans. If investors are not clear about the facts of the matter, they can easily make investment mistakes. We therefore feel that improvements are necessary in this regard.

Meanwhile, certain elements in our current system serve to underestimate a bank's actual profits. The main one is the business tax. China levies a "business tax" on commercial banks, and the basis for this tax is all of the interest income and fee income received by the bank. Irrespective of how much interest a bank itself has paid out, it must pay an 8 percent tax on all interest income it has received. This year the rate was revised to 7 percent but this is still extremely high, while the basis on which the tax is levied is not all that reasonable. In terms of the capital markets, this is another thing that might affect people's judgments about the financial standing and operating results of a potential investment.

China has made considerable progress in how it accounts for commercial and industrial enterprises, but we have a quite a way to go. When it comes to certain special industries, such as the financial industry, we feel we have much further to go. Indeed, having experienced problems listing the Minsheng Bank on the market last year, we feel we should increase the pressure to drive home major reforms in this area.

With respect to disclosure standards: how have we improved these, given our existing system of accounting standards? International accounting standards make special provisions for disclosure in the case of financial institutions. We are therefore requiring China's financial enterprises to disclose information according to generally accepted international accounting standards. China's accountants are unfamiliar with financial accounting, however, and they also are not familiar with generally accepted international accounting standards. When it comes to accounting services, we therefore feel that for a certain period of time we should allow "experienced" international accounting firms to undertake the auditing of financial enterprises. By the term "experienced," we mean either well-known international accounting firms or their joint-venture partners inside the country. This is the only way we are going to achieve progress on this front. This will necessarily impact our domestic accounting firms, but I feel we cannot worry about the little things and take bigger losses as a result. The stakes are high, since major investors and countries need to have a clear view of the operating results of our financial institutions. We cannot afford to present unclear financial statements to the world just in order to save the jobs of a few people. I'm afraid that is not acceptable.

Our efforts to deal with financial disclosure in this way have garnered fairly good overall results. We have accelerated the reform process in commercial banks, and at the same time provided investors with relatively accurate information.

This way of handling disclosure has also raised a couple of issues, however.

The first relates to the appended audit reports as performed by the experienced international accounting firms that we hire, which use generally accepted international accounting standards per our requirement. These reports are used as appendices when disclosure of financial conditions is required. The international evaluations differ from the accounting evaluations performed according to our domestic accounting standards. Not only do the discrepancies themselves raise many questions, but investors also now raise many questions. At times the situation becomes rather chaotic with everyone wondering how to resolve the differences. This happens particularly since financial interests are involved.

The second relates to when banks have high accumulated levels of nonperforming loans and cannot dispose of them through normal practices of drawing on reserves. First, there may be no more reserves for a portion of the bad loans. Second, excess profits that may have been accumulated in the past may already have been distributed out in dividends. The result, which came about in the past, may now appear all at once on the profit and loss and balance sheet statements of the bank. Two different accounting systems will thereby derive different financial data. Handling issues that have accumulated over the years is a very tricky business.

In the course of its IPO, the Minsheng Bank accounted for the previous accumulation of bad loans under the system that was in operation at that time. It put them to one side and decided that, if problems arose, the former shareholders would bear that burden. New shareholders were therefore not obliged to use money they were investing for the purpose of dissolving historical problems—covering the nonperforming loans themselves or writing them off after verification. This way of doing things allowed for a relatively clear distinction between the interests of new and old shareholders, but it still did not resolve all the problems.

In sum, such accounting-system problems will only be resolved through speeding up the pace of reform and making sure our accounting accurately reflects the underlying financial situation and operating results of an enterprise. Once that happens, we will face fewer of these issues until we finally are able to get rid of them altogether. That is actually the only real solution. What we are doing right now is a temporary fix. That is, we are simply allowing "disclosure standards" to be more stringent than "accounting standards."

Finally, I would like to say a few words about my own personal conclusions on this subject.

The first thing that I want to emphasize is that our capital markets can only become more "standardized" once we improve our accounting standards. Better accounting standards are a prerequisite. We have talked a lot about China's capital markets recently, and our debate has focused around the issue of "standardization" versus "growth." Which should come first? Some feel that we need to grow the markets before we try to regulate them. Others feel we need to regulate them or they will never grow properly. What I would like to mention, however, is the relationship between standardization and "infrastructure building." In one sense, building the infrastructure for capital markets is in the same category as growing markets. It means going from not having a market to having a market. Infrastructure includes such things as laws, regulations, accounting systems, accounting standards, and corporate governance structures. These are the most basic requirements. Only if we establish them properly will we standardize and thereby grow our capital markets.

Everyone should think back to just a few years ago, when China did not even have a *Securities Law*. Back a few more years, we did not even have a *Company Law*. If we are honest with ourselves, many of the rules we have to this day are not all that reasonable. How can we even think of "standardizing" in such a situation? Very hard to do! Accounting standards are critical and basic when it comes to growing our securities markets. With low-quality standards, we are not going to make much progress with standardizing our markets.

The second thing that I want to emphasize is that we have indeed made great progress on the accounting front with respect to our commercial and industrial enterprises. I personally want to applaud the outstanding efforts put into this by the Ministry of Finance and our accounting community. Some in the community say that we are close to being at the level of international accounting standards. The thing I want to point out, however, is that there are many other special circumstances that are not covered by these standards. There are still many specific issues that need to be addressed and for which we need to establish regulations. The number of years that we have put into creating a market economy is not all that great, and our experience is still quite modest. Because of that, we still have quite a few "side doors" or unorthodox approaches. The gap between these and a market economy is substantial. It is imperative that we learn from international experience in this regard.

Finally, China's future accounting standards must refer to those of mature market economies but must also take China's specific circumstances into account. In doing this, we should make the right distinctions, however. The "specific circumstances" we take into account may well be precisely those we want to get rid of, since they relate to our former traditional planned economy. They were not designed according to the needs of growing China's economy and achieving reform and opening up. We should therefore not declare that "accounting standards must comply with China's specific circumstances" in order to retain precisely those things that we need to reform. We must not retain things that are not in line with our current economic environment. We must therefore move closer to international standards. At the very least, this is an urgent requirement for our capital market regulators as they attempt to build up China's capital markets.

Note

1 This was originally a speech given by the author at the International Seminar on Government Budget and Accounting Reform. It was published in the April 13, 2001 issue of *China Securities Journal*. The article uses the example of the Minsheng Bank's initial public offering as an indication of the need to reform our accounting system and the need to internationalize our accounting standards.

11 Capital adequacy ratios and the need to take corrective action in time[1]

(September 12, 2003)

Technological advances in recent years have enabled major growth in the financial industry. Computer technologies, and particularly networking technologies, not only have taken the industry far from the old days of manual operations but have radically changed banking operations and banking models. They have improved the efficiency with which capital can be used through networked funds settlement and systems for remittances and transfers. At the same time, they have propelled the *de facto* globalization of finance. Derivatives are one of the notable results of modern-day financial engineering, particularly options and ways of pricing options. These have had a major impact on the financial industry. Financial engineering draws on scientific and technical advances to create highly innovative products. Derivative products have proliferated as a result, including such things as asset-backed security (ABS), mortgage-backed security (MBS), and collateralized debt obligation (CDO). These are used in banking operations around the world and play an important and positive role in reducing credit risk.

As everyone knows, China's bank loans have grown at a very fast rate this year. After studying these new products, if we are able to take advantage of them they may well help us reduce the risk of these loans and enable more sound economic growth. The astonishing advances in science and technology are creating a whole new context for finance, but meanwhile the financial condition of bank customers is also changing much faster than it did before. Financial institutions are exposed to much greater risk. Managing risk, and dealing with the whole issue of incentive mechanisms, is something that now deserves our close attention.

China's economic structure has gone through the process of shifting from a centrally-planned economy toward a market economy. Centrally-planned economies focus on having production meet quantitative measures, or quotas. Once such quantitative quotas are met, qualitative requirements may also be used as supplementary targets—such things would include consumption of energy. This then forms a complicated web of things that is actually very hard to execute, a so-called "system of economic indicators (technical targets)." The greatest defect of this whole system, however, is its lack of incentive mechanisms. That is, enterprises are not motivated to accomplish many of the objectives set forth by the system. In contrast, market economies are extremely focused on incentive mechanisms. Such mechanisms stimulate market players to move in the desired direction.

Despite reforms, our economy, and in particular our financial industry, still lacks incentive mechanisms. A phrase that we commonly use to describe our approach can be summarized as "whipping the stronger ox so that it will pull along the weaker ones in the yoke." We ask a company with good results to merge with or acquire one with poor results, and call it "One helping the other so that you have a Red Team." The result, however, is to pull down the good company.

The lack of incentive mechanisms leads to "negative incentives" and "moral hazard." The operating results of many of our financial institutions are already quite poor, and yet banks are greatly expanding their asset base. They have three things in mind as they do this. First, expansion shows that they are contributing to economic growth and they thereby earn political credits (in the form of preferential policies). Second, expansion helps dilute the severity of problems that arose in the past. Third, the bigger their "stand" is, the less likely they will be shut down or merged with others. This results in distorted incentives that work in the wrong direction. From a macroeconomic perspective, our intent is to have quality institutions expand faster than poor institutions, in order to improve quality overall. Our existing incentive system has the opposite effect. It cannot serve the goal of supporting outstanding institutions and getting rid of the bad ones.

Can the system that we used in the past, in our planned economy, serve the present? Can we use (old) performance criteria to try to solve the incentive issues in financial institutions? I feel that the problems in doing this are substantial. Since the start of this year, China's money supply has increased fairly rapidly together with the increase in loans. Some analysts feel that the reason is banks can lower their nonperforming loan ratio through rapidly growing the denominator in the equation. One of the main criteria by which banks have been evaluated in recent years has been precisely that nonperforming loan ratio. This performance criterion has indeed served a good purpose but at the same time it allows for loopholes and problems.

Because of that, some people are considering simply raising the nonperforming loan ratio requirement. The problem is that this performance criterion can never achieve its full purpose. Financial institutions have all kinds of policy loans on their books, the legacy of history. Any constraint on them becomes a kind of one-on-one bargaining instead of a powerful incentive mechanism overall. In this period of economic transition, it is actually quite hard to find clear incentive mechanisms that serve operating goals as well as the need to have constraints on behavior.

Internationally, the most comprehensive and effective incentive mechanisms were incorporated in the *Basel Accord* of 1988. The *New Basel Accord* has already been formulated and is being discussed, and has even more positive aspects to it. Why do we feel that the *Basel Accord* is a comprehensive system in terms of regulatory supervision and the auditing of internal operations? The reason is that capital adequacy ratios are its core substance. These embrace the operating targets of banks and profitability on the one hand, while still putting effective constraints on bank expansion on the other hand.

The numerator of the capital adequacy ratio indicates the degree of adequacy—that is, it shows how capable the institution is of withstanding risk. The more capital a bank has at its disposal, the greater its ability to cope. "Capital" is dynamic, and depends on the ability of the institution to build up profits. That is, if an institution hopes to rely on external sources of funds, to supplement its coffers, any external investor will first scrutinize the profit-making abilities of the institution. If they come up short, that external investor may well decide not to put in funds. Moreover, when a bank expands through the use of mergers and acquisitions, it must still live within its capital constraints.

This carries within it a hidden condition, namely that each country sets its own rules for acceptable levels of risk. Each classifies loans according to categories that meet its own system's specific needs, and the drawing down of reserves depends on the category of loan. The accounting for capital is thereby done on a more solid basis.

The denominator of the capital adequacy ratio provides a weighted coefficient of the risk of different kinds of capital. This coefficient system encourages banks to engage more in low-risk business and less in high-risk business. If they undertake high-risk business, then they need more capital on hand to cover. This helps control an excessive expansion of risk.

The *New Basel Accord* has introduced a so-called Internal Ratings Base standard (IRB). This encourages banks to conduct internal evaluations in determining the level of all classes of asset business, since the risk coefficient system encourages banks to engage in non-asset-type business. Such business includes the "intermediary business" that we often hear about. The *New Basel Accord* also indirectly promotes the practice of securitizing assets, since securitization lowers the risk for asset owners, which in turn brings down the required level of capital reserves. At the same time, this provides banks with methods of shifting, neutralizing, and lowering risk. Because of this, the capital adequacy ratio is highly comprehensive in terms of both incentive and constraint mechanisms. It also recognizes the benefits of all kinds of technical innovations in improving credit quality. It incorporates thinking about operations risk that will result in greater use of IT technology and further developments in IT technology.

If we are to apply capital adequacy ratios to China's banking institutions, at the present time we still have one major conflict to overcome. That is, the "historical legacy" of nonperforming loans that were built up over the course of reform is different for different institutions. It is hard to use one unified standard as a required way to measure liabilities. Instead, we must use more forceful reforms to resolve this historical burden altogether. Once that is done, we can apply more rigorous capital adequacy ratio requirements. Not only will this be to conduct regulatory oversight, but it will be to encourage banks to incorporate self-governance and operational controls as a core internal objective. We still have some basic work to do in this regard, but it should be said that the China Banking Regulatory Commission is highly in favor of using the capital adequacy ratio as a performance standard.

If the country does indeed summon the determination to resolve this historical-legacy problem, we will then be taking a new path toward the future. Once we have changed into new shoes, we will no longer walk the old path.

In addition to adopting the capital adequacy ratios of the *Basel Accord*, can we define explicit measures that will be taken if capital becomes too low? This is what is referred to as "Prompt Corrective Action." Some people also translate it as reform measures that must be taken within a specific timeframe. From an outside perspective, there must be measures that enable sufficient pressure to be brought to bear when risk becomes too great or the quality of assets becomes too low. These must serve to bring on corrective actions as soon as possible. They must, that is, give explicit incentive signals that say a worsening of capital adequacy ratios is unacceptable and will be subject to restrictions.

A classic example of this came with the FDICIA (Federal Deposit Insurance Corporation Improvement Act of 1991) in the United States. This defined Prompt Corrective Action steps that would be taken if capital adequacy ratios reached certain levels. A ratio of 10 percent meant that an institution was well-capitalized. When it went down to 8 percent, this meant the institution was not allowed to accept any brokered deposits, as mandated by law. If it went to below 8 percent, the institution would be classified as "under-capitalized," and a set of new Prompt Corrective Actions would be applied. These would include the inability to accept any brokered deposits, the inability to pay out any dividends or management fees, and the need to implement a capital restoration plan with capital growth being subject to limitations. Specific approvals would have to precede the establishment of new branches, any mergers-and-acquisitions activity, and the launch of any new business.

When the capital adequacy ratio of an institution drops below 6 percent, additional Prompt Corrective Actions are mandated which include adjusting capital structure, limiting associated transactions, limiting interest rates on deposits, and limiting the compensation of senior executives. When it drops below 4 percent, the institution is classified as critically under-capitalized and subject to severe restrictions. These include a stop to paying interest on subordinated forms of debt, restrictions on other business activities, and the appointing of an "asset manager" or a regulatory supervisor. If improvements have not begun within four quarters, a receiver will be appointed to take over the assets. Such actions in the United States significantly reduced the speed with which highly risky financial institutions were expanding in the past, and prevented the spread of risk. Many other countries have now adopted their own Prompt Corrective Actions.

Each country's legal system is different and the authorities of regulatory agencies are also different. The measures that are available depend on different parties, so a variety of means must often be used in order to achieve Prompt Correction Action. China's situation is that incentive mechanisms have been extremely weak in the past and we therefore need to pool the efforts of all sides if we are to create a well-functioning incentive system. Such coordination will enable us to be more effective in preventing adverse choices and moral hazard.

Through establishing an effective incentive system, we can bring greater pressure to bear on financial institutions. Such pressure must be comprehensive as opposed to being exerted in only one spot. It has to address the underlying issues. With sound incentive systems in place, financial institutions will be more motivated to use their own internal driving forces for change. They will adopt advanced technologies in support of their own financial innovations, and they will more fully use the innovations already brought forth in the world of modern economics and finance. Given a stronger foundation, they should be able to adapt more readily to the high risk levels of modern economies by setting up their own improved systems for risk management.

Note

1 This was originally a speech that the author delivered at the 6th China Beijing International High-Tech Expo.

12 Several issues to do with reform of State-owned banks

(April 16, 2004)

Favorable and unfavorable factors affecting the reform of China's State-owned banks

As with all areas of reform in China, reform to do with State-owned commercial banks involves certain prerequisite conditions. It can be said that the Asian financial crisis turned some of the unfavorable conditions affecting China's bank reform into more favorable conditions. The eruption of this crisis raised awareness among all parties about the importance of maintaining stability in our banking operations. It also raised awareness of the massive financial risk we face in having a weak and vulnerable banking system. It solidified the resolve of policy makers to reform our State-owned commercial banks.

China came through the Asian financial crisis smoothly. In the latter part of the 1990s, the country saw stable and sustained economic growth which further improved the conditions for reforming State-owned commercial banks. Sustained economic growth brought with it greater resources which made reform more feasible. What's more, the eruption of the Asian financial crisis made the attention of regulators focus on the whole issue of lowering banks' percentage of nonperforming loans. By now, nonperforming loans in State-owned commercial banks have dropped by nearly half from levels at the time of the crisis.

In the fourth quarter of 2002, and the first quarter of 2003, the nonperforming loans of China's State-owned banking system became the subject of tremendous international media attention. Foreign financial magazines and newspapers ran prominent articles saying that China's massive amount of nonperforming loans would impact sustainable growth. (These included *Times, Business Week, The Economist*, and the *Far Eastern Economic Review*.) Some people even estimated that the percentage of bad loans exceeded 50 percent, if you applied a scientific classification to our bank loans overall. As a result, people lost a great deal of confidence in China's State-owned commercial banks, which affected the amount of foreign investment coming into the country's financial industry.

The situation is much better at the present time, however. Reform of our State-owned banks has already entered a substantive phase and business results of State-owned banks are constantly improving. Statistics indicate that the percentage of their nonperforming loans is dropping at a rate of 3 to 5 percent every year.

China's central bank has been monitoring the condition of nonperforming loans in State-owned commercial banks since the start of reform and opening up, to evaluate the causes and structure of the problem. The central bank's analysis shows that poor bank management practices account for only a small percentage of nonperforming loans within the total. According to the central bank's analysis of its surveys, nonperforming loans that were formed in the past (historical legacy-type loans) can mainly be attributed to government interference, to a weak legal environment, and to improper management of client groups by State-owned commercial banks.

Looking at the situation more specifically, some 30 percent of nonperforming loans of State-owned commercial banks were caused by government interference at various levels of government, which includes interference at the central government level as well as at local (provincial) levels. Another 30 percent was brought on by loans to support credit of State-Owned Enterprises, 10 percent was caused by the absence of an adequate legal environment, an inadequate understanding of the rule of law, and the inability of some regions to enforce laws. Another 10 percent of nonperforming loans came about because the government closed, merged, suspended, or transformed some enterprises (including military enterprises) in the process of revamping the country's industrial structure. Generally speaking, only 20 percent of nonperforming loans were brought on by poor credit practices of banks themselves.

It is notable that the above causes saw great improvement in some respects after the 1997 Southeast Asian financial crisis, which made people focus on the issue. First, the government has already basically given up the practice of administrative interference in State-owned commercial banks. From a legal standpoint, government departments have already explicitly determined that commercial banks have autonomy over their own loan decisions. Second, policy regulations regarding credit support changed. In the 1980s and 1990s, policy guidance explicitly stated that State-owned commercial banks were required to extend credit support to State-Owned Enterprises. By the mid-1990s, however, the government had already begun to give up this kind of policy guidance way of thinking. By now, State-owned banks are not obliged to extend any kind of loans to State-Owned Enterprises.

The People's Bank of China undertook a survey of State-owned banks in 2003, and results show that at present more than 50 percent of their loans are made to non-State-Owned Enterprises and individual citizens. (These include loans to foreign-invested enterprises as well as people-operated enterprises, and mortgage loans for housing and individual consumer loans.)

Third, as reform of State-Owned Enterprises moves forward, some are being listed on the market. Improvements in the operations of these enterprises have raised the possibility that they will be able to resolve the problem of an overly high percentage of bad loans. Fourth, China has needed a well-rounded bankruptcy law for quite some time. Disputes have arisen regarding unjust rulings in loan cases in some parts of the country, while enforcement is not strict enough in other parts. The problem relates to local government interference in the court system. We should take note of the fact that laws and regulations are in fact being improved, with revisions of the *Bankruptcy Law*, the *Securities Law*, and the *Company Law* under way right now. Overall, the scale of China's nonperforming loans is still high, but there is hope for reform in relative terms. The reason is that the percentage of bad loans that State-owned banks are generating themselves is not too high.

Initial reform steps for State-owned banks

Reform of State-owned banks involves the issue of proper sequencing, which has always been a matter of strategic choices in the course of reform overall and which therefore requires historical analysis.

In the early period of reform, we decided to use our public spending and financial resources first on agricultural reform, State-Owned Enterprise reform, and reform of the foreign-trade sector. We compelled reform in these areas through the method of "granting benefits" (allowing profits to stay with the entity generating the profits). Reform in each of these areas consumed a large amount of resources. Since our treasury was quite constrained at the time, and since our systems overall were inflexible, our financial system bore the brunt of carrying these costs. The consequence has been that the banking industry accumulated a large amount of nonperforming loans. Meanwhile, this also delayed reform of the banking sector. When reform has progressed to a certain stage, however, we undoubtedly must shift the emphasis of reform to the financial industry and resolve this historical burden.

In reviewing how reform of the State-owned commercial banking sector has progressed to date, we can see it went through several main stages. First, in 1998, the Treasury issued RMB 270 billion worth of national debt in order to make up for the insufficiency of capital in State-owned commercial banks. Between 1999 and 2000, we stripped a certain portion of nonperforming loans off the balance sheets of State-owned commercial banks through setting up Asset Management Companies that took in the assets.

Second, after examination and verification, we cancelled out some nonperforming loans by mobilizing existing resources. The funds used for this purpose (theoretically) came from original reserve funds, operating profits prior to allocations for reserves, and originally held capital. Bank reserve funds could only cover a portion, however, given the scale of nonperforming loans. They have not even been enough to cover the category of "loan losses" in the five-part classification of loans. It therefore was obviously necessary to mobilize other funds to fill in the gap. Looking at the profitability of commercial banks in recent years, it should be possible, and indeed it is necessary, to start using some of the banks' profits to help bolster inadequate reserve funds. Using the above methods, two pilot-project banks have indeed basically been able to cancel out the historical losses due to bad loans.

Third, we mobilized some of our foreign-exchange reserves and gold reserves to register State capital in State-owned banks. It should be said that registering capital is only one step in the process of reforming the entire commercial banking system. If we truly want State-owned commercial banks to turn into real banks, we must comply with international accounting standards and the requirements of listed companies. We must continue cleaning up the internal assets of State-owned banks, improve internal risk-control systems, and put in place proper corporate governance structures. Under the new regime, we must make every effort to avoid a resurgence of nonperforming loans. The aim is to ensure that newly registered capital does indeed return a profit. Moreover, regulatory institutions must focus on compliance with capital adequacy ratios. They must create institutional mechanisms that ensure we do not have another large round of nonperforming loans.

Looking at the situation overall, we will not have well-rounded corporate governance structures in State-owned commercial banks until we achieve shareholding-system reform that has very well defined objectives. Only when that happens will it begin to be possible for reform to show results.

Potential controversies regarding reform of State-owned commercial banks

Controversial issues may arise on several fronts as we proceed to reform State-owned commercial banks. I would like to present my own views on two such issues below. We can discuss problems relating to other areas in the question and answer session.

Should we push forward reform by strengthening management (control over banks), or should we do it through reforming internal corporate governance and shareholding systems?

This is one of the hottest topics among all the controversies surrounding our policy options for reform. One view says that we should first focus on the issue of corporate management. Once that is settled, we can proceed with shareholding system reforms. If we look back on our reform of State-Owned Enterprises, we can see a similar debate. That is, do our problems arise from issues to do with management or issues to do with corporate mechanisms? Do we have a problem of people or of systems? If the leadership of banking enterprises isn't working out, can we just switch leadership and get better operating results, accumulate more profits before moving on to "corporatization" and shareholding system reform?

Years of experience have taught us that the results of this way of thinking have not been all that good with respect to State-Owned Enterprises. We have learned that the root problem of State-owned entities does not relate to unscientific management. Instead, the problem lies in the essential nature of the system. It was for this very reason that the Communist Party of China reiterated the proper orientation of enterprise reform in its 16th National Congress (2002) and its Third Plenary Session of the 16th Central Committee (2003).

In comparing State-Owned Enterprises and State-owned banks, it is not hard to find strong similarities. If enterprises were like government institutions in the past, to a degree banks were like government departments—or one could say they were "quasi-bureaucratic systems." They were not like commercial entities. The administrative ranking system as well as an intense sense of bureaucratic turf applied to all systems including personnel, compensation, employee benefits, social security benefits, and internal incentive mechanisms. The decision-making authority of the person actually responsible for business in State-owned commercial banks was often restricted, which made market-oriented operations difficult.

Meanwhile, bank branches at the grassroots level require different kinds of staff. In addition to needing tellers that take in deposits, they need the ability to attract and hire competent people who can discern and avoid credit risk. The differences in job descriptions should be substantial, but this is not reflected in the pay levels that banks are allowed to provide. Since internal incentive mechanisms are inadequate, and external pressure is also inadequate, merely strengthening management is not going to work. If we rely solely on that, I'm afraid that China's State-owned commercial banking reform will take a long time.

The Communist Party of China explicitly confirmed the orientation of shareholding reform at the 16th National Congress. It confirmed that we must truly change corporate operating mechanisms by changing corporate governance structures. This same thinking should be applied to reform of State-owned commercial banks. In essence, reform of State-owned commercial banks is the same thing as reform of State-Owned Enterprises.

Should we actively promote the idea of turning State-owned banks into publicly-held listed companies?

One view on this mistakenly equates listing on the market as the end-goal of reform. It believes that listing is done to satisfy the need for funds. It is done to supplement the inadequate capital of State-owned banks, and to resolve the problem of paying executives enough as an incentive. It should, however, be recognized that this is not the only purpose of listing State-owned commercial banks on the market.

Listing is only one stage in the process of reform. If we divide the entire process into segments, one could say that listing lies somewhere in the first half. In reality, since the State actually does have the ability to inject capital into banks, fund-raising is not the primary purpose of listing, nor is resolving the issue of internal incentives. The end-goal of reform is to set up a whole new set of market-oriented incentives and restraint mechanisms that contribute to the interests of investors and thoroughly break out of the old mold of a quasi-bureaucratic system. The goal is to change the operating objectives of the "bureaucratic turf" approach. Through reasonable performance incentive mechanisms and adequate risk-control and capital constraints, it is to turn State-owned commercial banks into truly market-oriented entities.

Since listing is indeed a major step, however, one of the key considerations will be resolving longstanding problems, particularly those that derive from institutionalized constraints that other departments impose on banks. For example, take the tax revenue issue. For a long time, China has handled the taxing of banks in ways that are not in accord with the laws of a market economy. Tax-revenue departments admit it themselves. Since the situation is complex, however, with many different kinds and rates of taxes, they always face a question of priorities. Before State-owned banks are oriented toward capital markets and public inves-tors, it is going to be very hard to put tax-system reform on the agenda. Only when State-owned banks start the countdown to being listed will this issue finally come to the fore and be resolved.

Such aspects as personnel, benefits, social security, autonomy in operating decisions, and so on, will follow suit. Only when State-owned banks face the urgent tasks of listing on the market will each department decide that cooperative behavior is in its own interests and that this should become the priority. The fact of the matter is that, without outside pressure, no department with any say in the matter will voluntarily relinquish the power in its hands. Without such outside pressure, reform will keep being put off.

In looking at the broader significance of corporate governance, commercial bank operations affect public interests. Because of that, governance mechanisms must serve to increase transparency and improve the ability of the public to exer-cise regulatory supervision. In the process of shareholding reform and listing on the market, State-owned commercial banks must satisfy various disclosure requirements for listed companies. Listing on the market helps create the condi-tions for true oversight by the public.

Because of this, any injection of capital by the government is aimed at helping set up financial intermediary mechanisms that are able to use savings deposits efficiently. Government funding is not done merely to improve the balance sheet of a bank. In a very real sense, improving corporate governance mechanisms through sufficient outside pressure and listing on the market will be the only way to cut loose from old operating mechanisms that served the organs of bureaucracy. It will be the only way to ensure the success of State-owned commercial bank reform.

Reform of some large State-Owned Enterprises can serve as a good model to follow in this regard, given the changes that they went through after shareholding reform and being listed. We have all observed that some of these large State-Owned Enterprises were also organs of bureaucracy prior to public listing. Their lack of a true "owner" (an empty seat at the top) led to a massive amount of insider control, low operating efficiency, and poor results. After shareholding reform and listing on the market, supervisory control no longer stopped at the level of gov-ernment organizations directly in charge. After listing, both public investors and institutional investors both within and outside China, as well as the demands of regulatory agencies both within and outside China, forced listed companies to take the interests of shareholders into account. This applied to information disclosure, business operations, and market strategies. It is fair to say that going public forced internal changes in corporations as well. Without shareholding reform and the outside pressure from shareholders, without the supervisory oversight of strategic institutional investors and the public, and without the adoption of an independ-ent board of directors, I'm afraid there would not have been sufficient internal pressure to change. That is, internal forces pressuring enterprises to reform themselves would not have been effective.

Commercial banks are the same. After listing, they will be forced to accept supervisory oversight from shareholders, regulatory agencies, the public, and other relevant stakeholders. They will have to undertake detailed information disclosure and follow improved accounting standards, and on this basis they will have to take the interests of shareholders into full account.

Therefore, only by pushing forward the listing of our commercial banks and strengthening corporate government will we be able to change "the rules" in a thorough manner. We want to create an effective way to avoid the phenomenon of moving forward one step and back two, returning to follow the same old repetitive patterns as we carry out reform.

Prospects for bank reform: potential strengths as well as problems

China's financial system is still in the preliminary stages of growth. Financial products are not well developed and the operations of financial systems are rudimentary.

On the positive side of the ledger, however, indirect financing via banks plays an enormous role in China. The M2 measure of money supply is nearly 200 percent of GDP. China has the advantage of a massive population. Given all these things, China's traditional banking business has enormous room within which to grow. Growth will be in the form of innovative new products, including intermediary business, cross-market financial products, consumer credit, and mortgage loans, among others. The interest-rate spread is considerable, which allows for profits from deposits. Overall, the prospects for profitable commercial banks are good.

On the negative side of the ledger, China lacks a sufficient cohort of professionals trained in the field of finance. In looking at how other industries are developing, it is not hard to see that Chinese people are industrious and eager to learn. Although it takes some time, human resources can be developed. The number of people now graduating from institutions of higher education is enormous, and in many technical fields we should be able to catch up with and overtake the competition. Right now, young people are highly enthusiastic about studying finance and I believe that the supply will be able to satisfy demand if we can provide the right incentives.

In the immediate future, it will be hard to cultivate people who are adept at financial innovations, but in terms of normal operations and financial engineering, we should be able to develop the human resources fairly quickly. I myself believe that the process of reform, and particularly the process of setting incentive systems in place, will enable us to attract sufficient talent, some of it from overseas.

China's longstanding veneration of knowledge and its excellent education systems will help resolve the issue of professionals in the field of finance. The problem will be put to rest in the course of reform. Naturally, right now we still need to address the problem of a lack of highly trained executives who are capable of handling both modern finance and international competition.

We should not underestimate the formidable nature of banking reform. From a global perspective, we can see that reform of financial systems is far more daunting than that of other areas. Whether we are talking about shock-therapy reform or incremental reform, both share the need to develop institutions that never existed before in the planned-economy system, institutions that must meet the needs of a market economy, including corresponding legal and regulatory systems. Institution building and establishing well-rounded laws and regulations takes time. Reform therefore faces the dilemma of being implemented in the context of immature institutions. The first problem is that banking, securities, insurance, credit, funds, and so on, are all, in themselves, immature. The second problem lies with customers. Customers to whom banks lend money, for example corporations, are still in the midst of reform themselves and therefore "immature." Both depositors and investors may not necessarily have the capacity to make correct judgments, or wise investment decisions given, as Janos Kornai has said, the whole issue of "soft budgeting constraints."

The third problem lies with setting up regulatory institutions. Such problems include straightening out systems, clarifying accountability, drawing together sufficient high-caliber personnel, ensuring that the institutions operate in a fair and incorrupt manner, and so on. In a transition period, all of these require a period of adjustment. Fourth, we need to reform accounting standards. The differences in accounting systems of centrally planned versus market systems are enormous. Given our lack of understanding and the paucity of qualified accountants, it will be hard to see the results of transplanting western systems directly over into China's situation. On the other hand, gradual reform has problems too, since each step taken in accounting reform may not be in time for overall reform of the system.

The fifth issue relates to setting up accounting firms, asset evaluation institutions, and rating institutions. This process involves going from absolutely nothing at all to having full-blown institutions, which again takes time. It also involves integrating entities we have cultivated internally with the process of opening up to the outside world. Sixth is the problem of evolving and enforcing our bankruptcy law. This involves reform of the judiciary as well as the administration. Lacking a good bankruptcy law and process means we will continue to suffer from a poor credit environment and high levels of nonperforming loans. Seventh is tax reform, and the believability of public finance, especially when it comes to the rates for both individuals and corporations, and irregular behavior at each level of government given "soft" constraints. Eighth is creating viable markets with specific regard to risk management. The financial industry must have market-economy ways to transfer and avoid risk.

Ninth, we must "grow" institutional investors. This is a necessary link in the process of growing financial markets and expanding financial product offerings. The process of developing institutions requires a considerable investment of time. It is not very realistic to think that when institutions are not yet fully formed we will have low levels of nonperforming loans, highly "clean" capital markets, information that is never distorted, and an insurance industry that is fully sound. We hope that institutions will develop in smooth fashion, but we do not want to be overly idealistic about it. Financial reform and institution-building are mutually dependent activities. Each will reinforce the growth of the other.

One short-term issue that we should be aware of is that competition for high-end customers will intensify once foreign-invested banks enter the market. Statistical analysis of this in some countries shows that high-end customers are the most important source of commercial bank profits. The top 10 percent of such customers bring in roughly 80 percent of profits. The primary competition between foreign-invested banks and China's State-owned banks is going to be in this arena. China's banks may have tremendous networks and client groups, but if they lose their high-end customers it is highly likely they will face serious problems.

Over the mid- to long term, we are optimistic about the prospects for China's banking reform. We also hope that more foreign-invested institutions will enter this market, stimulate greater competition, promote innovative and progressive services, and lend momentum to our economic prosperity.

13 Promoting further development of capital markets by improving corporate governance

(December 1, 2004)

The issue of corporate governance is highly important to China's development. The subject touches on a great many considerations and has a very broad impact. At the same time, it generates strong emotions. We began trying to introduce the concept into China only fairly recently, but even in such a short time we have encountered a number of problems. We first went through a stage of debating the most rudimentary issues, almost like holding discussions among school children. Nevertheless, after years of working on this, China's corporate governance is in fact making fast and very exciting progress.

Of course there are still many issues that remain to be addressed and that will require further concerted study. I would like to take this opportunity to propose 12 topics for such study. I hope we can address them during this forum and make some progress. Constructive opinions will be very helpful for China's efforts in this arena in the future.

Twelve topics for discussion

First, the concept of corporate governance was introduced into China from abroad, and our understanding and implementation of it has required a certain process. The Communist Party of China obliquely included the concept in its report at the Third Plenary Session of the 14th Central Committee in 1993. It noted the mutual constraints that "investors, the board of directors, management levels, and employees" place on one another, which could be seen as at least mentioning the basic concept of corporate governance. The formal introduction of the actual term did not happen until 1999, however, when it was written into the Party's major documents at the Fourth Plenary Session of the 15th Central Committee.

As for the guidance elements of corporate governance, we have adhered closely to international experience, but it would be best if the government clarified its attitude toward the *Five Principles on Corporate Governance* released by the Organisation for Economic Co-operation and Development (OECD) in 1999. The OECD places particular emphasis on how governments formulate the overall systemic framework for corporate governance, including how the legal system plays an important role. This was set forth in the OECD's *Revision of the Principles on Corporate Governance* in 2004. In recent years, some authorities in China, including the China Securities Regulatory Commission, China Banking Regulatory Commission and others, have put out their own excellent guidelines on corporate governance. One issue that should be further discussed, however, is what more the government can do to actually promote such guidelines.

Second, different models for corporate governance exist around the world, such as the Anglo-Saxon model, the Rhine model, and the Japanese and Korean model. Over the past decade or so, these models have tended to converge. They are more aligned on certain issues, but they still differ on many others. China must select options that conform to its own particular circumstances. In this regard, we should actively explore what kinds and what parts of models to adopt.

Third, the most important reason China began introducing the concept of corporate governance in the early 1990s was that we faced a severe problem of insider control and lack of accountability. To this day, this remains a major unresolved problem. It needs to be faced head-on and thoroughly discussed.

Fourth, another problem, closely related to that of insider control, has come about as a result of our practice of swapping out debt for equity. In 1999, we instituted this conversion of debt into equity on a massive scale. In the process, we had considerable distorting of the facts, while corporate governance principles were either simply ignored or openly violated. The leadership of the State Council has recently focused on this problem. The mistakes have already been made and the question now is what to do about them. Going forward, how do we handle the legacy of corporate governance problems that came about as a result of this debt-for-equity swap?

Fifth, as judging from China's own experience, the best practitioners of corporate governance have been listed companies. They have to follow the corporate-governance guidance of regulatory bodies, and they are subject to supervision by investors, the public, and the market. This experience of listing companies has made people begin to recognize that one of the primary orientations of our overall reform will be shareholding-system reform. The question now is whether or not we can make substantive progress in corporate governance if we do not push forward the listing of our large- and medium-sized companies. I am afraid progress may well be difficult if we do not list such companies.

Sixth, one of China's unique considerations is that of the Party. In addition to relationships among investors, the board of directors, executive management, and stakeholders, we need to consider the role of a corporation's Party committee in corporate governance. We should move forward in discussing and clarifying issues surrounding this subject.

Seventh, China has adopted much of the excellent experience of other countries with respect to corporate governance, but we have always evaded the whole subject of stakeholders. This is included among the *Five Principles* of the OECD's document on corporate governance, but we have never responded with either a positive or a negative opinion on the matter. The OECD's 2004 *Revision* puts even greater emphasis on the role of stakeholders in corporate governance. One of the key topics before us, therefore, is how to gain an accurate understanding of the implications of "stakeholders," and how to take advantage of the positive role they can play.

Eighth, one of the rather obvious deviations from good corporate governance that we still find in China is the way companies disregard the interests of shareholders. For example, some of our traditional State-Owned Enterprises have not paid any dividends to shareholders to this day. One of the topics we should address, therefore, is how we can improve China's corporate governance going forward via respecting the interests of shareholders.

Ninth, one very satisfying thing we have accomplished in recent years is the establishment of independent directors on the boards of companies. We have made enormous progress in this regard, since such a system of independent directors never existed before. At the outside, many people were doubtful about it, thinking that independent directors were going to be on boards merely for decorative effect. In fact, with experience and training, the positive role that these directors are playing in companies is increasingly apparent. One topic to address is how we can make even better use of independent directors in the future.

Tenth, a number of new institutional investors have begun to participate in China's capital markets in recent years. These institutional investors include closed investment funds, open investment funds, various kinds of venture capital funds, industrial investment funds, pension funds, and so on. Given that we still have pronounced problems in our corporate systems, namely no "owner" who can be held accountable, and insider control, should such investors adopt the American model, that is, passive investing, or should they be more actively involved? This should be discussed.

Eleventh, many of China's enterprises are very highly leveraged. They are highly indebted to banks, while the percentage of their own capital is quite low. Banks are therefore extremely important creditors. The role of creditors in corporate governance is something that the OECD focuses on intently. Mechanisms for the protection of creditors' interests and effective settlement frameworks are all included in OECD corporate governance principles. As creditors, what role should banks play in China's corporate governance? This is an extremely important topic that the banking community should discuss in depth.

Twelfth, China has made considerable progress in thinking about corporate governance overall, which is to say that we are taking up the topic with respect to our non-State-owned entities, and not only to our State-Owned Enterprises. In the past, our policy documents on this subject were written specifically with State-Owned Enterprises in mind. It was as though non-State-owned entities had no corporate governance issues to deal with. More recently, however, people have begun to recognize the commonalities of corporate governance for both. Such commonalities in enterprise reform also should be a topic for discussion.

I have presented twelve topics and welcome your views and recommendations.

We hope that all participants in this forum, but particularly representatives from China, will focus on the major progress made in the revised version of the OECD corporate governance principles.

Major progress made by the OECD's *Corporate Governance Principles (Revised) 2004*

In 1999, the OECD released *Five Principles on Corporate Governance* which attracted the attention of a broad range of people in China, including policy makers, investors, corporate personnel and corporate stakeholders. As time has gone on, new challenges relating to governance are now confronting these *Five Principles*.

For this purpose, the OECD started conducting global surveys and discussions in 2002, to look into how to ensure effective implementation of the *Principles*. It looked into such things as how to ensure independent decision making by the board of directors, how to strengthen the "right to know" of shareholders, how to strengthen the independence of auditors, how to improve transparency of ownership structures, and so on. Finally, in April 2004, the OECD issued the *OECD Principles on Corporate Governance (Revised)*.

Five major new advances have been made in the 2004 edition as compared to the 1999 edition.

First, the Revisions have added a chapter called, *"Ensuring a sound basis for the corporate governance framework."* This presents the role that the government should play in formulating overall systems and a legal framework within which corporate governance operates. It points out principles that the government should follow in doing this, including setting up compliance mechanisms and ways to ensure that corporate governance principles are thoroughly carried out. It also provides mechanisms to protect the rights of people who participate in corporate governance. At the same time, this chapter talks about how to avoid the costs of an excessive amount of regulation. With the addition of this chapter, there are now *Six Principles* as described in the 2004 OECD document.

Second, the 2004 *Revisions* strengthens protection of shareholder rights. The "voice of the shareholder" is now included in the following respects: (1) The board of directors should determine the compensation policies for senior executives, these should be made public, and levels should be linked to long-term results of the company. Meanwhile, shareholders have the right to know the compensation policies of members of the board of directors and senior officials, and any equity-related compensation must be approved by shareholders. (2) Shareholders have the right to change members of the board. Effective ways should be available to them by which they nominate candidates for the board and vote on board membership. (3) Institutional investors that are authorized as trustees should make public their own corporate governance policies, including the means of enforcing their right to vote, and how to implement that right to vote in the event of conflicts. (4) Any barrier to cross-border voting should be eliminated.

Third, the *Revisions* focus much more on how to resolve conflicts of interest. Based on the disclosure requirements as put forth in the 1999 *Principles*, with respect to conflict of interest, the 2004 *Revisions* requires that people with a conflict of interest make known how they intend to resolve that conflict of interest. The *Revisions*, moreover, takes note of the fact that many emerging market countries share the problem of a conflict of interest between large and small share-holders: (a) The *Revisions* add a *Principle* which requires that rating agencies and research agencies, which know the operating performance of the company, disclose such conflicts of interest within reason when they publicize information on the company. (b) The *Revisions* focuses on the responsibilities of the auditor and explicitly states that the auditor is accountable to the board of directors. (c) The *Revisions* focuses on the independence of the auditor and details the steps the auditor should take to manage and reduce potential conflicts of interest. (d) The *Revisions* puts more emphasis on protecting the interests of the small investor: "the interests of the small investor should be protected in the event there are either direct or indirect losses that result from actions on the part of the controlling shareholder. Moreover, effective remedy should be made to the small investor."

Fourth, the *Revisions* places much more emphasis on protecting stakeholders and whistle blowers. With respect to stakeholders, the role and the rights of both employees and creditors are given more prominence: (a) Explicit mention is made that, "mechanisms that improve employee participation should be made available." Stakeholders, including individual employees as well as any institutions that represent them, should be able to express their views freely to the board regarding any immoral conduct or violation of the law that might have occurred. Both the views that the employee expresses, and his right to express those views, should be taken seriously and protected. Channels should be made available for the secure transmission of confidential information so that it actually reaches the board of directors. (b) Efforts should be made to improve participation in cor-porate governance, so that any particular skills an employee has can be quickly transmitted to the company and put to good use in either direct or indirect ways. Examples of employee participation mechanisms would include: including an employee representative on the board of directors, implementing a shareholding plan by employees, ensuring that employees share in profits via their pension plans, and so on. Moreover, when pension-type funds are established, they should be put into a segregated fund and the fund managers should be separate from and independent of the management of the enterprise. (c) The *Revisions* empha-sizes the important role that creditors should have in corporate governance, and the role that creditors play in external supervisory oversight of the corporation's business. An effective and efficient settlement framework should be established, and effective mechanisms should be set up to enforce creditors' rights. These are important supplementary steps in making corporate governance effective. They serve to ensure that the rights and interests of shareholders are protected. The new edition of the *Principles* raises the emphasis on employees and creditors to a very high level.

Fifth, the *Revisions* goes further in emphasizing the responsibilities of the board of directors: (a) the board of directors must maintain high moral standards, must observe discipline and abide by the law, and must oversee internal corpo-rate controls and financial reporting systems; (b) the board of directors must be independent of both senior executives in the company and controlling sharehold-ers; (c) information on any transactions or activities that have a bearing on the company must be disclosed, including resolutions adopted by committees that are under the board of directors, meeting procedures and structure, and so on.

The 2004 *Revisions* of the OECD's *Corporate Governance Principles* further broadened our understanding of corporate governance in general. As China transitions towards a market economy, it has introduced the concept of corporate governance and is now taking initial steps to incorporate its *Principles*. We still need to go further in taking advantage of international experience, following up on the new advances made by corporate governance principles. We need to strengthen our understanding of corporate governance through forums and discussion so as to enrich our actual practice of corporate governance.

To a large extent, how well China develops a market economy will be determined by the quality of our listed companies. Meanwhile, the quality of our listed companies is intimately related to corporate governance. I personally have great confidence that China's capital markets will prosper as we build our understanding of corporate governance and put it into practice.

We have discussed most of the major issues relating to corporate governance and have become aware of the most important elements. We will gradually reach consensus with respect to some remaining issues. Our practice in resolving problems and the principles by which we resolve them will gradually be put in place. Improved corporate governance will then serve as a solid foundation for growing China's capital markets. It will also play a role in our efforts to create a better model for how banks and corporations relate to one another.

14 Improving legal systems and reforming China's "financial ecosystem"[1]

(December 2, 2004)

We have already put a great deal of resources into handling nonperforming loans, dissolving hidden risks, and preventing financial crises. We still have much to do in the next stage of financial reform, however. One of the most important steps will be to improve legislation relating to finance and especially laws relating to bankruptcy and loan fraud. This relates as well to relevant accounting standards. Legal issues directly impact our financial ecosystem. Crucial problems are emerging in this area. I would like to take this opportunity to exchange some initial thoughts with everyone, and hope we all can go further in studying and discussing these issues.

The forms that financial risk can take keep changing as we deepen our economic transition, and hidden risks that we have to deal with keep changing as well

The fundamental reasons financial risk develops are the following. First, the global context is changing rapidly, including economic, scientific, and financial developments. Many issues can no longer be dealt with by using our existing theory and practice. Financial stability is now facing grave uncertainties. Second, China's transition is still a work in progress. As we shift from a planned economy to a market economy, many mechanisms are still halfway between market and plan and are in conflict with one another. Third, many economic problems and crises are reflected in the financial system first, as a kind of mirror image. We experienced that in the Asian financial crisis. If hidden financial risks are not resolved in time, they are likely to build up and lead to a full-blown financial crisis.

Since the risks are uncertain, it behooves us to take the problems seriously, examine them thoroughly. We can only dissolve hidden risks by taking timely action. On a global basis, it is clear that the longer financial risks are allowed to mount up, the harder it becomes to resolve the problems.

Financial risks take different forms at different stages in the course of economic transition. The characteristics of hidden risks, and their key features, keep shifting. Problems that we encountered in the past are now no longer the main issues, while things that we dismissed as minor in the past may now become rather major. For example, for a certain period we had to deal with a massive amount of nonperforming loans. To do that, we issued RMB 270 billion worth of national bonds in 1998 in order to make up for inadequate capital in our State-owned commercial banks. In 1999, by setting up asset management companies, we stripped one trillion RMB worth of nonperforming loans off balance sheets. At the end of 2003, we began to carry out shareholding reform of the Bank of China and the China Construction Bank, as a pilot project. We used existing capital to cancel out nonperforming loans. After that, we registered State capital in the Bank of China and the China Construction Bank through the use of some of our foreign exchange reserves and gold reserves. Starting in 2003, we have pushed forward reform of the agricultural credit cooperatives, also through spending a certain amount of the State's resources.

In order to come to a thorough understanding of the nonperforming loan issue, in 2001 and 2002, we undertook a detailed sample survey that allowed us to feel out the contours of how these bad loans had arisen in the past. It was imperative that we undertook this fundamental work prior to designing the reform of State-owned commercial banks and trying to resolve the nonperforming loan problem. The results of the survey indicated that around 30 percent of the nonperforming loans were the result of "planning" and administrative interference. Another 30 percent came about as the result of loans that State-Owned Enterprises had reneged on, policy loans made by State-owned banks in support of the State-Owned Enterprises. Ten percent of the nonperforming loans came about because of structural adjustments made by the State, by closing down, merging, or shifting production of enterprises. Another 10 percent came from local-government interference, including inadequate protection of creditors due to judicial or enforcement problems. A final 20 percent of the nonperforming loans came about as the result of poor internal management within State-owned commercial banks themselves.

In addition, we have a severe problem of enterprises simply walking away from their loan obligations, given very poor credit practices in the country. We are still not able to implement rigorous accounting standards, and all of these things serve to interact with one another. It should be noted that most of the problems are connected with legal, judicial, and enforcement issues.

As we address all kinds of problems in the course of reform, we have found that the original conflicts then constantly transform into new issues. For instance, some of the causes of nonperforming loans in the past are being eliminated. We are, for example, gradually resolving such things as improper administrative interference, disconnects between central and provincial governments, the lack of internal controls in commercial banks, many of which came about because "government" had not yet been separated out from "enterprise."

In the early stage of reform, the relationship between central and provincial governments was characterized by the phrase, "administrative division of authority" (decentralization of authority). To a great extent, this influenced the results of the internal control systems of commercial banks. Authority to make loans mimicked the administrative division of authority, so that provinces, districts, municipalities, and counties were all allowed to decide on loans at their own level. Bank branches therefore took advantage of the phenomenon known as "three eyes," namely the oversight theoretically provided by the headquarters of the bank, the local government, and the local branch of the People's Bank of China, which served as the regulator. In the early period of reform, communications were not well developed and so daily regulatory oversight or "guidance" was in fact strongly impacted by local interests. Internal controls were, in contrast, quite weak.

To give an example, in the early 1990s I was working in a commercial bank and discovered that the official regulations governing internal operations were extremely detailed and complete. Superficially, the system seemed sound. In reality, as headquarters well knew, enforcement was quite another matter. To a great degree, the formulation and improvement of all kinds of regulations had become a way to allow for the shirking of responsibility.

Each branch organization took advantage of the "three eyes" of the system to do what they wanted. If things did not work out with a given loan, headquarters could claim it was not their responsibility.

We started focusing more intently on the problem of internal controls after the 1993 Third Plenary Session of the 14th Central Committee of the Communist Party of China. At the time, we were encouraging "specialized banks" to become comprehensive commercial banks. The idea was for them to move in the direction of being commercial corporations and no longer administrative institutions. They no longer would use administrative means to carry on business.

Change often takes longer than one expects, however. Not until we absorbed the lessons of the Asian financial crisis in 1997 did we hold a National Financial Work Conference to take up this challenge. Only then did State-owned banks begin to institute "vertical management systems" in terms of their business as well as personnel systems. That created the conditions for the banks to actually strengthen internal controls.

Other causes for nonperforming loans are also constantly changing, such as problems with the regulatory system, problems within State-Owned Enterprises themselves, and so on. With respect to these, risk factors are gradually being eliminated. For example, in the early period the problem with regulatory agencies could be put quite simply: they mainly issued birth certificates. That is, they focused on granting permissions and disregarded any subsequent regulatory oversight. Once the baby was born, they had nothing more to do with it.

After the Asian financial crisis, however, China's government basically discontinued administrative interference over State-owned commercial banks. From a legal perspective, government departments explicitly confirmed that State-owned commercial banks had the authority to decide upon loans by themselves. From the start of this century, the government also gradually relaxed the requirement that State-owned commercial banks "should be inclined to" extend credit to State-Owned Enterprises. As reform of State-Owned Enterprises has gone forward, some large entities have been listed on the market. Their business situation has improved, which brings with it the possibility that the asset quality of their loans with banks will improve.

In general, we are gradually resolving the old kind of nonperforming loan problem. However, our financial system is now facing a whole new set of problems as our economic structure enters a new phase of development.

To deal with these new problems, the research department of the People's Bank of China produced a report on the risk profile of our financial sector. This report divides financial risk into nine main aspects.

Specifically, risk factors are as follows. The savings rate and M2 continue to rise, which mean that an increasing amount of risk is concentrated in the banking industry. The stability of the value of the currency faces substantial potential pressure. On a global basis, operating in deficit mode is often a source of financial instability. The rigidity of China's exchange-rate system and a severe imbalance in the country's balance of payments is harboring a tremendous amount of risk. The relationship between the banking industry and its customers and the bank-corporation relationship is gestating obvious risks. Financial institutions are operating in a context that doesn't allow for self-determined pricing, or that doesn't have any scientific way to derive prices. This is incubating enormous financial risk. A lack of financial innovation systems is leading to financial rigidity which leads to the risk of being less competitive. The country's need to protect financial stability and its need to prevent moral hazard conflict with one another. And so on.

Among this list, many of the issues are closely related to the legal aspects of our financial ecosystem. For example, looking at the realities of the relationship between banks and corporations, we can see that China's corporations are very highly leveraged. The percentage of their own capital is quite small, and they rely to a large extent on bank loans for their capital needs. The question then becomes: can banks rely adequately on external information in evaluating these loans, or do they rely to a great degree on internal information? When corporations renege on loans, are legal arrangements sufficient to protect creditors, and reduce the extent of the losses?

Risk in a market economy is always going to exist, and the appearance of nonperforming loans is inevitable. In dealing with them, however, how much control do banks, as creditors, really have? Should the relationship between banks and enterprises be one of "control and guidance," or should it be one of "keeping a distance?"

The answers to all of these things in fact relate to legal conditions or the accepted way of handling things as established by case law. They also relate to accounting standards, external auditing, information disclosure, whether or not judicial procedures and enforcement are in fact very sound, and the ability to get valid market information. The relationship between banks and enterprises is one that is constrained by normal conventions, but ultimately it is also determined by a strong stick. That means it is determined by the extent to which a bank can use the threat of forceful action.

As creditors, banks hope that when enterprises run into trouble they will correct the problems as soon as possible. Some enterprises cannot turn around a bad situation, however, and in these situations the critical issue is whether or not the *Bankruptcy Law* can provide the creditor with effective and efficient guarantees of the creditors' rights.

Another issue is closely related to legal issues, and that involves the connection between preserving financial stability yet also preventing moral hazard. If there is no sound legal framework by which financial institutions can deal with bankruptcy closings and settlement, then the ways in which we actually do handle such situations may not be all that well grounded. Incidents may even occur that affect social stability.

That is, it may be hard to achieve "fairness and justice" since there has been no clear legal definition of the rights of depositors as opposed to the rights and duties of investors before a problem arises. The lack of such legal clarity also means that market participants cannot anticipate risks and cannot make choices based on foreknowledge of risk. Another issue that the law needs to make more explicit, therefore, is whether or not and how all participants in the market can place constraints on the financial markets and the structure of the financial system.

Controversial issues

In bringing up "controversial issues" yet again today, I mainly want to focus on three specific things: the *Bankruptcy Law*, loan fraud ("loan swindling"), and accounting standards as they relate to loan swindling.

Regarding the Bankruptcy Law

Financial reform and financial institutions have long awaited the birth of a new *Bankruptcy Law*. The 1986 version of the law, called a "trial version" was enacted in the early transitional period of reform. As our market economy has progressed, that version no longer fits the needs of a market economy in terms of coverage, settlement, bankruptcy restructuring, and so on. In the course of handling the bankruptcy case of the Guangdong International Trust and Investment Co., Ltd., we were able to use some amendments and judicial explanations regarding settlement procedures and restructuring. Our current laws and regulations are simply not sufficient, however, to guarantee the financial discipline and financial restraints that are required in the process of setting up a socialist market economy.

I have heard there are still some differences of opinion in the process of drafting the new *Bankruptcy Law*. Here, I would like to focus on four specific aspects.

The first topic being debated relates to settlement procedures. Among these procedures is the sequence of priorities in settling creditor's rights for mortgaged assets and other pledged collateral. One view says that these rights should come after the creditor's rights of the workers. Generally speaking, these are understood to mean payments in arrears for work performed. A broader interpretation includes unpaid basic social security costs, pension funds, unpaid medical bills, and even such things as resettlement costs and re-employment costs for workers.

If the scope of workers' creditor rights is not rigorously and explicitly defined, and such rights are given preference over creditors' rights to collateral, the results may well be that nobody gets much at all. Workers do not get paid, while recovery rates for any remaining collateral become extremely low. Moreover, such things as pension fund guarantees, healthcare insurance, re-employment conditions and so on are themselves in the midst of reform. All of these are still in a very amorphous stage and not well defined.

The second topic being debated relates to the conditions of bankruptcy. It seems legally logical to say that if a bank loaned money to someone and was not paid back, then the bank, as creditor, can threaten to file a suit to retrieve what it is owed. This implies that the creditor has a big enough stick to enforce the results of the suit, however. It implies the ability to "supervise and urge" the enterprise to return payment. If the enterprise does not oblige, then the creditor files a suit according to the terms of the *Bankruptcy Law*.

However, the first thing the courts will do according to the *Bankruptcy Law* is to appoint a receiver and to set up a creditors' committee. All authority previously vested in the executive management of the enterprise is now transferred to the creditors' committee. This procedure is of ultimate importance in protecting the rights of creditors. Experience has taught us by now that many bankruptcy suits are not filed for the purpose of forcing the enterprise into bankruptcy, but rather for two other purposes. One is to use the proceedings as the ultimate threat, to force the enterprise to return what it owes. The second is to provide greater opportunities for the enterprise itself by forcing restructuring proceedings. In the course of restructuring, creditors can reduce or exempt a portion of the debts, or extend payment terms, or other ways so as to help the enterprise be "reborn" after reorganization. In other words, the suit is not necessarily intended to dismember the enterprise and reduce it to a pile of scrap metal.

The effectiveness of bankruptcy proceedings will be much less effective, however, if "bankruptcy" includes simple insolvency, when assets are not sufficient to cover liabilities. This turns the *Bankruptcy Law* into something more ornamental than real. This is particularly so if the so-called insolvency is merely a matter of accounting, highly flexible figures or outright manipulation. I will discuss that in a bit. This relates to the question of whether the role of the *Bankruptcy Law* should be a matter of "hard constraints" or "soft constraints." It therefore relates to whether or not our entire process of reform can finally walk away from what Janos Kornai has termed a system of soft financial constraints.

The third subject being debated is whether or not the subject of bankruptcy is specialized enough to require strong legal measures that call for setting up a specialized court. From a superficial view of it, bankruptcy law seems rather simple: if borrowed money is not returned, the final resort is to go to court. If the case involves complex liability structures, however, including tax issues, labor problems, and restructuring, then it may be necessary to have quite professionalized expertise handle the case. For example, if there are different classes of preferential claims on creditor rights, claims on pledged or mortgaged assets, senior debt and subordinated debt, the sequence of settling claims on these may differ. Meanwhile, restructuring is similar to mergers and acquisitions in being a highly complex process. People may well doubt the ability of local courts to handle such bankruptcy cases, if the matter rests with the local judiciary.

The fourth subject relates to the bankruptcy of financial institutions themselves and whether or not this should be encompassed within the bankruptcy law. According to international experience and the opinion of international organizations right now, it should be. Another view, however, says that it should not be due to the breadth of considerations and people affected in Chinese cases. These may include both depositors and creditors, since at the present there is nothing to guarantee the deposits made by depositors. There is also nothing to ensure that investors will get any of their money out. Some people therefore advise not including financial institutions in the *Bankruptcy Law*, or at least "letting the State Council decide."

Would this not lead to yet another extended delay in establishing bankruptcy rules for financial institutions? What's more, would there not be all that much more obfuscating debate intended to block progress on deciding on ways to insure deposits and compensate investors?

Regarding loan fraud or "swindling"

China's actual situation right now includes fraudulent financial behavior that falls into two categories. One is aimed at gaining "illegal possession." The perpetrator carries out financial swindles through providing false information, that is, fraudulently withdraws bank funds by using false documentation. Examples of this would be fraudulent letters of credit, or promissory notes. China's laws on this type of swindling are quite explicit.

The second kind does not aim for illegal possession, but rather uses intentionally falsified financial data in order to commit loan fraud on behalf of an enterprise. In this kind of swindling, the perpetrator claims that the use of the money is real. That is, the fraud is ostensibly not done in order to pocket the funds. This is not therefore "illegal possession" and does not come under our current *Criminal Law*.

When a perpetrator uses false information to defraud a bank for purposes of getting a loan, that does not belong to the category of "financial fraud." Only when the loan is "illegally possessed" can the person be held criminally responsible. Otherwise, it becomes a matter for civil law and is tried under the *Contracts Law*, which provides radically insufficient deterrence against this second kind of swindling.

This fact is going to have a massive impact on our attempt to establish greater financial discipline. It is possible that we may see a huge resurgence in nonperforming loans on bank balance sheets as a result.

From data on international comparisons provided by KPMG, the scale of financial fraud that results from intentional falsification of financial data is alarming in all countries. Germany, the United States, and France have all put explicit language into their regulations making such activity a criminal as opposed to a civil offense. The aim is to combat and prevent such practices. Section 265b of the *German Criminal Code*, for example, stipulates that the following kinds of behavior are included in "the crime of obtaining credit by deception" if behavior is significantly carried out with the intent of benefiting the person receiving the credit and with the intent of influencing the decision or approval of the bank reviewing the credit application: submitting incorrect or incomplete documentation, providing reports in written form that are either incorrect or incomplete, not divulging any economically significant deterioration of financial conditions in documents or statements that are submitted as part of a loan application, and so on.

Title 18 of Section 1014 of the *United States Code* stipulates that falsifying applications for loans and credit is a crime. Behavior constitutes a criminal offense if a person intends to influence the bank's decision by providing information or reports that he knows to be false. The emphasis is on the intent of the perpetrator to influence the bank's decision. The case does not depend on whether or not the purpose was actually realized. In this situation, the term "loan" or "credit" incorporates all kinds of things including loans, loan commitments, or all kinds of bank guarantees. What's more, the period of time affected by Section 1014 includes not just the time of the loan application but an extended period if the loan is renewed and if further credit is extended.

England's *Financial Services and Market Act*, passed in 2000, also describes falsification of data as being a criminal act. Actions undertaken by a perpetrator may include influencing another person to sign an agreement, committing to sign a contract when one is knowingly concealing important information, providing declarations or forecasts that one knows to be false, making rash forecasts that include significant misrepresentations. The requirements of England with respect to the authenticity of information are similar to those of Germany and the United States but, in addition, a person may be criminally liable in England if he makes rash predictions without taking the consequences into account.

Accounting standards

Falsifying data in order to get a bank loan is in fact closely related to the whole subject of accounting standards. Fraudulent information falls into two categories. One involves utter fabrications, information that has no basis in fact whatsoever. The other involves accounting standards and principles as they relate to information. China's accounting standards have been improving ever since the country launched reform and opening up, but enforcement of those standards has not kept pace and is less than universal. Many smaller companies do not comply with or enforce our current accounting standards at all.

There is a clear relationship between the formulation and enforcement of accounting standards and the authenticity of or falsification of information.

Accounting standards are highly technical. People often think of them as being iron-clad rules, that is, "one is one, and two is two." Given the complexities of modern economics, however, some areas of accounting are subject to various understandings, judgments, even aesthetics. The yardstick is in fact flexible. In the early period of reform, we paid little attention to the whole issue of accounting standards. By 1993, accounting and financial systems in corporations had already reformed considerably and then the Asian financial crisis gave major impetus to further advances. We should give high marks to these outstanding achievements but at the same time we must recognize that there is quite a distance to go before we can meet the high requirements of a market economy.

It might be noted that the structure of China's accounting system is rather complex. There are a number of different systems for enterprises and for various industries, with substantial differences among them. For example, the enterprise accounting system requires drawing upon a depreciation reserve fund depending on the "recoverability" of assets. There are similar requirements under industry-specific accounting rules but they are far less secure than under the enterprise accounting system. Moreover, when a bank does due diligence with respect to the reliability of an enterprise's financial information, it generally does not even ask for an external audit in the loan application. The reason is that we still lack a very strong accounting industry, and external audits are simply ineffective.

From now on, banks may want to think of requiring audited information, and a legal evaluation that comes up to required standards in the course of granting loans. This may require having a research agency conduct an evaluation of collateral, and a rating agency look into rating a company's bonds.

It takes time to develop the expertise of such intermediary services, however, and it also takes time to develop the required levels of dependability, branding, services, and internal controls. Indeed, these things take decades. Meanwhile, is an audited financial statement necessarily all that reliable? Not necessarily. It all depends on the professionalism of the auditing firm, its internal controls, and so on. The development of our intermediary services industry also relates to issues of opening up to the outside world.

If we are not able to resolve these things effectively, the probability of fraudulent information and financial swindling is going to remain quite high.

It will be helpful if all of the experts and researchers who are present today can share your ideas on the above topics and sub-topics. I hope you can assist the central bank in coming up with further research into these things and recommendations.

The legal context for the financial ecosystem

The legal context has a direct effect on the financial ecosystem. To a certain degree, the fundamental question in transitioning from a planned economy to a market economy is "soft financial constraints." Whether or not these continue to apply relates in large part to how well we can change and improve upon our legal system. Many cases demonstrate this, and I would like to focus on such examples rather than the theory behind the whole issue.

The first example relates to the recovery rate of asset management companies. When we set up asset management companies to strip nonperforming loans off balance sheets in 1999, we invited a group of highly prestigious and experienced experts and officials from the World Bank and eastern European countries to help us conduct evaluations of the recovery rate of nonperforming loans. Their unofficial estimate was that China should be able to retrieve some 40 to 45 percent of the nonperforming assets.

Naturally, the prerequisites for this figure included such things as adequate legislation, judicial proceedings, enforcement, and so on, to support the recovery and restructuring tasks. The judgment at the time was that some enterprises, even though under-capitalized, would be able to survive and carry on production and sales if they could reduce the burden of such things as social responsibilities and historical debts. Now, looking at the actual results, we see that the recovery rate of asset management companies has not even been 20 percent.

The entire process of dealing with nonperforming loans is not yet finished but as time goes on that rate may go down rather than up. The quality of assets is declining, not improving. The recovery rate depends on many factors, including such things as how the diversification of ownership in the enterprise is proceeding. The most critical thing, however, still relates to the legal system within which the financial ecosystem is operating. Specifically, it relates to whether or not a properly functioning *Bankruptcy Law* is in place, and whether or not specific laws have been set in place that relate to asset disposal.

Examples in other countries include the *Financial Institution Reform, Recovery, and Enforcement Act* that the United States passed in 1989, which established a special legal framework for restructuring trust companies. They include the Polish law that grants quasi-judicial power to banks in the negotiations between enterprises and creditors regarding restructuring, in which banks as the primary "extra-legal mediator" have considerable legal authority. Sweden, Romania, and Bulgaria adopted similar measures to ensure that creditors are given priority in recovery and restructuring procedures. In China, questions remain that need to be answered in order to set up (viable) asset management companies and improve recovery rates. Should we establish a special court for this purpose? Should we cancel the process of foreclosure on mortgaged assets in order to simplify and expedite the realization of rights to mortgaged assets?

To address these issues, in 1999, when the four asset management companies were set up, we published a book called *Restructuring and Rebirth: The International Experience in Addressing Nonperforming Loans of Banks*. This reiterated the need to improve the legal structure and strengthen enforcement, in addition to emphasizing that banks must improve internal controls. We must explicitly define the rights and responsibilities of creditors and indebted parties in legal terms. This includes incorporating such definitions into the *Law on Guarantees*, the *Law of Negotiable Instruments* (notes and bills), and the *Securities Law*. Most importantly, the book emphasized that we must improve our *Bankruptcy Law*. In the real world of business, the percentage of bad loans that can be attributed to manipulating bankruptcy is extremely high. Some cases relate to fake bankruptcy and taking advantage of loopholes in the law, and some relate to administrative interference by government officials.

Naturally, there are other reasons the recovery rate of asset management companies is so low, including weak internal incentives in these companies, their "institutionalization" (dependence on government authorities), poor work performance, and so on. Nevertheless, we should not underestimate the influence that a lack of an adequate legal framework has on the recovery rate of asset management companies.

The impact on China's national economy of this lack of legal infrastructure is huge. Not only do we have the original amount of one trillion RMB in nonperforming loans, but we have another RMB 300 billion worth that are currently being disposed of as part of the financial restructuring of the Bank of China and China Construction Bank. At the estimated market price, these are being stripped off and given to Cinda Asset Management Co., Ltd., for wholesale disposal. In the future, the Industrial and Commercial Bank of China and the Agricultural Bank of China will face the same problem and undergo similar treatment. The difference between having a sound legal environment, a sound judiciary and sound enforcement, and not having these things, will cost the State upwards of one trillion RMB.

The second example I want to focus on has to do with when a bank packages nonperforming assets and sells them to the local government. At present, the real rate of return on these packaged loans is not too bad, around 30 percent, which is higher than expected. The reason may be that local governments are able to mobilize greater resources and accomplish things that banks cannot do. Local governments have increased the strength of their justice system, enforcement, and restructuring procedures. They have also been able to make arrangements for labor-type liabilities (such as organizing retirement, firing people, handling health care costs, and so on).

However, this way of handling things is somewhat controversial. This kind of packaging of loans presents two issues. First, the role of banks in this process is weak, with respect to their rights as creditors. They do not have a sufficiently "large stick" to hold over enterprises. Second, the force of administrative procedures takes precedence over the force of the market in this process. There is a saying in most such cases: one can always bring a suit, but the court won't necessarily hear it, or the court might decide to hear it but then be closed that day, or the court might hear the case but not pronounce judgment, or the court may pronounce judgment but it then will not be enforced. The result is generally that the bank "wins the court case but loses the money."

Some banks complain that this is particularly true in the case of bankruptcy suits. They say that the fact of the matter is you can't win. As a result, commercial banks and asset management companies rarely use the threat of bringing a suit as the last resort. Many unforeseen problems can result from this. For example, it leads to greater moral hazard. The enterprise may know that the case will be given over to the local government once it fails to pay back money it owes and the local government will then help it to restructure. This may lead to "ethical risk," and financial misconduct. In a market economy, the failure to pay back loans carries with it the risk of being forced into bankruptcy. There is no way to reduce debt unless the creditors agree, but that is not the case in our current system.

A second problem with this is that it contradicts our overall orientation of reform. The whole idea is for government gradually to reduce its management of enterprises and let market forces play their proper role. If the local government is successful in restructuring an enterprise in the hypothetical case above, and broadens the practice as a result, it may well be that the local government will then take a more active role in managing its local enterprises. Is that the direction we want to take? What's more, the very reason local governments are being asked to undertake these tasks is that they have more influence over their local court and enforcement systems. Is that really a good thing?

The third example I want to focus on relates to the professional nature of the judiciary. When a company begins to face problems, news of this travels on the market and suddenly you begin to see local court officials going to other provinces to try to freeze the accounts of that company. They talk to the securities branches of other provinces as well as commercial bank outlets. If these financial institutions do not agree to cooperate, they can easily be called to task for obstructing law enforcement. It is very possible that local governments are inclined to support their own local creditors in such cases. This ultimately makes dealing with them extremely difficult. Recently, a representative of the supreme court of a certain province came to the People's Bank of China and asked that certain financial accounts be frozen in other provinces. There are plenty of cases like this. They contribute to the desire on the part of people in the financial sector to have a specialized professional court handle these complicated matters.

The fourth example I want to focus on relates to policy-type bankruptcy. In the process of handling policy-type bankruptcy in State-Owned Enterprises, the Enterprise is allowed to first use assets to pay for "historical burdens" including resettling its former employees. Moreover, according to our current rules, the bankrupt enterprise may use its land-use rights for this purpose. (This holds whether or not the land-use rights have already been used as collateral for loans.) If such assets are not enough, then both mortgaged assets and non-mortgaged assets may be used, in the proper sequence.

The results of this practice mean that banks, as creditors, ultimately obtain an average settlement rate of less than 1.2 percent off such policy-type bankruptcies. This is ten times lower than what they normally might expect, which is quite disheartening to banks. If we allow labor-type creditor rights to take precedence over creditors' rights for which collateral has been pledged, and make such policy-oriented bankruptcy rules the universal practice for enterprises in general, banks will be forced to take counter measures. This will be highly detrimental to enterprises.

Microeconomic analysis of our financial ecosystem

The effectiveness of the legal system can influence the expectations of microeconomic entities to a significant degree. From a borrower's perspective, any loopholes or inadequacies in the law can be exploited to gain bank loans through fraudulent means, whether that includes conspiring with bank officials or taking advantage of the bank's inadequate information systems. If there has been no "illegal possession," then the bank has no grounds for bringing a suit against the borrower. If the bank tries to bring a suit under bankruptcy laws, the borrower can always avoid such a suit by "cooking the books," using our unprofessional accounting standards to say that the company does not qualify for bankruptcy since its assets can indeed offset liabilities. Even if the bank is successful in pressing a bankruptcy suit, the borrower can manufacture all kinds of "labor liabilities" that take priority in settlements. Prior to the bankruptcy proceedings, it can create such liabilities by not paying workers, by being in arrears on healthcare fees and pension funds, and even by manufacturing fake labor costs. In the end, the creditor is left with very little.

Any intelligent borrower can manipulate the system in this way. It can take advantages of legal opportunities to get out of paying debts. Obviously, this has a severely negative impact on our attempt to institute financial discipline in a market economy.

The effectiveness of the legal system can also influence the expectations of commercial banks. In the past, China's *General Rules for Loans* always emphasized that lenders should make the distinction between "credit" and loans backed by collateral (including mortgages, and loans secured by other pledged assets). The *Rules* stressed that loans should mostly be backed by collateral, in the case of trade letters of credit, for example, secured by the value of the goods being shipped. Loans that are secured by collateral (especially mortgage loans and pledge-backed loans) generally carry guarantees. If, however, the creditors' claim to such pledged or mortgaged goods is low on the totem pole in a liquidation process, this can create some consternation in the minds of bankers. They will wonder if all loans are essentially the same as unsecured credit. This then throws the whole loan business into confusion. In general, the banking community sorely hopes that the new *Bankruptcy Law* will be as close to international standards as possible.

If debts are settled with the priorities of labor in mind, this clearly has social and political implications. It should be noted that social security should by all rights be addressed by the social security system. It should be dealt with by setting up a sound retirement funds system, a sound healthcare system, and systems that cover basic social guarantees and unemployment. Such systems should be the way to ensure the rights and interests of workers. In contrast, it is reasonable to think that the bankruptcy law should standardize bankruptcy proceedings. It should focus on fairness in dealing with creditors' rights, and it should aim to protect the rights of creditors. Different problems must be resolved by relying on different standardized systems.

If rules are misapplied, if we give medicine to the third son in the Zhang family in order to treat the illness of the fourth son, we may well find that the problem of "soft financial constraints," which we tried so hard to fix in the early part of reform, comes back with a vengeance. If we do not treat the root of the problem, we may well continue to generate an untold number of nonperforming loans.

Macroeconomic analysis of our financial system

First, if nonperforming loans are high and continue to mount up, the situation will eventually lead to a financial crisis. As we know, Thailand developed problems first in the Asian financial crisis. Superficially, these related to exchange rates and foreign debt, but if we trace back we find they actually related to corporate governance in the private sector, to a mismatch of assets and liabilities given the use of different currencies for each, and to problems in the overall financial context of the economy, including the outmoded and distorted *Bankruptcy Law*.

Right now, our reform of China's financial system is a kind of last-ditch effort. We truly have our "back up against the water," and can no longer afford to issue huge amounts of nonperforming loans that exceed the normal levels for a market economy. If we do not reform our financial ecosystem properly, then the nonperforming loan ratio will increase and when it gets too high we will indeed have a financial crisis.

Naturally, when it comes to that, we can always try to strengthen regular macroeconomic measures to dissolve nonperforming loans if we do indeed have to avert a crisis. Such methods include expanding the interest-rate spread and increasing the provision for loans. With respect to interest-rate spreads, we cannot expect to compare with developed market economies. Instead, we should look to countries with financial ecosystems similar to our own, for example developing nations and transition economies. From that perspective, the differential or spread in China's interest rate structure is clearly on the low side. The net spread on one-year deposits versus loans is 3.33 percent, while for transitional countries it normally runs between 3.60 percent and 8.50 percent. In Latin American countries the range is between 3.82 percent and 45.11 percent. In major industrialized nations it is between 1.78 percent and 3.59 percent. Strictly speaking, there are many more refined categories that we use to address the concepts, caliber, and formulas for using interest-rate spreads, but I do not want to take them up here due to time constraints. In overall terms, over the medium-term to long-term, China's interest-rate spread is mismatched with its financial ecosystem. We hope to solve this problem by improving our financial ecosystem but we do not want to be overly optimistic about it.

In theory, we can help absorb nonperforming loans by widening the spread in interest rates. In practice, we need to distinguish between an ideal *Bankruptcy Law* and one that is not ideal, and raise the spread to the level needed to dissolve nonperforming loans. A conservative estimate would be to increase the spread by around one percentage point although some people feel it should be three percentage points. That is to say, if the *Bankruptcy Law* is imperfect, then we need a greater spread and the resulting economic turbulence will be very considerable.

For example, on October 29, 2004, we raised the interest rate on loans by 0.27 percent which was a tremendous shock. Increasing the spread can have a massive influence on the financial costs of enterprises as well as the entire economy. Right now, the overall profit level of our companies is quite good. If spreads increase, however, costs will instantly go up due to the highly leveraged nature of China's enterprises. This will have a substantial influence on the national economy.

Another possibility is that banks become reluctant to make loans if they are uncertain about their status as creditors and their degree of risk. One can see this in the case of Japan, where "loan reluctance" is having an impact on the economy. Such a phenomenon is universal in banks around the world. Last year, for example, Hong Kong's ratio of loans to deposits was less than 50 percent. Right now,

China's level exceeds 70 percent, and the actual ratio might even reach 80 percent if we include in it such things as development banks' subscriptions to financial bonds. If we lower that through new risk controls and regulatory supervision, out of concern for the financial ecosystem overall, the negative influence on our stated goal of creating a moderately prosperous society may be considerable.

In short, the result of our inability to widen interest-rate spreads by much, combined with an inability to reduce loans (out of fear of economic slowdown), may ultimately result in a re-accumulation of nonperforming loans. In that case, we may need to perform another surgical operation in the future.

The analogy commonly used when the subject of dissolving nonperforming loans comes up is that of cutting the cat's tail. The best way is to cut once and for all, and not cut the poor cat's tail segment by segment. That way, the cat will howl each time a cut is made. The unfortunate thing is that this is a matter of probabilities. Even in Hungary, where economic reform started fairly early on and where transitional economics was quite progressive, the "cat's tail" was already cut three times prior to banking reform in 1999. Few countries have been able to cut decisively, once and for all. Countries that did cut nonperforming loans decisively found that the cuts relied on high inflation, for which they also paid a painful price.

In sum, it is highly worthwhile to pay attention to the impact that our financial ecosystem has on our economy.

The gradually coalescing international consensus

In looking at how international standards have evolved, the legal issues surrounding financial ecosystems have always been a focus of international organizations. On November 20–21, 2004, Central Bank Governors and Finance Ministers within G20 (the Group of Twenty) held a conference in Berlin, out of which came a publication called "*Building systems in the financial sector*." This summarized the consensus of G20 on how to rank issues of primary importance. Among the many elements that were included, G20 emphasized a sound legal framework as being ultimately important in building financial systems. It pointed to such things as making sure property rights (for example, mortgaged collateral) could be realized and enforced through contractual obligations. It mentioned that enforcement of the law should contribute to the building of financial services and the improvement of financial markets. The publication emphasized that the training of trustees and judges was also extremely important as a way to combat corruption, in order to allow people to expect that their judicial system will operate properly.

G20 recognized that providing collateral for loans is one standard way to reduce credit risk and lower the cost of capital. In point of face, collateral is generally a requirement for getting any kind of long-term bank loan. One of the basic conditions for such collateral is that the overall system must guarantee effective means of settlement or of bankruptcy. To this end, deputy governors from G20 welcomed and appreciated the World Bank's efforts in drafting the "*World Bank*

Principles and Guidelines for Effective Insolvency and Creditors' Rights." They emphasized that the formulation of these principles should take the legal situations of various countries into account, as well as the special needs of emerging market economies.

The World Bank asked over 70 legal scholars to serve as consultants in the process of formulating these principles and guidelines. The purpose was to ensure that they would be sufficiently flexible and also economically feasible, while having a sufficiently broad base to reflect various legal systems. These legal experts came from both developed and developing countries. Starting in 2001, the World Bank began to evaluate a draft version of the *Principles and Guidelines* with respect to 20 different countries of varying legal and cultural backgrounds, in order to sum up the results and create a revised version of the document.

This revised *Principles and Guidelines* will soon be published. We already basically have achieved consensus on four main points. The revised version emphasizes the need to have simplified debt recovery procedures. It places more emphasis on the protection of creditors' rights and their priority in the liquidation process. At the same time, it recommends that settlement procedures and bankruptcy laws be applied impartially to all enterprises and companies, with as few exceptions as possible. To this end, the World Bank no longer recommends that financial bankruptcy should be dealt with as a separate part of bankruptcy law. The revised version also no longer calls for automatic freezing of a debtor's assets in the process of settlement or bankruptcy. Instead, it recommends "a sequenced and orderly process of freezing assets" in such cases, with public announcement by the courts.

International organizations, including the IMF, have always strongly emphasized the need for developing countries to have a sound bankruptcy law, established bankruptcy liquidation procedures, an effective judicial system, and effective enforcement. They have also emphasized the need for standard procedures in the case of "insolvency," when assets cannot cover liabilities. The World Bank presented 35 basic principles and guidelines in this regard in its 2001 publication, "*World Bank Principles and Guidelines for Effective Insolvency and the Protection of Creditors' Rights.*"

Among these, Principle Three emphasizes legislation to protect the rights and interests of assets put up as security or collateral. It recommends creating a legal framework for the creation, confirmation, and implementation of such security. Such security includes things like goods in inventory, accounts receivable, and proceeds from sales; it includes future assets or assets after an entity is merged or acquired. The Principle confirms that procedures should be respected on a global basis, that procedures be applied to interest income of both possessory and non-possessory parties, that they apply to debt obligations that the debtor has incurred both now and in the future. The Principle provides that prior public notice be given of any action, so that the existence of security interests is made known to creditors, purchasers, and the general public; it provides clear rules for the priorities of competing claims or interests in the same assets; it eliminates or reduces priority claims as much as possible.

Principle Four concerns how to record and register any rights to security or collateral. Principle Five relates to enforcing those rights. It points out that the enforcement systems should provide efficient, inexpensive, transparent, and predictable methods for enforcing rights to any security assets. The process should expedite realization of the rights as quickly as possible. It should ensure that the value of the assets be recovered to the greatest possible extent, and that both judicial and non-judicial means should be considered in order to achieve this.

Principle Eleven relates to governance structures. It is highly explicit in saying that the executive tier of a company that is undergoing liquidation proceedings should be replaced by qualified managers as determined by the courts. These managers should then represent the interests of creditors and they should have quite substantial authority to manage all assets.

Principle Sixteen relates to the rights and interests of creditors and how to handle priority claims. It points out that bankruptcy proceedings must protect the lawful rights and interests of creditors as set forth in commercial law, as well as their priority claims. This is done to guarantee the legitimate expectations of creditors and to promote the ongoing stability of commercial relations. Deviations from this general principle should occur only when factors combine to make it more in the interests of creditors to act otherwise, for example, when it is favorable to the restructuring of the company or when it helps maximize the value of fixed assets. At the same time, this clause also emphasizes that the *Bankruptcy Law* should recognize the priority rights of secured creditors to their collateral. When distributing any income to secured creditors, that is, those with rights over collateral, "the rights of the public shall be secondary to any individual rights and interests." At the same time, the number of people with priority rights over collateral should be kept to a minimum.

Principle Twenty-seven discusses the role of judicial institutions. It points out that either independent judicial organizations or relevant agencies should provide regulatory oversight over the handling of bankruptcy cases and should appoint experts to carry out all rulings. It states that the establishment of professional courts is absolutely necessary.

Principle Twenty-eight relates to measuring performance standards of courts, including the training of and qualifications of judges. It points out that a country should adopt standards to measure the competence, performance, and services of bankruptcy courts. These should then be the basis for evaluating performance and making improvements. Detailed qualifications for judges, training, and continuing education should strengthen the basis for such standards.

To sum up, I have chosen a number of issues relating to our financial ecosystem as my topic today, with the hope that we can enact a *Bankruptcy Law* that strengthens the process of reforming China's socialist market economy. At the same time, we all hope that China will pass a *Criminal Law* in the near future that includes revisions regarding financial fraud. We hope that this will then contribute to improving accounting standards.

I hope that all of you will help create the basic framework for a socialist market economy, that is, one with normal financial procedures and hard financial constraints. On behalf of the central bank, thank you for strengthening your research and cooperative efforts in order to accomplish reform of our overall financial system.

Note

1 This article was originally a speech that the author made at the Chang An Forum.

15 China's corporate bond markets

Experiences and lessons learned[1]

(October 20, 2005)

The corporate bond market includes a range of debt instruments, and developing the market for these instruments is something that we have wanted to do for quite some time. We made mistakes in trying to grow this business in the past, which led to an extremely depressed market that has not yet re-emerged. Our development of corporate bonds has therefore been quite a bit slower than the development of other financial instruments. This makes it difficult for us to take full advantage of China's relatively high savings rate, and the fairly large percentage of M2 to GDP (the broad measure of money supply as a percentage of GDP). These things are not playing the role that they could play in growing the national economy.

In addition to being stunted themselves, our immature bond markets are causing an irrational funding structure in our financial markets overall. This is creating very considerable hidden risk in the financial system and may have grave consequences for social and economic growth.

Naturally, the mistakes we made in the past, and problems we encountered, had to do with that period of time as well. We were in the early stages of transitioning from one track to another, and the "planned" nature of our economy was still quite pervasive. We had not yet established either the mentality or the environment for a well functioning market economy. In looking back at the past, therefore, I am not interested in placing blame on anyone but rather want to make sure that we all learn from our mistakes.

In 2003, the Third Plenary Session of the 16th Central Committee of the Communist Party of China adopted the "*Decision on various issues to do with improving the socialist market economy.*" As this Decision pointed out, we want to increase the amount of China's direct financing and set up a multi-tiered capital markets system. To do that, we need to actively promote the bond markets and put major effort into developing institutional investors. Only if we have a profound understanding of our past mistakes and past problems, analyze things clearly, will we be able to work out effective solutions to problems. Only then will we be able to turn the guiding spirit of the "Third Plenary Session of the 16th" into reality.

Problems in developing China's corporate bond markets in the past

We committed quite a few fairly substantial mistakes in our early attempts to develop corporate bond markets, that is, from the late 1980s through the first half of the 1990s. These mistakes led to an "about face" in the market from which it has not recovered. We therefore have to address these mistakes by discussing them in detail. To that end, I list 12 of them below.

1   Bonds were issued according to the dictates of "plans" as opposed to the functioning of a market economy. That is, both the quantity of bonds to be issued and the number of enterprises allowed to issue bonds were allocated by quota. Enterprise quotas were determined by each level of government. The State allocated a certain number to provincial-level governments, and provinces then re-allocated quota on down to lower levels of government.

2   When administrative entities allocated bond quotas to enterprises, they made decisions on the basis of the principle of "need." The most "needy" enterprises, those that needed "relief," were allocated bond quotas as a way to help them out. This meant that the lowest-quality enterprises were those that were allowed to issue bonds.

3   Due to the lack of any reliable credit rating system, there was no way to provide investors with a way to measure risk.

4   There was also no way to provide investors with any sort of "information disclosure" for use in analyzing a given situation. First, accounting standards were not in place at that stage of China's development. Neither internal corporate accounting nor external audits were valid, so that little useful information could in fact be provided. Second, we did not pay much attention to information disclosure at the time, nor did we warn investors that they should make investment decisions only after a thorough review of the information.

5   We controlled bond prices. That is, we determined prices through administrative fiat, which put a ceiling on them. This approach meant that prices could not reflect the degree of risk involved. It meant that neither the issuer of the bonds nor the purchaser had any ways to manage risk effectively.

6   Administrative requirements mandated that any bonds issued by an enterprise had to be backed by a bank's guarantee. Naturally, this was closely related to the problems noted above. Since issuance of bonds was determined by administrative allocation, prices were controlled, and there was inadequate information disclosure or credit rating, and since bonds were issued to a widely dispersed body of investors, naturally there had to be bank guarantees. The problem was that the minute a bank guaranteed the money, the product was no longer what one might think of as a corporate bond.

7   Bonds were issued to a market of dispersed retail investors, rather than to institutional investors with the ability to analyze quality, as per the international practice. That is, they were not issued to Qualified Institutional Buyers.

Given their inability to analyze risk, retail investors also did not have a very high ability to actually deal with much risk.

8   We had not yet set up effective market constraints. Market mechanisms play a self-constraining role when it comes to deciding on the number of bonds that a corporation will issue and how it will issue them. This works because of the ability of investors to evaluate and select what they want to buy. That is, the market itself should be what determines which enterprises should issue bonds, which should not, what the price should be, what the consequences are of violating terms, and so on. In the absence of sufficient market constraints, we place too heavy a burden on administrative management. That then generates a whole string of problems. Meanwhile, to allow the expression of market constraints, we should have a very flexible trading method that can respond to price judgments and risk evaluations via, primarily, an over-the-counter trading system.

9   We did not undertake adequate "investor education." At the time, many investors looked on bonds as a kind of savings account. The moment investors ran into problems, such as corporate default, they came running to the government to ask that it require the underwriter of the bonds to pay up.

10 We lacked and still lack an adequate *Bankruptcy Law*. Our current *Bankruptcy Law* does not give adequate protection when an enterprise violates its obligations, so that "bankruptcy" as a last resort is an insufficient constraint. That is, a creditor's rights are often not as protected as they ought to be under our existing *Bankruptcy Law*. If an enterprise truly goes out of business, at the very least the remaining assets of that enterprise should be traceable. In fact, however, our current situation is that many "left-over assets" disappear without a trace. The issuers themselves also disappear without a trace, without having gone through any legally-mandated procedures.

11 We did not correctly define the role of the underwriter. In the past, the whole process of underwriting had a strong flavor of "administrative control and administrative interference" to it, including the underwriting and redemption of bonds. Underwriters not only had to manage redemption of bonds, but were also responsible for any failure on the part of a corporation to redeem bonds. In fact, underwriters should not have been obliged to play that role. The responsibilities and functions of underwriting, consignment, and acting as an agent for redemption, should be separate from the accountability for redeeming bonds. The two involve different concepts. In our case, mixing up the two distinct concepts led to many difficulties down the road.

12 Administrative interference was a severe problem when it came to handling default on the part of the issuer. Mostly, default by an issuer was not dealt with by using the principle of market constraints. Given concerns about maintaining social stability, administrative interference was generally applied in a way that required the underwriter to do "follow-up issues." Essentially, governments shifted the responsibility for default onto the shoulders of the underwriter. As a result, underwriters became more and more bogged down.

The problems we see today with the liquidation and restructuring of securities companies are the result of this. They are the consequence of taking on the "historical burden of debt" in past years, underwriting corporate bonds on which an enterprise reneged.

The "main threads of analysis" with respect to past mistakes

All of the above mistakes are mutually interdependent. We cannot analyze any one in isolation but must apply a holistic approach to thinking about them all. In doing so, we can extract the main tenets of how to analyze and address the overall situation. I believe we can analyze the situation by applying the following three main lines of approach.

The first relates to our way of thinking, our mindset. For quite some time now, China has been in the midst of economic transition and a great deal of economic activity still adheres to our former planned-economy way of thinking. Problems do not get sufficient attention when they are just beginning to emerge and the reason for this is that we quite naturally analyze and address issues with a planned-economy mindset. In past, we approached many ways of doing things with this planned-economy mindset, including allocating quotas by administrative means, controlling prices, assigning functions in mistaken ways, not worrying about information disclosure, mishandling breach of contract, and so on. We were not very familiar with market economies or their overall business environment, nor did we understand the requirements of market economies. We put too little effort into research and understanding. By now, when we are confronted with problems, we must do our best to avoid over-simplifying issues. We must avoid repeating the mistakes of a planned-economy mentality.

The second relates to logic. It may well be that the logical source of a whole series of mistakes with respect to China's corporate bonds relates to a mistaken understanding of the positioning of the market. Corporate bonds by all rights should be sold to qualified institutional buyers because they have a better ability to analyze markets and to withstand risk. Instead, the way we issued bonds was often too fast and overly simplified. Given unsophisticated and dispersed buyers, this necessarily led to buyers then relying on governments. Local governments in turn shifted the risk onto banks. It is also possible that we lacked the ability to determine proper pricing, which is why we set prices by administrative means. Meanwhile, when dispersed customers had to deal with breach of contract, they had no proper means to protect themselves. Again, they put the responsibility on governments which, in order to avoid social unrest, used administrative interference-type measures to force underwriters to take the blame. Underwriters then were required to try to do follow-up redemptions of the bad bonds, leading to a series of further distortions and severe consequences. If we had asked qualified institutional buyers to invest in the bonds in the first place, we may not have faced the above linked series of problems. From a logical standpoint, therefore, the positioning of the proper investors may have been the key consideration.

As we issue new financial products, we should take into consideration how to enrich the product offerings that we can indeed make to individual customers, and what investment channels we should use for distributing these products. We should definitely develop or introduce from abroad such financial products as are suited to dispersed, individual investors, but this is not to say that all financial products are suitable for the ordinary investor. For example, from now on we may be issuing more complex derivative products. These may well not be appropriate for retail investors.

The international practice is to market corporate bonds mainly to qualified institutional buyers, and the great majority of such bonds are traded on the over-the-counter market. When sold, the issuer emphasizes the counterparty risks involved and the independence of the trading price. Naturally, a small amount of high-grade bonds may be traded on stock exchanges by automated matching programs. Such bonds are exposed to a low risk of default due to their excellent rating. In addition, stock exchanges often set a limit on the number of bonds that can be traded at any one time. Only small-lot trades are allowed, so that any larger quantities are traded over the counter. That is, the corporate bond business mainly operates through the over-the-counter mechanism.

In the United States, 90 percent of corporate bonds are held by institutional investors, while the remaining 10 percent is held by individuals. These individuals, however, are often quite wealthy and approach the status of institutional investors themselves. What's more, they generally buy very high-grade corporate bonds. One reason low-grade bonds are sometimes in a portfolio is that the rating of a company may deteriorate after bonds were purchased.

The third relates to the surrounding context. Just as with the financial ecosystem overall, corporate bonds need to exist within a certain environment. This mainly refers to institutional structures and institutional guarantees. Such things include adequate laws and regulations (which define the relevant aspects of corporate bonds in sufficiently clear ways), improved accounting systems (which provide necessary information to investors and do not attempt to mislead them), standardized information disclosure requirements, and improved bankruptcy laws.

If we have the right mindset, are logical in our analysis, and have an improved context for corporate bond business, we do not need all that much regulatory control. Qualified institutional buyers and the over-the-counter market will naturally guide the bond business in the direction of major advances. The task of regulators will be reduced in proportion to the strengthening of market-oriented constraints. However, once we begin to extend the reach of bond markets to small- and medium-sized enterprises, as well as innovative-type companies and start-ups, the task of regulatory oversight should increase. Innovative smaller companies in particular will try to capitalize on bond markets as a way to finance their growth. Once they are somewhat established, some will list on the market and then delist as a quick way to earn a return. This process is often not all that open or transparent. It is also subject to manipulative "packaging" as companies are listed. The experience of the United States in this regard with its high-yield "junk bonds" can serve as evidence of the practice.

Solutions

If we are clear in how we analyze problems, the path by which we arrive at solutions becomes fairly obvious.

First, we definitely must change our mindset and move from a planned-economy to a market-economy way of thinking. If we continue to allocate planned quota, use administrative "review and approval" procedures to grant permits, and engage in administrative interference, the future prospects for this corporate bond market are highly doubtful. In addition, we can no longer use our old planned-economy way of thinking to analyze the mistakes we made in the past. Some people attribute the failures of the bond market in the past to irrelevant causes, non-mainstream issues, and even extensions of other problems. That is why it is so important to have a conference such as this one, in order to discuss issues and get some clarity on them.

Second, we must ascertain the correct logical connections if we are to get a handle on finding solutions. Logically speaking, an excellent starting point would be to orient this market toward qualified institutional buyers, and use primarily the over-the-counter market. We should allow institutions with strong analytical ability and the ability to withstand risk to play the major role. We can neatly resolve quite a few problems by starting with qualified institutional buyers and the over-the-counter market. We then do not need such an elaborate process of administrative approvals for issuing bonds, or such close "administrative management." The permitting process would then not be controlled by examination and approval authorities. Instead, issuers and investors would rely on information disclosure and market constraints. Moreover, the process would not require that commercial banks serve as guarantor of the bonds. Were problems to happen later, were the company issuing the bonds to run into trouble or even renege on its obligations, the institutional investor should have enough discriminating judgment to prepare for risk contingencies. The government should not have to come in and save the day.

Third, improving the environmental context for a bond market is a necessary step, but systems-building is also an ongoing process. We have made enormous progress in this regard, but still need to keep up the effort. We have steadily improved our accounting standards over these years, so that they increasingly approach international standards. In terms of disclosure and regulatory oversight over disclosure, we have substantially raised reporting requirements. Our *Bankruptcy Law* is currently being revised and we expect the revised law to contain far greater protections for creditors' rights and interests.

In sum, the critical entry point in nurturing China's corporate bond market is to develop qualified institutional buyers and the over-the-counter market.

Finally, I would like to add a word about a related issue, namely how to finance the growth of small- and medium-sized companies. Right now, all of us are quite aware of the importance of nurturing small- and medium-sized companies, and we are fully aware of the problems such companies face in getting financing. We should avoid any over-simplification of the issue. There are, generally speaking, two possible approaches to this problem of financing small- and medium-sized enterprises.

The first is through making use of external considerations. That is, through making commercial banks focus on extending loans to small- and medium-sized enterprises. International experience shows that when larger and more successful companies start to finance themselves more in the bond markets, banks naturally orient themselves more in the direction of small- and medium-sized companies. They begin to provide financing services for a different client base. That is, market segmentation is achieved by or "squeezed into existence" by competitive mechanisms. Right now, our commercial banks view loans to large enterprises as a way to improve their asset quality and lower their nonperforming loan ratios, so our four major banks, as well as some stockholding-system banks, are focusing on them. This is a correct assessment. However, the moment these larger and better companies shift their business in the direction of funding through bond markets, commercial banks will get the signal. They will begin to set up business units that focus on smaller customers. They will put more effort into researching how to finance the business of these customers. In practice, the results of this approach are quite apparent.

The second possibility is to develop a bond market for issues of small- and medium-sized corporations. Such bonds typically are high-yield high-risk type vehicles. In actual practice, they carry a high degree of risk and easily run into problems. Even with adequate preparation, the right kind of market positioning, and accurate pricing mechanisms, issuing such bonds is not an easy thing to do. We will find it hard to ensure we don't have problems if we are too hasty about it. This process relates in part to the overall understanding of bond markets in general on the part of the public. If we start out with issues that are below investment quality, and carry a high risk, is that likely to work? In reality, this also relates to how we sequence the process of developing China's bond markets. That is, should we first develop a relatively high-grade corporate bond market, and then after that gradually develop credit-type issues that are below investment grade? Or should we try to develop the two markets simultaneously? We should research this in more depth. Many countries have not yet been able to develop small- and medium-size corporate bond markets with any success. The only one with any real success is the United States, but even the United States had the Michael Milken incident. The development of junk bonds can be a two-edged sword. I personally feel that we should thoroughly study and understand the Michael Milken phenomenon before we go developing such a market.

Overall, developing a corporate bond market in China is going to take a great deal of time and effort. This is indeed the proper orientation, but first we must be fundamentally clear about the lessons that our recent experience has provided.

Note

1 This was originally a speech that the author delivered at the "Summit on developing China's bond markets."

Major works by Zhou Xiaochuan

1 (With Wu Jinglian) *The Integrated Design of China's Economic Reform*, China Zhanwang Publishing House (Beijing), 1988.
2 *Collected Works of Zhou Xiaochuan*, Heilongjiang Education Press (Heilongjiang), 1989.
3 *On China's Foreign Trade System Reform*, China Zhanwang Publishing House (Beijing), 1990.
4 *Controversial Problems in Economic Reform* (translator and editor), China Foreign Trade Publishing House (Beijing), 1990.
5 (With Yang Zhigang) *Problems of China's Fiscal and Taxation System and Solutions*, Tianjin People's Publishing House (Tianjin), 1992.
6 (With Xie Ping, Xiao Meng, and Yang Zhigang) *Making Renminbi Convertible*, Economy and Management Publishing House (Beijing), 1993.
7 (With Ma Jianchun) *The Way Towards an Open Economy*, Tianjin People's Publishing House (Tianjin), 1993.
8 (With Wang Lin, Xiao Meng, and Yin Wenquan) *Enterprise Reform: Mode and Supportive Design*, Economic Press China (Beijing), 1994.
9 (With Wu Jinglian and Rong Jingben) *The Road to a Market Economy: Comprehensive Framework and Working Proposals*, Central Compilation & Translation Press (Beijing), 1996.
10 (With Yang Zhigang) *Transition of Mode of Thinking for an Open Economy*, Shanghai Far East Publishing House (Shanghai), 1996.
11 *Reconstruction and Rebirth—International Experience of Redressing Bank's Non-performing Assets*, China Financial Publishing House (Beijing), 1999.
12 (With Wu Jinglian, et al.) *Corporate Governance Structure, Debt Restructuring and Bankruptcy Procedures—Rethinking of Jinglun Conference in 1994*, Central Compilation & Translation Press (Beijing), 1999.
13 *Economic Analysis and Polices in the Transition Period*, Economic Press China (Beijing), 1999.
14 *Dealing with Risk in the Transition Period*, Guangdong Economic Publishing House (Guangdong), 2001.

Index

For Product Safety Concerns and Information please contact our EU
representative GPSR@taylorandfrancis.com
Taylor & Francis Verlag GmbH, Kaufingerstraße 24, 80331 München, Germany

www.ingramcontent.com/pod-product-compliance
Ingram Content Group UK Ltd.
Pitfield, Milton Keynes, MK11 3LW, UK
UKHW021613240425
457818UK00018B/542